Magical Epistemologies

Forms of Knowledge in Early Modern English Drama

Magical Epistemologies

Forms of Knowledge in Early Modern English Drama

Anannya Dasgupta

AAKAR

Magical Epistemologies: Forms of Knowledge in Early Modern English Drama
Anannya Dasgupta

First Published 2020

ISBN 978-93-5002-664-9

Published by
AAKAR BOOKS
28 E Pocket IV, Mayur Vihar Phase I
Delhi 110 091 India
aakarbooks@gmail.com

Laser Typeset at
Sakshi Computers, Delhi

Printed at
Sapra Brothers, Noida

To Ajay and Jaideep

for reminding me of the magic of persistence and friendship

Contents

Introduction

This book will be of interest to those interested in the early modern English dramatic form of popular Renaissance dramatists such as Marlowe, Shakespeare, Jonson and that of Milton, the poet, who wrote a masque early in his career that prefigured some of the philosophic concerns in his later magnum opus. The arc of dramatists and texts that this book draws between *Doctor Faustus*, *The Tempest*, *The Alchemist* and *Comus: A Masque at Ludlow Castle* offers a sustained examination of the epistemologies of magic in the context of early modern knowledge formation. The premise of this book begins with a simple question: when readers such as us encounter the term magic or figures of magicians in early modern texts, dramatic or otherwise, are we to read them only as fantastic representations of humanity's desire to transcend limitations of mortality and the laws of nature? Between fantastical longing and the actual work of producing, translating and organizing knowledge by historical figures like John Dee, who identified themselves as magicians, we are reminded to reexamine our ways of reading magic as only metaphor. How were the categories of knowledge, that now answer plainly to science or technology, talked about before the terms science or technology existed? How can we parse the term magic, which refers to and draws from a range of social, cultural, religious, economic, legal, and medical modes of intersectionalities in the early modern period? The plays that have been chosen as the starting points of this examination provide occasion to delve into these different forms of knowledge, but in each case, the reading of the play transforms in sense and significance for having paid attention to that particular aspect of knowledge and the ways of knowing it. The premise of this book then is magic as a form of knowledge and a method of knowing in the Renaissance.

Did magic have a Renaissance? Michael Bailey asks in his essay on the periodization of the history of European magic (18).[1] The revival of classicism and the rediscovery of Platonic, Neoplatonic and Hermetic texts profoundly influenced the Renaissance inheritance of classical and medieval magic. However, as Bailey points out and as the scholarship of Richard Kieckhefer and Karen Jolly demonstrates, the founding structures of the meaning of magic stabilized in medieval Europe.[2] The Catholic Church was instrumental in crystallizing and condemning magic as a demonic perversion, but it was equally instrumental in accommodating and recuperating pagan and folk practices of magic by forging and legitimizing Christian apotropaic charms and rituals. While the Church systematized magic in demonologies, the influx of texts from the Islamic world aided the formation of magic as a complex discipline of secular scholarly pursuit in astrology, alchemy, optics, mathematics and complicated rituals of conjuration.

The classical revival of magic in the Renaissance developed the basic structures of medieval magical thought. It replicated the pattern of simultaneous condemnation and selective legitimation of different aspects of the practices of magic. A renewed access to Platonism and Neoplatonism in the Renaissance by scholars like Ficino and Pico made possible a synthesized view of *Prisca Theologia* that traced Christianity in continuity with pagan religion and classical magic. It allowed Ficino and Pico to reintroduce the idea of natural magic based on the astrological theories of Neoplatonism, Orphism and Hermeticism into the intellectual circles of the high Renaissance.[3] At the same time the Reformation, by breaking from the Catholic Church, sought a complete break of religion from every kind of magic that played out dramatically in the reformers' rejection of the 'doctrine of transubstantiation'. Keith Thomas' ground-breaking social history of seventeenth-century England, which narrates the decline of magic, takes the disenchanting impact of the Reformation as its starting point and makes a thorough going case for the ways in which Protestantism would eventually wean the early modern English public from their automatic cognitive reliance on magic, religious and the secular, to alleviate their troubles.[4] He argues that the Protestant emphasis on systematic belief in providence, prayer, and the "affirmation of potentialities of human labor... encourage[d] men to seek a technological solution to their problems rather than a magical one (278)." The Reformation attempted to drive out magic by persecuting its practice, as the surge in witchcraft persecutions testify, but also by encouraging the language of technology to take over from the language of automatic efficaciousness of magic. The Renaissance development of medieval magic can be summed up as intensifying the process of the legal repression of magic, along with furthering the creative diversification of narratives that allowed for spaces of continued magical thought.

This book focuses not on the decline, which Thomas pronounced for magic, but in the spaces and narratives of its continuities in the early modern period. Recent historians of science, music and theater have most fruitfully re-negotiated the spaces of its continuity by arguing for the significance and difference of magic as a discourse of knowledge that cannot be either dismissed as trivial or completely subsumed in explanations of mechanics or science. The otherness of magic as a discourse, which Gary Tomlinson treats in *Music in Renaissance Magic: Towards a Historiography of Others*, does not come only from the post-enlightenment rational perspective of looking back at a pre-enlightened time to find a mode of thought that has since been declared outmoded; otherness is, in some ways, characteristic of early modern magic.[5] Magic claimed to be, even in its most ordinary calling, a way to access the extraordinary in order to extend ordinary experience. The otherness of magic was also constituted by its relationship of continuous contention with religion and by extension to secular authorities as well. In early modern Europe magic was controversial largely because as a discipline of knowledge it grew from and reflected pre-Christian, Greco-Roman, Judaic, Islamic and folk traditions of knowledge that continued to develop outside the ecclesiastical curriculum. Even though magicians usually placed their ideas and practices squarely within Christianity, Christian thought and rituals found their way into the work of magicians and remained an uncomfortable but inevitable alliance. Magic invites but exceeds normalizing narratives. Magical epistemologies are then, literally, the ways in which the early moderns made sense of their world and established how they knew what they knew.

Historians of science and literary critics studying the proto-scientific methods and mentalities in the early modern period, no longer dismiss magic in favor of a triumphant narrative of scientific revolution that marked the progress from magic to science, and yet most scholars tend to study early science not magic.[6] Scholars devoted to understanding the early modern structures of thought and practice are working with the rubrics and vocabulary of science. Magic as a category is still too discomfiting, too varied, and too esoteric to be drawn seamlessly into any conversation of continuity with the present. The question that arises is, whether there is anything to be gained from studying magic as magic, other than in preserving a part of the past that has irrevocably passed. Perhaps the solution lies in pressing the study of magic beyond the triad of religion, magic, and science. While magic overlapped most significantly with religion and science, the impact of its practice and persecution can be registered in almost every aspect of early modernity. Magic is a window into the intellectual and cultural mechanisms of the early modernity.

This book considers the intersecting discourses of magic, religion, mechanics, law, and healing as mediated by the discursive space of early modern drama. Theater with its make-believe world and reliance on wonder existed in close proximity to the issues and concerns of early modern magic that has already been receiving scholarly attention. Barbara Traister's *Heavenly Necromancers: The Magician in English Renaissance Drama* (1984), John S. Mebane's *Renaissance Magic and the Return of the Golden Age* (1989) and Ian McAdams's *Magic and Masculinity in Early Modern English Drama* (2009) study early modern magic through its representation on the early modern English stage. Traister's study traces the representation of the magician on the English stage as shaped both by the fantastic literary magicians of the medieval romances and historical philosophic magicians of natural magic: Agrippa, Giordano Bruno and John Dee. Traister's comprehensive survey of minor and major magician figures in Elizabethan and Jacobean drama culminates in her argument that the magician on the English stage responds to the "questions of how much achievement, power or knowledge is permitted to man, what are his possibilities and his human limitations" (67). Traister analyzes Friar Bacon, Faustus, Bussy D'Ambois and Prospero as representative magician figures whose success in negotiating magic depends on the level of their self-knowledge. Faustus is the least successful in this scheme because he is self-deluded and distanced from the goals of Renaissance magic, whereas Prospero is the most successful because he is the most self-aware especially of his own limitations. Traister's reading of the magic of stage magicians represents a standard view among magic scholars: that magicians were exemplary figures who represented the most elevated aspirations that stretched their ability and personality to encompass the best or worst of the spirit of their age.[7]

John. S. Mebane's book develops the context of philosophic magic and the magician's cult of personality further along the lines of Francis Yates' suggestion that Neoplatonic and Hermetic practical magic was a precursor to the disciplines of science.[8] Mebane argues that:

> philosophical occultism carried to its logical extreme the humanists' affirmation of the power of human beings to control both their own personalities and the world around them... magic became the most powerful manifestation of the growing conviction that human kind should act out its potential in the free exercise of its powers on the social and natural environment; moreover, those who explored "natural magic" often asserted that the quest for truth should not be limited by traditional religious, political, or intellectual authorities".(3)

Mebane's account of Renaissance magic as inaugurating a "golden age" of knowledge by freely formed individuals who were aware of their creative power and freedom shapes Mebane's reading of the stage magicians. Accordingly, his Faustus is self-deluded but heroic and Prospero's magic is the magic of restoring "love and faith" in humanity. Mebane's book is a useful survey of the multiplicity of philosophic traditions that inform the discourse of Renaissance magic, but seen from the context of legal and social persecution of magic, the challenge for early modern magicians and dramatists appears to be one where, they have to forge the cogency of magic rather than be able to take it for granted as Mebane suggests.[9]

Ian McAdam's examination of early modern magic and drama takes on a radically different approach to tackle the individuality of the magician. He argues that despite the Protestant dismissal of magic, magical self-empowerment retained an artistic and cultural hold over the early modern English society because of a crisis in masculine identity that was exacerbated by the Reformation (1-2). McAdam offers a psychoanalytic reading of the impact of the reformation on the male self identity which appropriated magic as masculine control. Magical discourse often centers on the material and symbolic value of the human body which claims the center stage in the spectacle of punishment in the persecution of magic. In that context, McAdam's study extends the vocabulary to discuss the power and anxiety about the body within the discourse of early modern magic.

My analysis of the representation of magic in the early modern plays is indebted to the works of these and other scholars who have identified not just the intellectual and philosophic contexts that informed the magic in Renaissance drama but have marked the key tropes and concerns that appear across the magic plays of different dramatists who occupied the English stage. My work departs from Traister, Mebane and McAdam's approach in one significant way: it shifts the focus from the magician to the evolving discourse of magic which scripts magicians, both on and off-stage, as the magicians find new ways to locate and narrate magic. This relocation, I argue, is precisely where forms of knowledge can be seen reflecting different epistemologies. My work takes up the existing interdisciplinary scholarship on early modern magic to re-read some canonical early modern plays: Marlowe's *Doctor Faustus*, Shakespeare's *The Tempest*, Jonson's *The Alchemist* and Milton's *A Masque at Ludlow Castle.* Rather than pursue a single idea through these plays, as Traister, Mebane and McAdam have done, I read these plays for the interconnected but several different aspects early modern magic that each play addresses. This is to suggest that the forms of early modern knowledge grew out of the intersections that early modern magic brings to light. Such gravity as the title of this book highlights, draws from a moment in Shakespeare's *The Tempest.*

At the beginning of *The Tempest*, Prospero gives Miranda the reason for raising the sea-storm (1.2.177). He tells her that by a strange accident Fortune brought his enemies close to his shore, but it is by his prescience, or power to foresee, that he knows that the astrological conjunction of the stars are just right for him to turn his fortune around (1.2.179-183). As he speaks, he seamlessly casts a sleeping spell on his daughter, and commands Ariel before the speech ends. Prospero joins his prescience to the providence of bountiful Fortune. Knowledge as providential and knowledge produced through skill are the bookends that hold between them most of the intellectual and social iterations and manifestations of early modern magic. Providence and prescience complicate the nature of knowledge and the knowledge of nature. It is a moment when epistemologies become magical. This moment is also important because it brings Prospero back in close proximity to other people on the barely inhabited isle. Because magic is alienating, its representation in Renaissance drama occasions reflections on ideal and idealized forms of community–its governance, its sharing of natural and material resources, its hierarchies of authority and legitimacy, its perception and punishment of non-conformity in its figuration of evil. These concerns form the thematic threads of analysis in each chapter with which the narrative of early modern magic is woven. Magic can be seen as a way to articulate and gain access to the inaccessible and dwells in its attendant paradoxes. Thus, if we are to map early modern ways of knowing and forms of knowledge, then the study of the stage representation of magic becomes an important component of early modern intellectual history.

In the opening chapter, "Cunning for a Soul": Religion and Magic in *Doctor Faustus,"* I examine Marlowe's treatment of the most influential formulation of early modern magic–a pact with the devil. This chapter explores the rhetoric and politics of the dichotomy between magic and religion. Where miracles were seen as the province of God and the Church, magic was the devil's art that registered the changing nuances of Christian theodicy. Pre-Reformation Europe sustained magic in a strategic combination of condemnation and recuperation but the Reformation shook that equation. Protestant demonologists stressed the absolute opposition of magic and religion, to the extent that magic as evil was not just contrary to God's miracle but *necessary* in its apostasy and continued transgression to make evident the goodness of God and the righteousness of the Protestant Church. In the process of attacking the Catholic Church as magical, the reformers made a scapegoat of the magicians. Marlowe's rendition of the popular Faust legend in *Doctor Faustus* delves into a scholar's aspiration for the devil's art and exposes the untenable simplicity of seeing magic only as "contrarie opposite," in King James' words, to religion. Marlowe plays with the possibility of a different provenance of magic, one that is outside the scope of Judeo-Christian theodicy, in the figure of Mephistopheles–the play's devil who, I suggest, takes on the role of a mentor and radically revises the relationship between a commanding magician and his submissive familiar spirit. The cautionary intent of the Faust legend would appear to mock Faustus' mortal education by pointing to the betrayal of his immortal soul, but Marlowe subverts the cautionary tale by shifting the emphasis from Faustus' damnation to Faustus' tragic death. Marlowe sacrifices Faustus at the altar of the orthodox view that magic is the "contrarie opposite" of religion. In Marlowe's rendering, the Faust figure becomes an embodiment of ways of knowing.

The second chapter, "Magical Theatricality in Shakespeare's *The Tempest*" maps the narrative shift from magic as a pact with the devil to magic as mechanics. In the seventeenth century the mechanical arts, of which theater was one, were inaugurating a new culture of knowledge formation that grew from artisanal or mechanical practice and transformed some foundational assumptions about knowledge: such as knowledge as *made* rather than *revealed.*

However, the movement from potentially damning demonic magic to secular mechanical philosophy was not one of linear progression. Theater, as a mechanical art, thrived in the tantalizing space of simultaneous anxiety and admiration produced by wonder. In this chapter, I argue that theatrical mechanics serve as a possible alibi for Prospero's magic. *The Tempest* tentatively negotiates an alternate language for demonic magic through the mechanical spectacle of theater. Prospero's magic is no different from Faustus', yet he harbors the hope to return to Milan as rightful Duke where Faustus could only beg for a finite limit to his eternal suffering. I argue that Prospero occupies a middle ground between the English magician John Dee, long held to be Prospero's historical prototype, and Francis Bacon as he produces a "probable explanation" for his work that deflects the risk of magic without compromising the effect of wonder. Prospero uses theatre not as metaphor but as device for his magic. The magical theatricality of the play makes visible the invisible mechanical aspects of theater and reflects on its effects as a response to the debate of the times between the ontology of magic and the status of the mechanical arts as a form of legitimate knowledge that Prospero hopes will serve his purpose as well. Faustus and Prospero attempt to forge legitimacy for magic as intellectual and probable; however, Jonson's satire presents a world of popular magic where the threat of magic is not that it is diabolical but that it is fraudulent.

Chapter 3, "Fraudulent Magic in Jonson's *The Alchemist*" examines the charge of fraudulence in the context of popular magic. Scholars have suggested the relevance of the context of vagrancy in understanding the genesis of Jonson's rogues. However, I suggest that the context of popular magic and the witchcraft laws is equally relevant. An overlap in the witchcraft and vagrancy laws, that has gone virtually unnoticed by the critics, played a crucial role in the association of fraudulence with the cunning men and women–the practitioners of popular magic who hovered between the rogue and witch in the early modern imagination. The play announces at the outset that there is no magic in it except the fake magic that three rogues sell to cheat people out of their money. Magical fraud shifts the focus of the play from the ontology of magic to the epistemology of credibility. Jonson offers that even metaphysical credibility is rooted in materiality. The rogues engage the credibility of their gentle gulls by simulating gentility in "words and fashion" and with a briefly borrowed house in Blackfriars. The magic that the rogues weave lays bare the fantasies of their social superiors. Although Jonson has the rogues' tricks exposed at the end of the play, he lets them escape unpunished albeit without their loot. The rogues' loot goes to the gentleman aristocrat, the owner of the house, in an ironic move where his class position gives him the authority to excuse the rogues' enterprise as "wit" and "invention". The business of magical gulling, his face changing manservant announces, will continue as long as the audience pays and returns to watch the play. Fraudulent magic does not empty the English stage of magic but complicates its representation.

In the final chapter, "The Virtue of Magic in Milton's *A Masque at Ludlow Castle*", I argue that Milton reforms the representation of magic in the court masque. In the court masque, as developed by Jonson and Inigo Jones, magic is derived from Neoplatonic rituals for attracting the influence of celestial bodies through the ritual charms of song, dance, and emblems with the aim of establishing an earthly harmony in court. In the courts of King James and Charles I, the masques produced the aura of political power in the process of representing it; and the body of the king, or the representative courtly authority, served as the corporal and symbolic core of magical power in the masque. Instead of assuming the aesthetic of intersecting political and magical power, Milton makes the question of power the subject of his masque. His masquers are three children who learn about the exercise and transforming effects of power. The corporal core of Milton's masque is the body of an adolescent girl and a figuration of chastity, popularized in Queen

Henrietta Maria's cults of chastity at court that Milton ultimately deems inadequate in it its magic. The magic in Milton's masque hinges on the idea of sympathy and the power of sympathetic magic in the figure of Sabrina. The emphasis on sympathy changes the generic expectations of the masque as it transcends the binaries of the traditional masque form for instance between the pastoral and masque. Milton's highly aesthetic masque empowered by a synthesis of Christian and magical thought is the concluding point of this book as it plays out the possibility that Faustus had only looked upon longingly at the end of Chapter 1.

NOTES

1. Bailey reformulates Joan Kelly-Gadol's famous question about women in the Renaissance to say that magic did have a renaissance though it only amounted to shifting and emphasizing focus on different aspects of medieval magic. Baliey disagrees with Keith Thomas about the extent of the disenchanting effect of Protestantism on the English mental attitudes.
2. See Kieckhefer's *Magic in the Middle Ages* and *European Witch Trials* and Karen Jolly's "Medieval Magic: Definitions, Beliefs and Practices" in *Witchcraft and Magic in Europe: The Middle Ages.* Eds. Bengt Ankarloo and Stuart Clark and *Popular Religion in Late Saxon England* for the meanings of magic before the Renaissance.
3. Paola Zambelli argues in *White Magic, Black Magic in the European Renaissance* that the Renaissance innovation with magic was its attempt, by scholars such as Ficino and Pico, "to claim the possibility of a purely natural tradition of magic" with no recourse to conjuration (3) that did not, however, go unchallenged. Zambelli returns attention to astrology, as Eugenio Garin did in *Astrology in the Renaissance*, as the founding premise of magic that is both natural and ceremonial.
4. In *Religion and the Decline of Magic* Thomas develops his position on the impact of the Reformation on the magical rituals of the Catholic Church in Chapter 2. For a discussion of how Protestantism sought to fill the logical gaps left by magic see Chapter 9.

5. Tomlinson closely interrogates the study of Renaissance magic as the process of understanding something alien to our perception. He borrows from the self-scrutiny of anthropologists to argue magic is best approached in "dialogical hermeneutic" so that it is not "silenced, effaced or absorbed" in the hegemonizing narratives produced to understand magic. He is critical especially of those histories of magic that approach it with the "prejudice of superiority" (11-14).
6. Brian Vickers' introduction to *Occult and Scientific Mentalities in the Renaissance* (1984) and his essay in it are an interesting case in point. Vickers does not see scientific mentality as a progression from magic but he does see magic and science as two incompatible traditions that need "level-headed" and "measured" treatment that can only come from approaching magic in relation to science. His essay in the collection "Analogy versus Identity: The Rejection of Occult Symbolism" outlines the rejection of occult thought by the scientific mentality is based on the premise that occult mentality does not make a clear distinction between words and things and is, in effect, a primitive mode of thought (95). Recent scholars of early modern science, who engage in an equally vigorous enquiry of early modern scientific thought, do so without relying on its discrediting of magic. Although Steven Shapin famously rejected the idea of a scientific revolution, Deborah E. Harkness' *The Jewel House: Elizabethan London and the Scientific Revolution* (2007) argues for one, but in her reckoning magic and science where not separate mentalities. She recounts, for instance the story of Giovan Battista Agnello a Venetian trader and alchemist, who was tapped by William Cecil who was hopeful about the uses of alchemy and metallurgy that could be backed as a business enterprise.
7. In the "The Magus as a Renaissance Man", Frank Brockhardt takes a grim view of the elite tradition of high magic especially because it grew to be too esoteric and isolated. He pauses on moments of disappointment expressed by historical practitioners of magic to argue that literary representations of the magi by Shakespeare, Marlowe and Goethe recognized this separation from humanity as a great deficiency of magic (76).

He argues that literary representation of magic produced the myth of the magus as an exemplary Renaissance figure, where in reality practitioners of magic in Europe between

8. See Francis Yates's *Occult Philosophy in the Elizabethan Age.*
9. See Michel Bailey's "The Meaning of Renaissance Magic" for a survey of the different narratives of coherence produced about magic by Renaissance magicians and by interdisciplinary scholars of magic since the nineteenth century.

Chapter 1

Cunning for a Soul: Religion and Magic in *Doctor Faustus*

The demonization and persecution of witches overshadow any discussion of magic in early modern Europe. The perception of evil in the form of the devil looms large over an art that was understood, in its most commonplace association, to be a result of a pact with the devil. Tied to the activities of the devil, magic was formulated by the changing notions of Christian theodicy in medieval and early modern Europe.[1] Although Catholicism considered magic to be the art taught by the devil in defiance of God, the vilification of magic was renewed as a part of the Protestant self-definition. The reformers seized upon the Catholic Church's somewhat ambiguous approach to magic in order to condemn the Catholic Church as magical. The severity of the witch hunts in early modern Europe testifies the extent to which magic was a troubled and troubling category of knowledge in discourse and practice.

Religion, both Catholic and Protestant, was instrumental in defining magic in the early modern period. Keith Thomas and Richard Kieckhefer have documented the ecclesiastical involvement in developing a range of the charms designed to attract God's blessing on secular activities and in exorcisms and reversing of enchantments.[2] However, the same medieval Church also authorized the writing and publication of the most influential demonology–*The Malleus Malificarum* in 1486 by Heinrich Kramer and Jacob Sprenger–meant to aid the identification and conviction of witches. The medieval Church's contradictory involvement and denunciation of magic suggests that the real problem with magic was not about whether or not it was a credible system of thought, but about who controlled it and authorized its exercise. Accordingly, the Church distinguished between its own "white" magic as enabled by prayer and the "black" magic of the lay people as witchcraft enabled by the devil.[3] This tendency to construct magic as a challenge to religion resulted in a discourse of opposition, contrariety, and contradiction that the reformers emphasized in their much more severe distancing from *all* magic. The demonized alterity of magic, to which Emily Bartels has drawn our attention, was made the repository for all kinds of non-conformity, transgression, and rebellion; it was achieved by wielding the stake over the body and eternal damnation over the soul.[4]

Christopher Marlowe's *Doctor Faustus* written and performed between 1591 and 1593 dramatizes the religious and academic polemics generated around the question of magic and its relation to religion. In this chapter, I argue that the representation of magic in *Doctor Faustus* challenges the oppositional discourse within which reformation Christianity had cast magic. *Faustus* has inspired a long scholarly tradition of reading the play precisely as dramatizing opposition between the "humanist aspiration" and "orthodox framework" of religion where critics have taken sharply polarized positions about the ultimate moral to be drawn from Marlowe's play.[5] But Jonathan Dollimore suggests that contrariness is a part of Faustus' deeply divided world and Faustus is "constituted by the very limiting structures that he transgresses" (110).[6] In his thesis of "subversion through transgression", an identifiably Protestant transgression, borne out of despair and without the hope of liberation, reveals the limiting structures of Faustus' universe (107, 118). Emily Bartels pushes the subversiveness of Faustus' transgression even further by suggesting that Protestant ideology "imposes a transgressive identity on [the] subject from without" (126). Faustus thinks he is in charge of his transgression but it is actually Mephistopheles and Lucifer-Protestantism dressed as devils, who manipulate him.

Dollimore's and Bartels' Faustus is heavily scripted from within and without and the critique that Marlowe offers in this tragic narrative is the impossibility of the individual to imagine a subjectivity outside these limiting inscriptions. The limiting inscriptions were scripted in part by the reformers, including Luther and Melancthon, who contributed to the Faust legend that grew around the life of a historical George Faustus by making it a story about transgression and punishment by damnation. So far as Faustus is considered a metonym for Renaissance magic, this scripting of Faustus implies a scripting of magic by religion. My contention is that although Marlowe's Faustus is shaped by the limiting structures and narratives of magic as contrary to religion, he finds that in practice magic exceeds the oppositional relationship with religion. His use of magic in the course of the play and the enactment of his damnation highlight not just the limiting structures but the process of constructing of those limitations. Marlowe's Faustus implodes the limits that circumscribe him by taking his subjection to the limiting structures quite literally. What John Cox says of the devils in the play applies to the entire play, "Marlowe recreates a simulacrum of familiar oppositional thinking in order to deconstruct it" (113).[7] The insistence of the demonological and theological writing that magic is necessarily opposed to religion is like the ghost inscription that appears and disappears from Faustus' arm.

The Devil's Art

"The history of the Devil", complains Nathan Johnstone, "has tended to be the history of the demonization of witches" (173).[8] He argues that Protestant demonization points not to an automatic oppositional discourse but one that is carefully constructed (177). While Johnstone's project is to recover the devil from his alienation onto marginal transgressors and place him in the heart and hearth of the ordinary Protestant's spiritual struggle, the corollary to his argument is quite relevant to the history of magic. The history of magic has tended to be the history of the devil. The following brief sketch of three key moments of theodical thought highlight the evolving conception of evil that impacted the demonology of transgressive magic as it was locked down in a relationship of confrontation and opposition to religion. In the words of the authors of the *Malleus Malificarum*: "S. Augustine says that the abomination of witchcraft arose from the foul connection of mankind with the devil" (29).

Following from Plato and the NeoPlatonists, and influenced by the theory of generation from opposites, St. Augustine dwelt both on the contrary and correlative aspects of good and evil.[9] In *The City of God* (c.417) he describes evil as an essential antithesis that sets off the goodness of God:

> For God who would never have created any, I do not say angel, but even man, whose future wickedness he foreknew, unless He had equally known to what uses in behalf of good he could turn him, thus embellishing the course of the ages, as it were an exquisite poem set off with antithesis. (Book XI.18.361)[10]

The idea of evil as necessary antithesis that is subsumed in the goodness of God leaves open the possibility of tainting God with evil which in early Patristic theodicy is countered by the idea of evil as privation. St. Thomas Aquinas stressed on the idea of evil as a condition of privation. Following Aristotle's lead, Aquinas deduced that all good necessarily demanded its privation; therefore, the devil and all evil following from him are defective in goodness. In *On Evil* (c.1263) Aquinas gives goodness the order of precedence over evil:

> It remains then that good is the accidental cause of any evil. But evil which is a defective good, may also be a cause of evil; nevertheless it always comes back to this that the first cause of evil is not evil, but good. (21)[11]

The *a priori* existence of goodness makes it possible to apprehend evil as the absence of goodness. In one of his iterations of hell, Mephistopheles describes the post-apocalyptic hell as the absence of heaven: "...when all the world dissolves,/and every creatures shall be purified,/All places shall be hell that is not heaven" (2.1.127-29). It is important that Aquinas, the most influential Catholic theologian, places the experience of goodness before the experience of evil because the Reformation theologians invert this order.

In the hands of the Reformation theologians, evil as privation became absolute; they made the individual responsible for the incidence of evil in the world by emphasizing the element of willful opposition to God. Aquinas' formulation where the positive logically made the existence of the negative possible, was inverted by the Reformation Protestants, especially Calvin. In *The Institutes of Christian Religion* (1536) Calvin's definition of original sin "as a hereditary corruption and depravity of our nature" made depravity and evil the first and inescapable experience of the human condition (292).[12] He goes on to add that, "our nature is not only utterly devoid of goodness, but so prolific in all kinds of evil that it can never be idle" for all of man from "intellect to will" and "soul to flesh" is "nothing else than concupiscence" (293). In Calvin's formulation, evil is both a hereditary condition and a willful persuasion of the human nature that is inherently prone to breeding further evil. Original sin as the first experience of existence needed rectification through the necessary sacrifice of Christ which did not, however, guarantee the availability of salvation to all, as Marlowe's Faustus will plainly come to realize.

The demonologies, given over the study of the devil and his minions–the witches and sorcerers–grew directly out of theodical thought. The devil is the enemy of mankind because he apes God and presents privation and antithesis. He is the tempter who manipulates the weakness of the hereditary condition of humanity's sinfulness by tempting people to damnation. The demonologies describe the falling into magic as the abandoning of oneself to the devil. Pope Innocent VIII's Bull of 1484, that delegated Heinrich Kramer and James Sprenger to the work of compiling the *Malleus Maleficarum*, articulates the Catholic Church's indignation over losing its laity to the devils in terms strongly resonant with the trajectory of Marlowe's Faustus:

> ...many persons of both sexes, unmindful of their own salvation and straying from the Catholic faith have abandoned themselves to devils... they blasphemously renounce their Faith that is theirs by the sacrament of Baptism and at the instigation of the Enemy of Mankind they do not shrink from committing the

> foulest abominations and filthiest excesses to the deadly peril of their own souls, whereby they outrage Divine Majesty and are a cause of scandal and danger to very many (xliii)[13]

For the Church, magic was mainly demonic because it challenged God's world and work but not without God's permission. Right at the outset *The Malleus* seeks to establish the three essentials of demonic magic–the witch, the sorcerer, and the permission of God (1). Through the text the interlocutor brings up the logical problem of this proposition by returning to the ideas of Augustine and Aquinas: "Why is it erroneous to say that God wishes evil to be and to be done..." (68).[14] The long-winded response draws on the Augustinian proposition that antithesis of the devil is meant to bring out the goodness of God: "it is not God's purpose to prevent evil, lest the universe should lack the cause of much good" (69). The authors of *Malleus* are unequivocal in denouncing the devil's magic, but it emphasizes the Augustinian paradigm of locating evil within a structure of goodness where the devil enacts opposition for the service of good.

Demonologists were instrumental in translating the relationship between God and the devil through the language of magic. In their zeal to mark the distinction between God and the devil in terms of religion and magic, the demonologists worked themselves into the logical trap of making the belief in witches necessary for the belief on God. As King James I, an orthodox demonologist did in his *Daemonologie* (1597), written to refute Reginald Scot's skepticism about the real power of witches. In the following dialogue from King James's *Daemonologie* Epistemon explains to Philomathes that there is no better way to know God but through "contrarie opposites".

> Phi: Since yee are enterted now to speake of the appearing of spirites: I would be glad to hear your opinion on the matter. For manie denies that anie such spirites can appear in these days as I have said.
>
> Epi: *Doubtleslie who denyeth the power of the Devill, woulde likewise denie the power of God, if they could for shame. For since the devil is the very contrarie opposite to God, there is*

> *no better way to know God, then by the contraries*; as by the ones's power (though a creature) to admire the power of the great Creator: by the falsehood of the one to consider the trueth of the other, and by the injustice of the one the justice of the other...and so foorth in all the rest of the essence of God, and qualities of the Devill. (38)[15] (Italics for emphasis)

In this exchange Philomathes's question alludes to Reginald Scot's skepticism about the validity of witchcraft accusations that King James refuted in his preface. Epistemons's response presents the devil as the "contrarie opposite" of God. This formulation is representative of the doubly emphasized relationship of opposition that defined not just the devil in relation to religion but also magic as a contrariety.

Stuart Clark demonstrates the centrality of "contrariety" in the linguistics and semantics of early modernity and consequently its crucial role in understanding the language of demonology. He suggests that *contentio* or antithesis as the verbal and syntactic patterning of sentences reflects the divided and oppositional cosmology of God and the devil.[16] Reformation religions especially articulated their perpetual relationship with magic as a conceptual inversion in the order of good evil. The early modern theologians were obsessed with the trope of inversion as a means to make sense of a disorderly world. Inversion was seen as the characteristic of the fallen world since the original sin was the first and decisive act of inversion. Magic is perceived as the inversion of legitimate religious ritual. Thus the witch's pact with the devil inverts the covenant with God, and is ritualized in a series of parodied sacraments such as rebaptism and a renewed confirmation with the devil. Marlowe's Faustus will undergo not one but two rituals of confirmation with the devil that parodies the covenant of redemption with God.

Magic as the devils' art draws attention to the way in which religion and magic are carefully constructed in opposition to one another. Marlowe's Faustus responds directly to this constructed opposition. It came not just from religious tracts and demonological treatises but also specifically in the way that the reformers used these ideas of opposition to give shape and credence to the Faust legend. The legend and the inadvertent history of the two markedly different extant texts of Marlowe's play are evidence for the continued grappling of the contrariness of good and evil in religion and magic and its material impact on the shaping of stories and the reshaping of texts.

Order for a Disorderly Tale: The Faust Legend and the Extant *Faustus* Texts

The idea of magic held together in *contentio* with religion would have shaped Marlowe's inheritance of the Faust legend. The Faust legend came together as disparate and some unconnected stories over a very long span of time. Its origins are traced in the Bible, and later through antiquity to early modernity that carried into theater and film in the nineteenth and twentieth century. The Faust legend illustrates how the idea of damnation and contrariety of magic gradually accrued to make Faust the cultural archetype of a damned magician that Marlowe inherited and significantly reshaped.

The earliest association of Faust is in a biblical story of St. Peter's counter-magic against Simon Magus of Samaria who had changed the likeness of Faustus' face to his own.[17] In that story Faustus is not a magician but a man tricked into bearing the imprint of a magician's face. The Apostle Peter's intervention with his ability to reverse the magic served to foreground the question of legitimate and illegitimate magic and the role of the Church in claiming the magical powers that magicians claimed to have. In *Confessions* St. Augustine mentions another Faustus, a Manichean Bishop whose eloquent speech was so full of faulty reasoning that it propelled Augustine towards Christianity–a movement that Marlowe's Faustus experiences in the reverse.[18] But the legend gathered real force around the exploits of an astrologer, physician and a rebel-rousing showman called George Faustus who lived in Germany.[19] His reputation for conjuration combined with his pompousness annoyed scholars of magic and the Protestant reformers alike though they reacted very differently to it. Abbot Trithemius, the well known philosopher of magic and teacher to such practicing magicians as

Agrippa of Nettisheim and Paracelcus, called Faustus a "braggart, pederast and a fool".[20] But the reformers added the pact with the devil and denounced him as damned. Martin Luther called him the "devil's brother-in-law" in *Table Talk* and Melancthon described him famously as a "shit house full of devils".[21] Melancthon is credited with embellishing the tale with a description of Faustus' corpse to indicate the fulfillment of the devil's pact–neck broken and head twisted around. A graphic bodily dismemberment is enacted at the end of Marlowe's extant B-Text. The printed German Faust Book *Historia Von D. Johan Fausten* of 1587 grew directly out of Melancthon's account and other widely circulating oral tales and myths; the editor Johann Spies describes his editorial intervention as giving an orderly fashion to a disorderly tale.[22]

The English translation *The Damnable Life and Deserved Death of Doctor Faustus* or The English Faust Book that appeared in England in c.1588 is regarded as Marlowe's source text. The English translator gave the idea of damnation a pride of place in the title as its first perhaps unintended gesture of departure from the German original. The title of the book is followed by an advertisement which reads: "Newly imprinted and in convenient places the imperfect matter amended according to the true copy printed at Frankfurt, translated by P.F. Gent. Seen and allowed". The correction of "imperfect matter" is usually read as P.F.'s claim to being close to the German original or as evidence for a prior undated and lost version of the translation that some scholars claim Marlowe had access to.[23] In his book *Faustus and the Censors*, William Empson suggests that the advertisement refers to the corrections made in the story in order to pass it through the censors. Empson goes on to suggest that the same censorship was the probable cause of the "textual mess" in which the extant versions of Marlowe's *Faustus* survive.[24]

The printed version of the play survives in two different versions, the A-Text published in 1604 and the B-Text in 1616.[25] The continuing editorial debate that surrounds the state of the texts and the consequent instability of its meaning can be read as a continuation of the conflict between religion and magic.[26] The

A-Text notes at the end of Faustus' first soliloquy that "A sound magician is a mighty God/Here, Faustus, try thy brains to gain a deity" (1.1.60-61). The B-Text's variation of the same line is: "A sound magician is a demi-God,/Here tire my brains to get a deity" (1.1.60-61). In the A-Text Faust sees magic as gaining divinity; he does not see his art as a turn to the devil. Magic is the work of God and magic as a process of intellection enables the apprehension of divinity.[27] The variation in the B-Text marks a different tenor in how Faustus understands magic in relation to God. A sound magician is only half-a-God; exhausted and disappointed by his intellectual attempts to approximate God, he turns to something different-magic.

The struggle between religion and magic was felt in the mechanism of censorship. William Empson reads the A- and B-Texts as material evidence of the direct impact of censorship on the production and publication of Marlowe's play.[28] Even if we do not go so far as Empson to claim that in Marlowe's uncensored version Faustus had escaped hell and therefore invited the direct wrath of the censors, it is still possible to see the effect of censorship on the texts. For instance, a 1606 Act of Parliament forbade the use of the name of Jesus Christ, Holy Ghost or the Trinity onstage. This is borne out by the corrections made to Mephistopheles' advice to Faustus. In the A-Text he says, "The shortest cut for conjuring/Is stoutly to abjure the Trinity" (1.3.54-55).[29] The B-Text which is dated after the Act of the Parliament rewrites the line as, "the shortest cut for conjuring/Is stoutly to abjure all Godliness" (I.3.50-1). There are no surviving documents detailing *Faustus*' brush with the censors; the only way to read it is to see how far the texts themselves bear the burden of the proof.

Is Faustus being willfully contrary to religion? Emily Bartels suggests that Faustus actually does not make a connection between his magic and damnation till Act 2 when Mephistopheles makes it for him.[30] Does he take on the dominant narrative magic and religion as contrary because it was an available narrative? Is he a careful scholar attempting to study a new subject that he will invest his utmost to master, but is sabotaged by zealous and possessive opponents? Can we retain one meaning and footnote the other or read each as evidence for uniqueness of each text that ultimately tells a different story? The differences in the A- and B-Texts point to redactions in the narrative that suggests that the material texts were shaped by the cultural expectations growing out of the struggle between the narratives of religion and magic. It also shows how Marlowe's editors, publishers and readers have wanted to see Marlowe's play as they interpreted and shaped the material text.

The publication history of *Faustus*, over which Marlowe had no control since he was murdered in 1593, exerts subliminal influence on how the central narrative of the text, the relationship of religion and magic, is perceived. What has become a part of Marlowe's text is itself a result of the complex negotiation between the dominant and subversive narratives of religion and magic. The conflict between religion and magic is more than just a thematic interest in the play. The evidence of the variable texts may be circumstantial but it is a fortuitous instance of the ineluctable intertwining of text and context that is addressed by the play's plot. The images that appeared on the title pages of each of the extant texts further the argument that the conflicting relation of religion and magic was the uppermost concern for those who were involved in the production of these texts.

The title page of the 1604 quarto (A1) edition of the A-Text of *Doctor Faustus* shows Faustus outdoors in a tunic with his left arm weighed down by a heavy stone while a pair of wings attached to his right forearm, lifts his right hand towards the skies. Correspondingly his left foot is planted firmly on the ground while his right foot is raised as if ready to fly. There is a dragon to his right spanning the distance between the sky and the earth. On the left side between the clouds is God with an arm outstretched. This entire sketch is enclosed in a simply embellished circular frame which is designed to look like an emblem or the imprint of a seal and it takes less than a quarter of the title page. The title page of the 1616 edition of the B-Text shows Faustus dressed in the robes of a scholar standing inside a magic circle that is embellished with astrological signs for planets. He holds an open book in his left hand, appears to have taken a step forward with his left foot, and in his right hand he holds down a magic staff. The scene is inside a study which has books and a globe. On the floor, in front of Faustus is an indistinct diminutive creature with a head and a beard like a man but his hand looks like a wing with talons. Each illustration captures what might have been taken to be the most abiding moment in the story of *Doctor Faustus* as it subliminally guides the interpretation of Faustus' transgression.

The A-Text sketch visualizes a line in Faustus' last speech: "O, I'll leap up to my God! Who pulls me down?" (5.2.77). It shows Faustus in his moment of deepest despair when he desires salvation but finds himself unable to repent. Despair is associated with the left hand of God, so the illustration has Faustus' left hand weighed down.[31] This moment of struggle between redemption and damnation epitomizes the story of Faustus as a cautionary tale about the dangers of over-reaching, except for a puzzling detail in the illustration. The dragon stands to the right of this figure associating itself with the uplifted part of Faustus, and God seems to have been relegated to the incapacitated and burdened down side of him. His tunic could be a sign of his suffering and desire for penitence but it is also reminiscent of the garments of the ancient Greco-Romans. The emblem does not point directly to magic; it just highlights his despair within an ambivalent narrative of religion.

Unlike the A-Text, The illustration on the B-Text memorializes Doctor Faustus as a scholarly magician at the height of his accomplishment. The illustration takes up a third of the page and Faustus is seen in a moment of triumph when he has successfully conjured a devil. The devil is diminutive, indistinct and demuring to the power of the magician who has forced him to be there. It has been suggested that the emblem on the A-Text could have been a generic emblem of despair that Marlowe represented textually in the play.[32] The 1616 title page represents the attempt to rewrite the image of Faustus as the epitome of despair with his moment of triumph as a magician. The title accompanying the illustration promises its readers "The Tragicall History". The A-Text illustration encapsulates the moment of tragedy in the idea of misplaced grace and damnation that might have been averted. The two images suggest the two ways to read Marlowe's *Faustus*: as a triumphant magician whose story is ultimately tragic or a cautionary tale meant to be read as a warning because despair is a form of hubris.

The dominant narrative of "contrary opposition" is played out at the level of religious and cultural discourse evident in the Faust legend and the subsequent print history of the extant manuscript. The thematic engagement of Marlowe's Faustus is much more ambivalent in its acceptance of the narrative of contrary opposition. In my reading, Marlowe's treatment engages with the idea of magic as a contrary and devilish art in order to exceed it. The magic that spills out of the tight containment of the damnation narrative is comical and entertaining. It strategically undercuts the doctrinal seriousness invested in the devil's pact. Marlowe's narrative sticks to the traditional narrative of the Faust legend in presenting the story of a scholar who transgressed and was punished but the telling of the tale tells a very different story. Unlike his source texts, Marlowe makes use of history and the elements of a cautionary tale to craft a tragedy.

Faustus' Fortune Good or Bad

In a retelling of a favored cautionary tale, Marlowe's Chorus appears to but does not take a firm stand of condemnation against the magician who sold his soul to the devil. The choric prologue begins famously by recounting what the play is not about. It is not about the "proud audacious deeds" of embattled Kings or about the dalliance of Gods. It is about "the form of Faustus' fortune good or bad" (8). The Chorus leaves the final judgment of the Faustus' fortune to the audience as it recounts his life up to the point at which the play begins. His early life is mapped in terms of how far he rose above his "base stock" with his success at the university in Wittenberg where his chief study was "divinity" in which he was "graced". The word grace is repeated twice in the prologue; the fortunes of the abundantly graced doctor of divinity will stand in stark contrast to when he thirsts for just a drop of grace at the end of the play. The ambivalence of his "good or bad" fortune is made further ambiguous when the Chorus presents his hubris compared to Icarus.

> Till swoll'n with cunning, of a self-conceit
> His waxen wings did mount above his reach,
> And melting, the heavens conspired his overthrow.
> For, falling to a devilish exercise. (1.1.20-23)

The comparison with Icarus allows the Chorus two different ways to read Faustus' fall into devilish exercise. Daedalus, who had invented the "waxen wings" and flown to safety but his son Icarus borrowed the wings and attempted to see how high it would take him. The Chorus' judgment is not against the creation of the "waxen wings" or the attempt to fly but Icarus' suicidal inability to foresee the limits of this art. The second explanation for Icarus' fall and therefore also Faustus' is that it is a "conspiracy of the heavens". In Icarus' case, it is the sun or the literal "eye of the heaven" that melted his waxen wings to cause his literal downfall. In Faustus' case, it is a reference to the conspiracy of Christian doctrine which cast magic in opposition to itself as a "devilish exercise" and used the threat of damnation to contain it.

The "devilish exercise" is specifically named as "necromancy": the knowledge that lies beyond the purview of "learning's golden gifts". Faustus chooses, like Eve did, the sweetness of the tree of knowledge that holds the possibility of knowing what is beyond the tried and tasted:

> And glutted more upon with learning's golden gifts,
> He surfeits upon cursed necromancy;
> Nothing so sweet as magic is to him,
> Which he prefers before his chiefest bliss.
> And this be the man that in his study sits. (1.1.20-28)

The sweetness of the apple from the tree of knowledge is indirectly invoked in the consumption of golden learning as the Chorus reframes Icarus' fall with tropes and references to the fall of Adam and Eve. The transgression and overreaching of the first fall had compromised eternal salvation and had become a point of particular reckoning for Reformation theology. The redeeming grace for the "chiefest bliss" or salvation was neither automatic, nor deserved, nor could it be earned as the Catholics believed. But Faustus in his study, graced in divinity, prefers the study of magic either with the knowledge that his redemption is secure or from knowing that redemption cannot be secured.

Faustus mulls over the question of sin, death, and salvation before turning quite dramatically to magic. He reads from Jerome's Bible, the Latin Vulgate which was the most popular bible of the medieval church. Scholars have pointed out that Faustus misreads the Bible by quoting only half the text each time; he leaves out the promise of mercy while recounting the reward of sin (Romans 6:23), and ignores the justice of God in acknowledgement of one's sin (John 1:8). While the original text of Romans 6:23 and John 1:8 uses the figure of antithesis to establish God's mercy, Faustus dwells on only one half of the binary to emphasize the inherent sinfulness of his existence and the logical conclusion of his sin as everlasting death not salvation.

> When all is done, divinity is best.
> Jerome's Bible, Faustus, view it well.
> [He reads] *Stipendium piccati mors est.* Ha!
> *Stipendium*, etc.
> The reward of sin is death. That's hard.
> [He reads] *Si peccasse negamus, fallimur*
> *Et nulla est in nobis veritas*
> If we say we have no sin,
> We deceive ourselves, and there is no truth in us.
> Why then belike we must sin,
> And so consequently die.
> Ay, we must die an everlasting death.
> What doctrine call you this, *Che sera, sera*,
> What will be, shall be? Divinity, adieu. (1.1.37-50)

Faustus reads the Bible like a Calvinist theologian except that he concludes on a note of impatience and exasperation and not renewed humility. His logic is one of inversion: truth, in acknowledging one's sinfulness, leads one to further sin. It is not deception that keeps one in sin but the acknowledgement of truth. He alludes to the providential nature of the doctrine of election in the final line which appears as a question in the A-Text and a statement in the B-Text. Faustus' eventual rejection of divinity makes the pun in his use of the word "will" explicit.

The issue of individual will, and especially its role of willing salvation was hotly contested between the Catholics and the Protestants. A medieval divine reading of the Vulgate would have concluded, with the help of Augustine, that human will is the handmaid of divine grace, and a willing acknowledgement of one's sins prepares one to receive salvation via God's grace. The reformers also argued for the servitude of the will but they insisted that the will had little to do with the willingness of the individual; it was entirely subject to God's grace–the *primum mobile* that directed the individual will towards repentance, rectitude and salvation.[33] In this context "What will be, shall be" could refer to the divine will, or it could refer to Faustus' own will that informs the course of action that culminates in what appears as the wholly determined "shall" of the future. Faustus begins by reading the Bible as a Reformation theologian but succumbs to the ambiguity of free will in the last line. The variation of the punctuation in the A-and B-Text suggests a desire to see Faustus as either inquisitive and ambiguous and never entirely resolute in his decision to trade his soul for his cunning or as firmly damned from the start. I contend that Faustus is never entirely convinced of the reality and possibility of damnation because he does not see the boundaries of magic and religion as entirely distinct and opposed.

Having dismissed disciplines of scholarship and divinity, Faustus closes his first soliloquy with a turn to his magic books: "These metaphysics of magicians/And necromantic books are heavenly" (1.1.79-80). The obvious gesture here involves the irony of a misplaced epithet which works in two ways. The first irony plays on the spectator's pop-culture knowledge that the Faust legend was popularized as a Protestant whipping horse as an exemplum of a scholar proved foolish because he treated the boundary between heaven and hell frivolously. The irony lies in recognizing that despite the imperious cheeriness of his tone, this decisive turn to magic is Faustus' first step towards fall. The more provocative irony lies in the recognition that "heavenly" is not a misapplied epithet for magic on more than one account. Astrology often used as a synonym for magic was a significant aspect of all branches of magic and involved the study of the heavens thus making the study "heavenly". However, the more significant dramatic thrust of Faustus' choice of adjective is that it brings the discomforting alliance of religion and magic to the fore. The "metaphysics of magicians" is "heavenly" because it is the same metaphysics that the divines employ in their study of religion. His "necromantic books" are likely to be grimoires: handwritten and consecrated magic manuals but could also apply to the "Hebrew Pslater and New Testament" that his friends instruct him to bring with him for the conjuration. It indicates the role that the Catholic and Protestant churches played in defining and stabilizing magic as its "contrary opposite".

Faustus' provocative (mis-) alignment of "heavenly" with "magic" takes us directly to the play's central conflict between religion and magic that Faustus experiences and challenges. Faustus' approach to magic, as made apparent in his first soliloquy, is shaped by the narrative of its opposition to religion. This narrative of opposition can be described as the "basic, limiting structure" that Jonathan Dollimore identifies as constituting Faustus even as he transgresses it (110). Faustus' defiance, which begins with the single act of calling magic heavenly, culminates in his desire for "power", "honor" and "omnipotence and a "dominion that stretcheth as far as doth the mind of man" ends with his vision of magic as exactly the kind of control that God exerts over the visible universe: "A sound magician is a mighty god" (1.1. 60-62).

Necromancy: Crossing Christianity Magically

Faustus' transgression is that he turns to a form of magic that allegedly perverts a miracle that is only attributed to God–bringing back the dead to life. In his opening soliloquy he had indicated the limits of his art as a physician that delayed but did not cure or reverse it: "Wouldst thou make a man live eternally?/Or being dead, raise them again to life again?" (1.1-24-25). Necromancy, the "devilish exercise" to which he falls, is a form of magic that involves raising the dead. Richard Kieckhefer gives the following definition for necromancy:

> Originally the word had meant divination (mantia) by conjuring spirits of the dead (nekroi). Circe was the classic necromancer of the Greco-Roman tradition, and the witch of Endor the archetypal necromancer of the Bible. When medieval writers interpreted such stories, however, they assumed that the dead could not in fact be brought to life but that the demons took on the appearance of the deceased persons and pretended to be those persons. By extension, then, the conjuring of demons came to be known as necromancy; this was the ordinary meaning of the term in later medieval Europe. Necromancy was explicitly demonic magic. (152)[34]

Necromancy is both the conjuration of devils and the art of raising the spirits of the dead and as such, as Kieckhefer's description suggests, it conflates the two activities in one fell swoop of demon calling. However, Marlowe makes use of the possibility of splitting necromancy into two different functions. The first is in the conjuration scene–a decisive step of black magic in calling the devil; the second is in the spectacular entertainments of raising demons to imitate the insubstantial forms of dead paragons. The conjuration takes on the dominant narrative of magic as the perverse reversal of Christianity from the point-of-view of the practicing magician; and raising the dead in royal courts undermines the doctrinal fuss by the distancing act of theatrical entertainment.

Faustus' conjuration of Mephistopheles is quite by the book. Like Subtle's alchemical jargon in *The Alchemist*, the "Lines, circles, signs, letters, and characters", that Cornelius and Valdes instruct him in, are to be found in conjuration manuals of such practicing magicians as Agrippa of Nettesheim who Faustus means to emulate in form, function and fame (1.1.53). The conjuration begins at midnight with a paean to the pitch darkness of the sky that will be echoed by Milton's sorcerer Comus. Faustus enters holding a book. He begins his incantations having "prayed" and "sacrificed" to the devils in an obvious reversal of those gestures of supplication (1.3.7).

> Within this circle is Jehovah's name
> Forward and Backward anagrammatized
> The breviated names of holy saints
> Figures of every adjunct to the heavens
> And characters of signs and erring stars
> By which the spirits are enforced to rise
> Then fear not, Faustus, be resolute
> And try the uttermost magic can perform. (1.3.8-15)

This conjuration scene does not pit religion against magic although Mephistopheles will insist later that magic is the abjuration of religion. This conjuration scene has to be understood in terms of the distinction between a prayer and a spell that the medieval Church proposed even though in practice they themselves routinely blurred the distinctions. Keith Thomas sums up the difference between a prayer and a spell as follows.

> The essential difference between the prayers of a churchman and the spells of a magician was that only the latter claimed to work automatically. A prayer had no certainty of success and would not be granted if God chose not to concede it...A prayer was a form of supplication; a spell was a mechanical means of manipulation. (41)

Having turned his prayer to the devil, Faustus' actual conjuration is meant to "enforce" the spirit to rise. David Ormerod and Christopher Wortham's Introduction to their edition of *Faustus* and Gareth Roberts essays point out the intricacy and complexity of this conjuration that is about much more than an impetuous crossing of religion.[35]

Ormerod and Wortham's lucid explanation of how lines, circles and numbers as "Figures of every adjunct to the heavens" and "erring stars" is meant to compel the demons hinges on their reading of Faustus' magic as an academic and intellectual exercise within the magic tradition that Agrippa of Nettesheim came to exemplify. Gareth Roberts claims that Marlowe had read Agrippa and his conjuration scene is more accurate and detailed than any other sixteenth-century play or the *English Faust Book* which is Marlowe's source text.[36] Roberts explains the presence of "Jehovah's" name as well as the saints and other plainly religious terminology, motifs, and gestures, such as images of Christ in apocalypse, signs of the cross, blessing with water, that Faustus employs all appear in the conjuration books and are meant to "protect" the conjuror and are not in defiance of religion. Accordingly the Latin incantation translated by Bevington and Rasmussen, reads as follows: "Let the threefold power of Jehovah be strong".[37]

Cornelius and Valdes ask Faustus to be "resolute"; Faustus constantly talks himself into not being afraid; the holiness evoked in these conjurations is meant to quell the fear and aid the process of a resolute commitment that is admittedly very difficult. Critics mostly agree that scholarly magic in the Renaissance was not seen by its practitioners as a contradiction of religion. Faustus' turn away from the study of divinity to the study of magic is at the crux of the two discourses that shaped every historical and fictional renaissance magician–the religious discourses that were only willing to admit such a turn away as a turn *to* the devil instead of God, and the discourses of the magicians themselves who saw the devil as an instrument of their control in God's universe.

Faustus' successful conjuration of Mephistopheles reiterates the contention between magic as spiritual compromise and technique. Flushed with the success of his technique, Faustus seeks affirmation from the devil himself: "Did not my conjuring speeches raise thee? Speak," (1.3.46). To which the devil advocates the narrative of "contrarie opposition" of religion and magic:

> That was the cause, but yet *per accidens*
> For when we hear one rack the name of God
> Abjure the Scriptures and his Savior Christ
> Nor will we come unless he use such means
> Whereby he is in danger to be damned.
> Therefore, the shortest cut for conjuring

> Is stoutly to abjure Trinity
> And pray devoutly to the Prince of Hell. (1.3.47-55)

Faustus did not actually rack the name of God or Christ; the Biblical exegesis in his first soliloquy is controversial but he does not abjure the scriptures. But Mephistopheles also refuses acknowledge the conjuration as a skill; he also refuses to do any of Faustus' bidding because he is the servant of Lucifer (1.3.41-42). Mephistopheles as the corollary representative of the Protestant faith makes it his business to guide Faustus' narrative of magic into the narrative of transgression, damnation and fall. The dead seriousness of black magic, as Mephistopheles presents its here, for which Faustus must die is not presented unequivocally in the text. It is one reading, reflecting the dominant Protestant theology, among others in the plurality of magical opinion infused in the text.[38]

Mephistopheles' mouthing of the dominant religious narrative of magic as evident in his claim that the abjuring of the Trinity is the only necessary act in conjuration is undercut in the sub-plot. Faustus' servant Wagner effortlessly conjures "Balliol and Belcher" to torment Robin; and later Robin conjures Mephistopheles himself with some "Dutch fustian" out of a book stolen from Faustus. Mephistopheles' irritable reaction to being thus summoned from Constantinople is: "How am I vexed with these villains' charms" which marks a stark contrast to his grave pronouncements to Faustus (3.2.32). The comic sub-plot of the antics of Wagner, Robin and Rafe plays the additional role of maintaining a thematic continuity to the burlesque in the main action that seems, once again, quite out of place with the gravity of Faustus' conjuration. David Bevington makes the case that alternating high seriousness and the debased practical joking in the play comes from the popular traditions of English drama, particularly the Christian homiletic tragedy, to which Marlowe was indebted (252).[39] It makes the comic scenes of the sub-plot and the main plot a part of an established pattern of alternating seriousness with grotesque caricature to distance the audience from any sympathy for the protagonist. However, the farcical elements of Faustus' use of magic–the absurdities at the

Pope's palace in Rome, placing horns on the Knight, cheating and frightening the horse courser–can also be read as not distancing but engaging the audience's sympathy through laughter and entertainment. In fact the entertainment value of magic makes it less frightening and earns it a different context of legitimacy.

The latter part of Faustus' career is devoted to the entertainment of Kings and Dukes at their courts where Faustus is rewarded with applause and money for performing necromancy. Magic, as cursed necromancy, is neutralized and normalized as spectacle.[40] The Chorus also succumbs to the visual lure of necromantic spectacle and excuses itself from its function to speak and describe:

> Now his fame is spread forth in every land.
> Among the rest his Emperor is one,
> Carolus the Fifth, at whose palace now
> Faustus is feasted 'mongst his noblemen.
> What there he did in trial of his art
> I leave untold, your eyes shall see performed. (4.12-17)

King Carolus requests the "entombed" Alexander and his paramour to be raised from the "hollow vaults below" by the "cunning of [Faustus'] art" (4.1.35-38). Faustus responds with modesty about what makes the spectacle possible.

> If it like your Grace, it is not in my ability to present before your eyes the true and substantial bodies of those two deceived princes, which long since are consumed to dust. ... But such spirits as can lively resemble Alexander and his paramour shall appear before your Grace, in that manner that they both lived in... which I doubt not shall sufficiently content your Imperial majesty. (4.1.47-57)

In a description that does not stray at all from the definition of necromancy as reflected in Kiekhefer's explanation at the beginning of this section, Faustus foregrounds his inability and the deficiency of his art. Necromancy as an art can only perform the likeness of things, and not the thing itself. It is an art of representation and not the miracle of bringing the dead back to life.

The anxiety in the idea of automatic efficaciousness of rituals is powerfully allayed by the idea that magical spectacle is carefully stage-managed. Magic is seen as analogous to theater where theater partakes of the wonder associated with magic and magic finds a safer refuge, most of the time though not always, in the theatrical analogy of performance. An instance of such a reading is Sara Munson Deats' essay "Mark the Show" which draws on the "salient similarities that bind magic and drama in the period" (14).[41] Keeping this aesthetic-metaphoric reading in mind, I suggest that magic had a much more literal function in its association with Court Theater.

The religious persecution of early modern magic with a determined narrative about its damning alliance with the devil is off-set by the refuge that royal patronage and language of theatrical spectacle offered to magic. Shakespeare's Prospero produces a similar "vanity of [his] art" in a wedding masque for the newly betrothed Ferdinand and Miranda (4.1.41).[42] Ferdinand offers to be bold in suggesting that the majestic and harmonious vision is being performed by spirits to which Prospero's tone is unapologetic in response unlike Faustus: "Spirits, which by mine Art/I have from their confines call'd to enact/My present fancies" (4.1.120-122). Court spectacles and masques became the legitimate grounds for magical thought and entertainment, as will be discussed in greater detail in Chapter 4. However, in the present concern if the bulk of Marlowe's play is given over to farce and entertainment, especially as it alternates in structure with the darker and more tragic aspects of Faustus' spiritual agony and doubt, it opens up a space for the audience to doubt the necessity of his damnation, as I claim that Faustus himself does.

The Magical Epistemology of Mephistopheles: Ways of Knowing

Faustus wants to conjure a devil because he wants access to knowledge that he does not have as a doctor of divinity. Other than the entertaining buffoonery with which Mephistopheles assists Faustus, he is also charged with making any knowledge available that Faustus desires. On top of the list of Faustus' reasons for turning to magic is to be "resolved of all ambiguities" (1.1.82). Even the Evil angel primes Faustus towards learning more about "nature's treasury." Faustus' desire for empirical knowledge about the physical world around him is apparent in his conversations with Mephistopheles. The central problematic of Faustus' turn to magic then seems to lie in the way that his quest for knowledge is viewed. Catherine Belsey outlines the two conflicting systems of knowledge in the play as "discursive knowledge" of salvation centered on God that implies the dissolution of the self and "empirical knowledge" about the book of nature (166).[43] Hillary Gatti adds that the opposition to the dogmatic religious approaches to the problem of gaining new knowledge was developing in "provocatively heretical terms" (84).[44] I suggest that in addition to the well worn image of Faustus as caught between different traditions of knowledge, it is Mephistopheles who is Marlowe's real heretical move. Mephistopheles is made Faustus' informant both for the "discursive knowledge" of God through hell but also for the "empirical knowledge" that drew Faustus to magic.

The first thing that Faustus had asked of Mephistopheles was to be reassured of his skill with conjuration that Mephistopheles sententiously denies. Mephistopheles disabuses Faustus of any notion that magic is an art or cunning. He wants instead for Faustus to believe that it is a state of cursed damnation. Mephistopheles gives the example of his own suffering: "Think'st thou that I that saw the face of God/And tasted the eternal joys of heaven,/Am not tormented with ten thousand hells/in being deprived of everlasting bliss? (1.3.79-82)". Margaret O'Brian documents the source of Mephistopheles' suffering in Aquinas' *Summa Theologica*.[45] The corresponding passage from Aquinas suggests that the turning away of the intellect from the divine light is the most extreme form of unhappiness: "And this is the chief suffering of the damned. It is known as the punishment of losses".[46] Mephistopheles' poetic evocation of suffering and damnation, that Faustus takes lightly, are a part of the cautionary tale function that Mephistopheles fulfills. He fulfills the functions of leading Faustus away from his salvation not by lying but by telling him the truth. But Mephistopheles' exceeds the function of a devil in a cautionary tale and becomes Faustus' mentor.

Mephistopheles rewards Faustus with a book for gifting his soul to Lucifer. The book is meant to teach Faustus conjuration—to get wealth, to control the elements, and enslave men to do his bidding. All things that Faustus had led his audience to believe he wanted, but he asks Mephistopheles for more.

> Faustus: Thanks Mephistopheles. Yet fain would I have a book wherein I might behold all spells and incantations, that I might raise up spirits when I please.
>
> Mephis: Here they are in this book.
>
> *Turn to them.*
>
> Faustus: Now would I have a book where I might see all characters and all planets of the heavens, that I might know their motions and dispositions.
>
> Mephis: Here they are too.
>
> *Turn to them.*
>
> Faustus: Nay, let me have one book more, and then I have done, wherein I might See all plants, herbs and trees that grow upon the earth.
>
> Mephis: Here they be.
>
> *Turn to them.*
>
> Faustus: Oh thou are deceived.
>
> Mephis: Tut I warrant thee. (2.2.170-182)

It is important that this exchange follows the signing of the deed, which ensured Faustus' commitment to study magic. The Mephistopheles in these lines appears to be different from the stage devil that the audience would expect him to continue being. He no longer thinks that it is enough for Faustus to abjure God in order to become "conjuror laureate". He takes on the role of mentor and teacher to guide Faustus through the quest that he has chosen to follow. He instructs Faustus to "peruse the book thoroughly" but also guides him repeatedly to return to it and read it when Faustus refuses to believe that all the information that he seeks is in the one book that he has received. A.D. Nuttall argues that this persistent pursuit of empirical knowledge in the play is a form of gnosis "transformed from transcendental knowledge to physical power ... [that] leads from thaumaturgy through conjuring to natural science" (59).[47] This phase of the relationship between Faustus and Mephistopheles–twenty-four years of magic before the damnation–is devoted to learning magic as a form of knowledge.

After many learned disputations with Mephistopheles, Faustus flies into the cosmos to learn all the secrets of astronomy. In Act 3 Wager reports on what Faustus exploits thus far:

> Learned Faustus,
> To know the secrets of astronomy
> Graven in the book of Jove's high firmament
> Being seated in a chariot burning bright
> Drawn by the strength of yoky dragon's necks
> He is not gone to prove cosmography. (3.1-7)

Faustus' reputation as a necromancer is only rivaled by his reputation as a scholar. At the beginning of Act 4 the Chorus steps in to speak of Faustus' fame among scholars at home after he returns from his travels: "They put forth questions of astrology,/ Which Faustus answered with such learned skill,/As they admired and wondered at his wit" (4.9-11). Mephistopheles is far from the devils and vice figures on stage in the popular English dramas. Mephistopheles is an odd devil. He fits the Christian paradigm of devilry perfectly and then he exceeds it. The devils that appear in Marlowe's play are either documented in grimoires or demonologies.[48] All except Mephistopheles who is a new devil invented specifically in the Faust story; there is no prior record of a devil named Mephistopheles before the German Faust Book. He is a literary devil whose influence on Milton's Satan is evident, but even Milton left him out from his list of subordinate devils in *Paradise Lost*. His name gives a clue to his ability to reach beyond the ironies of his role that Marlowe exploits much more than the others who told the stories of Faustus and Mephistopheles in the source texts.

In an article devoted solely to tracing the etymology of the name Mephistopheles, Julius Goebel makes two exciting suggestions.[49] The first that "according to Hebrew noun-composition *mephiz-tophel* would mean "destroyer of lies"" (149) and later from a study of fifteenth and sixteenth century magic-books that it refers to the planet Mercury:

> The spirit of the planet Mercury, or rather the demon Mercury should be called Ophiel=serpent God, is explained by the fact that Mercury-Hermes was represented during the later Hellenistic period with the caduceus.[50] The caduceus is above all the symbol of Herems Trismegistos or Maximus Mercurious, the guardian God of the magicians, alchemists and astrologers. I do not doubt for a moment that Mephistopheles is a corrupted form of Megist-Ophiel, and that Mephistopheles is originally identical with Hermes Trismegistios. (152)

In a recent essay "*Doctor Faustus* and Renaissance Hermeticism", Andrew Duxfield argues that Hermetic philosophy "attempts to reconcile the pursuit of knowledge through faith" (107).[51] He embeds Faustus' aspirations within the gnostic text of the *Corpus Hermeticum*. What Duxfield does not see or say but that can be said on the basis of Goebel's etymology of Mephistopheles is that in an ironic turn Mephistopheles alternates between being the Protestant devil and a hermetic teacher and mentor to Faustus.

The exchanges between Faustus and Mephistopheles represent Faustus as the eager and curious student who demands more from his teacher who is happy to comply. There are instances of intimate and affectionate address between the two that seems excessive of their contractual engagement. Even before he signs the pact, Faustus says, "Had I as many souls/as there be stars/I'd give them all for Mephistopheles" (1.3.104-105). Later, as he prepares to sign the pact he claims, "Lo, Mephistopheles for the love of thee/I cut mine arm..." (2.1.53-54). Mephistopheles seems to count on such affection, when he refuses to grant Faustus' wish for marriage, a sacrament that is beyond the devil's access: "If thou lovest me, think no more of it" (2.1.155).[52] Faustus often addresses Mephistopheles with the possessive 'my' and Mephistopheles promises to teach him more than Faustus even knows to ask. When Faustus asks him if he will be able to raise spirits, Mephistopheles responds with a promise of greater things: "Ay, Faustus, and do greater things than these" (2.1.87). The Hermes-Mephisto figure emerges briefly in the text to suggest a different context and a potential for the magician that is not viewed solely as the anti-thesis of religion.

Damning a Doctor of Arts: Making *Faustus* a Tragedy

The subversive crux of the play lies in the enactment of Faustus' damnation. On the surface of the play, the damnation confirms the orthodox narrative of magical transgression as punishable by eternal death. However, as the play takes apart the assumption of the oppositional relationship between magic and religion, the damnation at the end of the play is hardly free of irony and doubt. Marlowe presents Faustus' damnation as a necessity, which is not doctrinal but politic and grows out of a literal document: Faustus' written pact with the devil. In a moment of doubt when Faustus asks Mephistopheles, "Why, thinkest thou then that Faustus shall be damned?" Mephistopheles points to the freshly acquired deed of gift to say "Ay, of necessity, for here's the scroll/Wherein thou hast given they soul to Lucifer" (2.2.132-133). The force of Faustus damnation comes not from the act of conjuration but from a pact, a literal document of a deed of gift that he makes after he has conjured Mephistopheles. The pact with the devil combines the tragic and comically parodic elements of the play. Faustus cuts his arm to draw his blood for ink: "Lo Mephistopheles, for the love of thee/I cut mine arm, and with my proper blood/Assure my soul to be great Lucifer's" (2.1.53-55). But his blood congeals and Mephistopheles scurries off to fetch a chafer of coals to unfreeze the blood. "Is not thy soul thine own?" (2.2.67), which of course he knows it is not, at least not in the same way that his body is his own. It is for this reason that the devils can torture the Old Man in Act 5 physically, but cannot touch his soul. After Mephistopheles makes the blood flow again by warming it up, Faustus signs the deed with the last words spoken by Christ on the cross: *Consummatum est*, it is finished.

The literal and literary commitment to the devil is a parody of the covenant of redemption with God. If Faustus is conscious of the parody, and from his choice of words to end the bill it would seem that he is, then it devalues the pact with the devil and makes a mockery of its validity in favor of the real covenant with God. But Marlovian protagonists are propelled by the expectations of their archetype, and even though Faustus wrenches a moment of interiority with a moment of conscious parody, the parody soon turns against him. From a parodist he becomes the object of parody as the authority of Faustus' character passes on to another's hand, quite literally. As he had used his blood as ink, so his body is turned to parchment and an inscription appears on his arm "*Homo fuge*". But the writing disappears no sooner than it had appeared. "My senses are deceived, here is nothing writ/I see it plain, here in this place is writ/"*Homo fuge*!"" (2.1.77-80). It is significant that the signing of the pact with the devil is immediately followed by an instance of a ghost inscription which is substantial just like his pact with the devil only in so far as Faustus thinks it is. If this warning for Faustus to flee the devilish contract is of Godly agency then it reinforces the idea that Faustus can still flee the contract; he is not beholden to a parodied deal. But Faustus says to himself, in his third person address that makes his decisions sound both prophetic and prescriptive: "Yet Faustus shall not fly" (2.1.81).

Faustus never entirely believes that he will be damned, till as late as the end of Act 4 he comforts himself that Christ called upon a thief on the cross, thereby saving him in the very last minute.

> What art thou, Faustus, but a man condemned to die?
>
> ....
>
> Despair doth drive distrust into my thoughts
> Confound these passions with a quiet sleep
> Tush, Christ did call the thief upon the cross
> Then rest thee, Faustus, in quiet conceit. (4.1. 139-144)

Faustus may not be the only one to doubt the adequacy of the written pact to actually determine the damnation. Oddly enough Mephistopheles makes Faustus sign a second pact. It is interesting that Faustus has to make his commitment to damnation two times; it points to the possibility that there might always be a chance of his redemption. Marlowe subversion of the tale in its telling comes from moments like this when Faustus appears to have to work much harder to stay damned than repent and get grace.

Among the events that lead up to the damnation of Faustus in the last act is the entry of an Old Man who exhorts Faustus to repent. The suggestion of repentance is not a new element in the final Act of the play. Through the play we see Faustus wavering in his allegiance to the devil for instance in the soliloquy in the beginning of Act 2: "Now Faustus must thou needst be damned,/ And canst thou not be saved" (2.1.1-2). In the B-Text these lines appear as two questions instead of two statements which change the import of the lines considerably. Depending on the text being followed, this could be the crucial moment that Faustus decides to transgress without regret or it could mean that he is still debating the chances that he will escape damnation. Through the play right up to Act 5 Faustus repeatedly brings up the issues of repentance and despair. However, in Act 5 especially after the Old Man's interjection, an increased urgency and sense of suffering permeates Faustus' language. The success of the play as a tragedy depends on the audience being convinced of Faustus' suffering in Act 5. Faustus' last soliloquy demands a powerful, heart wrenching performance that successfully solicits audience sympathy:

> See, see where Christ's blood streams in the firmament!
> One drop would save my soul, half a drop. Ah, my Christ
> Ah, rend not my heart for naming of my Christ!
> Yet will I call on him... (5.2.78-81).

The teasingly proffered blood of Christ that is withheld Tantulus like makes the torture, according to Fred B. Tromly, a mocking torment of the idea of saving grace (151).[53]

As the audience commiserates with Faustus' imminent fate, Marlowe achieves a moment of unsurpassed dramatic irony where spirit and letter of the idea of repentance are wrenched chillingly apart. Faustus' genuine suffering and poignant calling out to Christ suggests that he is ready to repent; yet, in his eleventh hour speech instead of repenting, he asks for more time to repent. Earlier in the play Faustus had drawn a parallel to the Pharaoh's fate in the book of Exodus and had claimed that he could not repent because his heart was hardened (2.3.18-19). However, unlike the Pharaoh, Faustus is moved to tears, which Mephistopheles notes in lines that appear in the B-Text. Faustus' spiritual state is presented as a dilemma:

> Accursed Faustus, where is mercy now?
> I do repent, and yet I do despair.
> Hell strives with grace for conquest in my breast.
> What shall I do to shun the snares of death? (5.1.63-65)

Repentance and despair are paired up with hell and grace to formulate the options that Faustus has, even at this stage. It is worth noticing that Faustus seems to be in a spiritual dilemma that is theologically dubious both for the Catholics and the Protestants. According to Catholic doctrine, if Faustus is willing to repent he can deserve God's grace that can save him from damnation. According to the Protestant doctrine of both Luther and Calvin, the individual lacks free will so any inclination towards repentance and willingness for mercy is already a sign that God's grace is at work. Since God's grace does not work in halves, if Faustus feels grace in his heart he should logically be saved in the end. Thus Faustus' claim that he can repent and despair at the same time, or that he can feel a contest between hell and grace presents the audience with the dilemma of seeing the suffering of a protagonist whose damnation is not doctrinally necessary but dictated by the necessity of the Faust story as a cautionary tale. According to Clare Harrraway, "Faustus has always been free to be saved...Faustus is eventually damned not because he has signed away his soul but because he believes he cannot be saved." (47).[54] Faustus even cries out, "O I'll leap up to my God! Who pulls me down?" (5.2.77).

What pulls him down is the orthodoxy of belief that a magician cannot be saved. For as long as it is possible to accord Faustus some agency, choice and free will, it is possible to argue that he brings the tragedy upon himself because of his sins. However, a crucial admission by Mephistopheles that appears only in the B-Text makes Faustus' death akin to sacrifice not punishment.

In the A-Text at the end of Faustus' speech the devils come and leave the stage with him even as Faustus promises to burn his books and calls out painfully to his one constant companion in the play, "Ah! Mephistopheles" (5.2.124). The B-Text elaborates this ending, dwelling on the spectacle of his death preceded by a crucial admission from Mephistopheles.

> I do confess it, Faustus, and rejoice.
> 'Twas I that, when thou wert i' the way to heaven
> Damned up the passage. When thou took'st the book
> To view the Scriptures, then I turned the leaves
> And led thine eye. (B5.2. 97-101)

Mephistopheles' admission takes away all agency and semblance of free will from Faustus; all Faustus' moments of doubt and wavering appear heroic in the face of a pre-determined damnation. Faustus' damnation does not establish the unquestioned authority of religion it questions it. Alan Sinfield's argues that "*Faustus* is ...*entirely ambiguous*...the theological implications are radically and provocatively indeterminate" (176).[55] The B-Text at the end of the play Faustus' limbs are torn asunder and scattered on the stage as a mark of the devil's handiwork. Faustus' death appears as an over determined excess in the B-Text, unlike the poignant "Ah! Mephistopheles" at the end of the A-Text.[56]

The Choric speech that ends the play compliments the one with which the play had begun. The last line of the Chorus's epilogue exhorts the "wise" and the "forward wits" to not "practice more than the heavenly power permits":

> Faustus is gone: regard his hellish fall,
> Whose fiendful fortune may exhort the wise
> Only to wonder at unlawful things,

> Whose deepness doth entice such forward wits
> To practice more than heavenly power permits. (4-9)

These last five lines of the epilogue appear without variation in the A-and B-Texts. Magic is unnamed but described as the unlawful practice that is in excess of what is permissible by heavenly powers. The ambiguity of the use of "heavenly" as referring to astrology and divine power noted in the opening Choric speech is repeated again in the epilogue. But in a play that just damned a magician for confusing the meaning of "heavenly" it is curious that in its final pronouncement the Chorus alludes to once again, the same ambiguous conflation of religion and magic. The equivocation with the term heavenly is only one example for the Chorus' subtle but consistent manipulation of its function to declaim the moral behind Faustus' damnation. The Chorus' speech suggests awareness in the text about an external censorious and censoring authority that the play is negotiating.

In that context perhaps the "heavenly powers" do not refer to God at all but to the earthly deputies who claim to have authority sanctioned by the heavens. It relocates the turf for the struggle between religion and magic from it metaphysical status to being a worldly contest for power. The last line of the play is hardly decisive in its condemnation of magic. The Chorus identifies those that are likely to exceed or disregard the bounds of permission: "the wise" and "the forward wits". The word "such" would indicate that "forward wits" describes the ambitious nature of the wise, thus detracting from the quality of their wisdom. However, the phrase "forward wits" could also refer to the university wits, such as Marlowe himself was, as a group of people who did more than just wonder at magic from a distance. The "forwards wits" could dabble in magic by questioning its epistemological status and by questioning the narrative that religion provided about magic, for instance in the way that the performance Marlowe's play just did.

Conclusion

The three strands of my argument in this chapter–the particular history of the way theodicy developed the conceptual framework of how evil is to be understood in relation to good; how censorship around the stage representation of what was considered heretical impacts the publication history of the play text of *Faustus*; and how the re-reading of both the chief devil Mephistopheles and the doctrine of grace upends the simple narratives of damnation–aims to re-read this literary classic of Marlowe's for the complexities of ways of knowing. It is not enough to read the multiple narratives of the Faust story for an uncomplicated opposition between religion and magic. The dramatic representation of magic in Marlowe's *Faustus* serves to evoke the dominant narrative of magic as the demonic perversion of religion. It highlights the politics of Reformation religions that projected a narrative of negative inversion onto the discourse of magic. More importantly the play also serves as a specific example of the intellectual engagement with that narrative. The specificity of the play, as an individual instance of an encounter with the dominant narrative, produces innumerable fissures and excesses that the dominant narrative aims to but cannot contain. Consequently *Faustus* is an important text that reveals conflicting and potentially subversive narratives that are also available and at play.

As a tragedy, growing out of the Christian homiletic plays, *Faustus* is constrained by the demands of its genre that requires a tragic ending for its protagonist although Marlowe comes close enough to indicate that the tragedy is ultimately gratuitous. However, it would be a mistake to consider Faustus' tragic end merely a matter of generic requirement. Practical magic was persecuted and the consequences for the practitioners were not unlike Faustus' fate. The play touches upon a genuine anxiety about the inability to find a vocabulary for knowledge about the empirical world in a language outside the discursive language of religion.

In this chapter I discussed that Faustus not only discovers the limits in the language of knowledge but he discovers that the limits are culturally constructed. Magic as spectacle in the courts, for instance, provides occasion to neutralize some of the vicious opposition to it. The play briefly opens up the world of empirical knowledge as the underlying reward for venturing into unsanctioned territories of knowledge discourse. However, it is a fleeting vision in Faustus' world. Faustus is still poised between Icarus and Eve and is damned either way. Faustus does not escape the devil but points to a narrative that is struggling to find a voice. Icarus' wings still need a vocabulary that does not automatically only cast it in narratives of downfall. The technology of Icarus' wings is played out in Shakespeare's Ariel in the next chapter. The narrative of early modern magic is about encountering the limits in the vocabulary of experience and finding a new language to accommodate and express it.

NOTES

1. For early Christian theodicy and the development of the devil in the New Testament see Jeffery Burton Russell's The Devil: Perceptions of Evils from Antiquity to Primitive Christianity. Also see Darren Oldridge, *The Devil in Early Modern England.*
2. See Keith Thomas *Religion and the Decline of Magic* and Richard Kieckhefer's *Magic in the Middle Ages.* Possibly the two foundational texts for early modern magic studies.
3. Eamon Duffy recounts the dubious distinction between prayer and magic.
4. In *Spectacles of Strangeness: Imperialism, Alienation and Marlowe*, Bartels argues that the magician was the alien at home whose inscrutability as a European subject was a result of an imposition of the transgressive subjectivity from without.
5. Bevington and Rassmussen.
6. See Jonathan Dollimore *Radical Tragedy.*
7. See John Cox. *The Devil and the Sacred in English Drama.*
8. See Nathan Johnstone. "The Protestant Devil: The Experience of Temptation in Early Modern England".
9. *Thinking with Demons: The Idea of Witchcraft in Early Modern Europe* is Clark's seminal work on demonologies. In it he elucidates how "contrariety" coming from religious discourse becomes a crucial component of decoding the language and sense of demonic magic. The through line of the evolution of evil from Augustine to Calvin that I draw here is partly in debt to Clark.

10. All quotes from Augustine are from Marcus Dods Tr. *The City of God by Saint Augustine.*
11. All quotes from Aquinas are from Jean Oesterle. Tr. *St. Thomas Aquinas On Evil.*
12. All quotes from Calvin are from Henry Bevridge. Esq. Tr. *Institutes of Christian Religion by John Calvin.*
13. All quotes from *The* Malleus are from Montague Summer's Tr. Ed. *The Malleus Maleficarum of Heinrich Kramer and James Sprenger.* New York: Dover Publications, 1971.
14. And S. Augustine in the *Enchiridion:* "In all things good and evil consists the admirable beauty of the universe. So that what is said to be evil is well ordained, and kept in its due place commends more highly that which is good; for things good are more pleasing and laudable when compared with bad. S. Thomas also refutes the opinions of those who say that although God has no wish for evil (since no creature seeks for evil, either in its natural, or its animal or its intellectual appetite, which is the will, whose object is good), yet He is willing that evil should exist and be done, not wishes it not done; and this is good for the perfecting of the universe. Why is it erroneous to say that God wishes evil to be and to be done...?(68)."
15. All quotes from King James' Demonology are from James Craigie and Alexander Law Ed. *Minor Prose Works of King James VI and I.*
16. Clark develops this idea in Chapters 4-7 in *Thinking with the Demons.*
17. In *A History of Magic and Experimental Science* Vol. 1, Lynn Thorndike notes the earliest mention of Faustus in a religious romance known as the Pseudo-Clementine literature popularly known as *Recognitions.* Pope Clement I alludes to the Biblical story (Acts 8.8-24) of Simon Magus, a magician from Samaria. In *Recognitions* Faustus is Clement's father. Simon Magus uses a magic juice to change the likeness of Faustus' face to look like his own so that he could escape by leaving Faustus to be killed by the mobs who thought him to be the magician. Luckily for Faustus, St. Peter intervenes and is able to reverse the magic and return Faustus' own face to him. Simon Magus's association

with Marlowe's Faust is central to A.D. Nuttall's reading of a Gnostic reading of the play.

18. In Book V, Ch. 14. *The Confessions of St. Augustine* Translated by Rex Warner.
19. This Faustus liked to be known by a rather pompous title "Magister Georgius Sabellicus, Fasutus Junior, fons necromanticorum, astrologus, magus secundus, agromanticus, pyromanticus". Marlowe's Faustus has a similar moment of elevated self-regard when he successfully conjures Mephistopheles for the first time.
20. See John Henry Jones' Introduction to *Faustus and the Censors* and The Introduction to the Revels edition to for sources and materials associated with the historical George Faustus.
21. Quoted in John Henry Jones as well as the Revels Edition.
22. The German Faust Book considerably embellished and expanded the story that appeared with a preface by the Lutheran propagandist Johann Spies. He stressed the purpose of publishing such a story:

    "The multifarious exploits of Dr. Johannes Faustus, the famous sorcerer and black magician, have been the talk of all Germany for many a year. Everywhere at parties and social gatherings, there is great enquiry for a biography of this Faustus... I have often wondered that, as yet, no one has presented this terrible tale in an orderly fashion and published it as a warning to the whole of Christendom" (13). Spies testifies to the popularity of the story and his editorial intervention in presenting the tale in an "orderly fashion". Spies would have had to deal with the disorderliness of a story that was still growing- as popular legend and in its reprehensible moral disorder (). The book had a sensational reception, was translated into other languages including English, and had to be reprinted five times before the end of the year. Augustine Lercheimer, a student of Melancthon, published Christian Synopsis of Magic (1597) in order to point out wrong facts in Spies' version of the story: such as the fact that Faustus is reported to be a doctor of divinity at Wittenberg which placed unearned laurels on Faustus. Lercheimer realized that Spies' ordering of the story might not serve the purpose of warning effectively enough. The "multifarious exploits" of the magician was attractive enough to sabotage the moral of the story.

23. This is necessary since there is no consensus on the composition dates for EFB or Marlowe's play, some possible dates suggest that Marlowe's play is earlier than the date of the published translation, which would make it difficult to argue that he dramatized the EFB.
24. William Empson. *Faustus and the Censor: The English Faust-book and Marlowe's Doctor Faustus*. Ed. John Henry Jones. See especially Chapters 3 and 5.
25. Editors have struggled to find the rationale for the additional scenes in the B Text, the logic of truncation in the A Text, and finally have attempted to answer the difficult question of which text is more authentic to what Marlowe and his supposed collaborator originally wrote. The earlier critical trend to argue the virtual merits of one version over the other was followed by the editorial practice of creating composite editions of the play where editors wrangled over what lines were to be kept and what had to be relegated to the appendix or the footnotes, till it was convincingly and powerfully argued that the two versions need to be seen as individual texts, written to embody and address distinct issues and ideologies. See Michael Warren, "*Doctor Faustus*: The Old Man and the Text" and Leah Marcus, "Textual Instability and Ideological Difference: The Case of *Doctor Faustus*".
26. The variations in the two texts have inspired a rich tradition of Faustus scholarship around the questions of early modern print and book history which account for the material impact of the idea of devilish magic. Two of the newer essays that pursue this line of enquiry are Sarah Wall-Randell's "*Doctor Faustus* and the Printer's Devil"and Georgia E. Brown's "The Other Black Arts: *Doctor Faustus* and the Inky Worlds of Printing and Writing" in *Doctor Faustus: A Critical Guide*. Ed. Sara Munson Deats.
27. William Empson, A.D. Nuttall, and Andrew Duxfield develop this line of criticism where Faustus' apparent academic arrogance is located within the alternate Gnostic and Hermetic traditions that were not opposed to Christianity but their language for the approximation of divinity did not share the Protestant sense of humility born out of the despair of the first fall.

28. "All these complaints [about the inconsistencies in the play] are met by one explanation: the play was disrupted by an explosion of censorship. There is a real likeness to the ruin left by volcanic action, where a specially hard pillar of rock often marks the place where the hole used to be, through which the molten lava forced its way. The insistence in the B-Text to send Faustus to Hell marks the source of its trouble; in Marlowe's play he had escaped." (44) *Faustus and the Censors.*
29. All quotation from the play by act, scene and line numbers are from the A-Text of Bevington and Rasmussen's *Doctor Faustus.* Quotations from their B-Text are identified specifically whenever they appear.
30. Bartels 129.
31. For instance, see Susan Snyder, "The Left Hand of God: Despair in Medieval and Renaissance traditions".
32. By David Wooton in his Introduction to his edition of *Doctor Faustus.*
33. Martin Luther, "Bondage of the Will" (187). *Martin Luther: Selections from his Writings.* Ed. John Dillenberger.
34. Richard Kieckhefer, *Magic in the Middle Ages.*
35. David Ormerod and Christopher Wortham Eds. Dr. Faustus The A-Text and Gareth Roberts "Necromantic Books: Christopher Marlowe, Doctor Faustus and Agrippa of Nettesheim" in *Christopher Marlowe and English Renaissance Culture.* Also See "Marlowe and the Metaphysics of Magicians" in *Constructing Christopher Marlowe.* Eds. J.A Downie and J.T Parnell.
36. Roberts, "Necromantic Books: Christopher Marlowe, Doctor Faustus and Agrippa of Nettesheim".
37. Bevington and Rasmussen 26. n16-23.
38. Roberts, "Marlowe and the Metaphysics of Magicians," p. 67
39. David Bevington. *From Mankind to Marlowe: Growth of Structure in Popular Drama of Tudor England.*
40. Scholars, such as Douglas Cole, who read the play as "thoroughly Christian in conception and import" read the entertainment scenes as the thorough debasing of the man who wanted to be a mighty god. (194, 216). *Suffering and Evil in the Plays of Christopher Marlowe.*

41. In *Placing the Plays of Christopher Marlowe: Fresh Cultural Contexts.*
42. Frank Kermode Ed. *Shakespeare's The Tempest.*
43. Catherine Belsey. "Doctor Faustus and Knowledge in Conflict" in *Marlowe* Ed. Avraham Oz. In this elegantly argued essay, Belsey suggests that Faustus' tragedy is in being "poised between two problematics, a discursive knowledge which does not lead to power, and an empirical knowledge which is not yet certain of its own project or its authority" (170).
44. Hilary Gatti. *Renaissance Drama of Knowledge: Giordano Bruno in England.*
45. O'Brian, Margaret 'Christian Belief in Dr. Faustus'.
46. From the *Compendium of Theology* 188.
47. A.D. Nuttall, "Marlowe: Raising the Devil" in *The Alternative Trinity: Gnostic Heresy in Marlowe, Milton, and Blake.*
48. Hand written manuals of magic that were consecrated and passed down from master to pupil. These were usually not published. These manuals contained spells, charms, protocols for the magician as well as astrological and planetary signs with the symbols for their accompanying spirits. They also list names demons and spirits with descriptions of their specialization so that the appropriate demon is conjured for the job at hand.
49. 'The Etymology of Mephistopheles'.
50. The wand carried by an ancient Greek or Roman herald. *spec.* The fabled wand carried by Hermes or Mercury as the messenger of the Gods; usually represented with two serpents twined round it. The OED documents its earliest use in English by Spenser.
51. Andrew Duxfield. "*Doctor Faustus* and Renaissance Hermeticism" in *Doctor Faustus a Critical Guide.*
52. Ian McAdam reads homoerotic passion between Mephistopheles and Faustus to be in keeping with the early modern association of sorcery with sodomy but also sees it as alienating Faustus from his natural world (93) in *Magic and Masculinity in Early Modern English Drama.*
53. Fred. B. Tromly. *Playing with Desire: Christopher Marlowe and the Art of Tantalization.*
54. Clare Harraway. *Re-citing Marlowe.*

55. Alan Sinfield. "Reading Faustus' God" in *Marlowe* New Casebooks.
56. In *Faustus and the Censor* William Empson reads this moment not as Faustus succumbing to his fate but as escaping it. "Nothing happens except that... he dies in the arms of his deceitful friend with immense relief, also gratitude, surprise, love, forgiveness, and exhaustion. It is the happiest death in all of drama" (122).

CHAPTER 2

Magical Theatricality in Shakespeare's *The Tempest*

This chapter explores the relationship between magic and theatricality in early modern drama in the context of an increasingly intelligible epistemology of the mechanical arts. I hope to demonstrate the inter-connectedness of the discourses of magic, theatricality, and the mechanical arts and tease out the implications of their overlap for the English Renaissance stage. Shakespeare's *The Tempest* (1611), well known for its meta-theatricality, simultaneously engages attention to itself as a representation and to the semiotic and mechanical processes of its theatrical representation. Prospero's "Art" suggestively but ambiguously consists of magic and theater; instead of reading one as a metaphor for the other, as is a common enough practice amongst critics of the play, I will read the play for ways in which theater held a stake in the social, religious and intellectual broils that involved early modern magic.

In the previous chapter, I argued that Marlowe's Faustus is caught in a linear narrative that progresses from a diabolic pact to damnation. Faustus' attempts to distract himself from damnation are ultimately futile for his mortal life though its significance for readers and audiences far exceeds the embodied action on the stage. Unlike Faustus, Shakespeare's Prospero is devoted to producing an alternative narrative of magic designed to deflect the damaging charges of conjuration. Early modern scholarly magicians often found themselves accused of diabolic magic that they refuted, some less successfully than others. In this chapter, I am particularly interested in the narrative of explanation as a way of knowing, and as a way of working with ambivalence in a way that deflects accusations of conjuration.

Critics have characterized Prospero's magic as black or white and therefore as either malevolent or beneficial.[1] I argue that Prospero makes use of the ambivalence between black and white magic to produce himself as a magician. Underlying his triumph in Act 5 is a possibility that his position at the end of the play is much more vulnerable to implications of malevolent magic than is customary to associate with Prospero. If the play were to allow such a reading where Prospero finds himself cornered and forced to explain himself, what could Prospero say? In this chapter, I read the play as a probable narrative of explanation that Prospero might offer his auditors. Prospero's art strides the world of early modern magic and early modern science. His social fortune and intellectual predicament places him somewhere between the English magician John Dee and the purported progenitor of the scientific revolution Francis Bacon.

John Dee (1527-1609), long recognized as the historical prototype for Prospero, was a magician in Queen Elizabeth's court who faced accusations of conjuration. He lost favor in court and found himself especially disadvantaged when King James succeeded to the throne. He spent the last years of his life writing apologies in defense of himself and his art. As Dee was losing favor, Francis Bacon (1561-1626), found his fortunes rising in the same court; he dedicated *The Advancement of Learning* (1605) to King James where he explicitly denounced magicians, of the sort that Dee was, and classified the different branches of learning purged of their magical past. This seemingly straightforward narrative of progression from magic to science is, however, complicated by its very details.[2] The first time Dee was accused of malevolent magic was in 1547 when, as reader in Trinity College, he created a flying mechanical scarab for a theatrical production of Aristophanes' *Peace*.[3] This suggests that things mechanical looked magical. It also suggests that theater is especially predisposed to thrive on the epistemological ambivalence of magic and mechanics. What complicates the picture further is that Bacon's overt dismissal of magic in the *Advancement* is accompanied by a covert recuperation of magic as a mechanical art.[4]

In the early modern period, theater was considered a mechanical art.[5] Henry Turner describes theater as a "practical epistemology, a way of coming to knowledge through representation" where the "mode of representation is nothing less than a process of doing and making" (27).[6] Similarly, Elizabeth Spiller emphasizes that *The Tempest* both depicts and participates in the transition from one form of knowledge making to another (25).[7] However, a particular paradox of theatrical mechanics is that while mechanical and technical knowledge that both Turner and Spiller describe is meant to demystify physical phenomena and rationalize wonder, theatrical mechanics are meant to produce wonder and amazement–the effects of magic. Technical and mechanical knowledge in early modern England was only tenuously beginning to emerge as a distinct empirical discipline that would eventually be completely distanced from its origins in the ranks of Renaissance magic.[8] In the early seventeenth century it is worth pausing on the moment when the inscrutability of technology and its secular context cannot yet be taken for granted.

Instead of presenting a neat transition from one system of knowledge to another, *The Tempest* dramatizes the inter-connectedness of newly forming discourses and epistemologies that Dee and Bacon exemplify. It is in this context that *The Tempest* lends itself to a re-reading. I propose to read the theatricality of *The Tempest* in the context of an ongoing process of forging legitimacy for magic in terms of mechanics. In this chapter, I would like to argue that *The Tempest* makes visible the invisible mechanical aspects of theater and reflects on theatrical effects as a response to the contextual debates on the ontology of magic and the status of the mechanical arts. The play participates in a current and topical tension between the empirical explicability, for instance, of theatrical production and the necessary inexplicable wonder of its effects.

The Myth of the Magus: John Dee, Francis Bacon and Prospero

Francis Yates is one of the earliest critics to have mined the connection between Dee and Prospero thereby contributing to what has come to be known as the Renaissance myth of the magus. In her book, she describes the fate of this much maligned English magician and sees the character of Prospero as a defense of John Dee: "Her [Queen Elizabeth's] philosopher, the white magician doctor Dee, is defended in Prospero, the good and learned conjuror, who had managed to transport his library to the island" (160).[9] Yates is referring to Dee's return to England in 1589 after a six-year sojourn in the Polish court where he had gone with his scryer Edward Kelly to practice angel calling. He returned to find his library in Mortlake pillaged and his reputation tarnished in the English court. In a section entitled "Disgrace and Failure", Yates describes Dee's return as follows:

> Shunned and isolated, Dee was also confronted with a growing witch-hunt against him. The cry of "conjuror" has always been sporadically raised but in the old days the Queen and Leicester had protected his studies. Now the enemies were increasingly vocal. Dee felt obliged to defend himself in a letter to the Archbishop of Canterbury. (89)

Yates re-creates the scenario of hostility surrounding Dee's return to England fuelled by, among other things, John Foxe's mention of Dee as a conjuror in the early editions of *Actes and Monuments.*[10] Dee's reception in England testifies that neither James's court nor early modern Anglican England held an unproblematic view of a magician-scholar. Since the post-colonial debunking of Prospero's politics when Prospero's sway is no longer impressively intimidating for his readers and audiences, perhaps, it is easier to see an alternative to Yates' view that Prospero is a "good and learned conjuror" who lends credibility to Dee.

The historical scenario that Yates creates could be used to argue the opposite of her claim: an association with John Dee undermines and destabilizes the figure of Prospero as a magician on the English stage. The connection that I want to highlight between Dee and

Prospero comes from the latter part of Dee's life that scholars have not connected to Prospero. Dee made several fervent attempts to explain himself and his art to, among others, the Archbishop and King James. In 1599 Dee petitioned the Archbishop of Canterbury in "A letter, containing a most briefe discourse apologeticall with a plaine demonstration, and feruent protestation, for the lawfull, sincere, very faithfull and Christian course, of the philosophicall studies and exercises, of a certaine studious gentleman: an ancient seruant to her most excellent Maiesty royall".[11] The address of his letter makes it clear that he is attempting to redress some wrongful allegations. Dee calls his letter an "apology" or defense of the "studies and exercises" that he identifies as "lawful" and "philosophical". He uses his connection to the authority of the Queen Elizabeth as a subliminal leverage for his suit. Dee begins his letter with a strategic humility: "Most humbly and hartily I craue your Graces pardon, if I offende any thing, to send, or present vnto your Graces hand, so simple a discourse as this is..." He goes on to describe the "simplicity of his discourse" as: "to make some part of my former studies, and studious exercises (within and for these 46, yeeres last past, vsed and continued) to be first knowne and discouered vnto your Grace... afterwardes, the same to be permitted to come to publique view". Dee divides his audience into two distinct groups: The Archbishop and the others in power whom he addresses directly because they have the authority to influence public opinion and then the general public who need to be ultimately appeased. In the play, Prospero also adopts this strategy of presenting his case differently to different groups of his audience.

In a letter sent to King James I on June 5, 1604, Dee intensifies the language of humility and self-deprecation: "In most humble and lamentable manner beseecheth your Royall Maiestie, your Highnesse most distressed Seruant, Ionh Dee".[12] Dee is straightforward in his suit; he seeks the King's intervention to be cleared of the charges of conjuration. He ascribes the slander to rumor that has continued in print. He also mentions his own attempts at publishing diverse and earnest apologies against it which had clearly not turned the tide of public opinion.[13] Towards the end of his letter he makes the dramatic move to seek the King's attention by offering himself for a witchcraft trial and punishment of death if he was found guilty. His suit ends on a final appeal to justice and mercy:

> So long, hath his vtter vndo | ing, by little and little, beene most vniustly, compassed. The Almightie and most mercifull God, alwayes direct, your Maiesties royall heart, in his wayes of Iustice and Mercy.

It is significant that Dee's apologies make strategic use of the rhetoric of humility, supplication and debility. A similar tone of humility, with calls to justice and mercy, is audible in Prospero's abjuration speech and the epilogue that is meant to serve a purpose not unlike Dee's. The rhetoric of humility is meant to soften the readers and prepare them to be sympathetic and more receptive to his explanation. In his letter to the Archbishop, Dee clarifies the nature of his work. He seeks to assure the Christian readers that he has been a faithful and constant student in his study of "the most meruailous frame of the *whole World*, philosophically viewed, and circumspectly wayed, numbered, and measured (according to the talent, & gift of God, from aboue alotted, for his diuine purposes effecting)." Dee emphasizes his faithfulness as a Christian and then outlines his method for understanding the world in very quantifiable concepts of weight and numbers. Dee stresses the empirical aspect of his study and qualifies his work in explicitly material, quantifiable, mathematical and mechanical terms which is well represented by his Preface to *Euclid's Elements of Geometry* wherein is "disclosed certain new Secrets, Mathematical and Mech[...]icall".[14]

Dee scholars have long wrangled over how to account for all of Dee's magico-scholarly pursuits. Recent Dee scholars have dispelled the "distorting effects" of the "myth of the magus" while re-inventing him as an eclectic scholar with a "schizophrenic" range of interests whose contributions to his age was that he made "knowledge–especially new forms of knowledge a political commodity...".[15] Much of Dee's scientific contributions in navigation, cartography and mechanics have been acknowledged. However it must also be acknowledged that for Dee mathematics and mechanics were still "a maruailous Arte" not base as things natural and but partaking the mystique of the supernatural which gives the practitioners powers above the ordinary: "Thus can the mathematical minde, deale speculatiuely in his own Arte: and by good meanes, Mount above the clouds and sterres [...] And thirdly, he can, by order, Descend to frame Naturall things, to wonderfull vses..." ("Preface"). Forced by social circumstances, Dee attempted to but could not ultimately disambiguate his magical scholarship such that it completely satisfied his early modern evaluators.

Dee is not the only scholar magician to have had to explain himself. Agrippa denied magical scholarship as vanity and Bruno met his fate on the stake. Dee's recourse to mathematics and mechanics as a way to deflect attention away from angel calling directs attention towards the shifting and expanding paradigms of knowledge. Francis Bacon's clarion call for the "mechanical arts" in the *Advancement of Learning* responds to and furthers Dee's project in a way that would at first glance seem counter-intuitive. Although they would appear to be on the opposite ends of the spectrum of early modern thought, there is a language of overlap between Dee's project–a scholar magician seeking immunity from charges of conjuration–and Bacon's project to rid "natural philosophy" of the confusions of magical discourse.

Ronald Levao has argued that Bacon's projected interest in distinguishing between true and false knowledge draws its energies from the instabilities in the late Renaissance culture and thought.[16] Although Bacon often presents, what Levao calls, blunt dichotomies, it is possible to see his scientific realism in continuation with the magical thought of John Dee. Francis Bacon's objective in *The Advancement of Learning* is to separate natural philosophy from theology and the natural from the supernatural.[17] In doing so, Bacon co-opts natural magic in his exposition of the "mechanical arts". Bacon's reclassification of knowledge shifts the context and vocabulary of magic. Instead of a default evocation of spiritual damnation, magic is subsumed in a branch of learning that emphasizes utility, practicality and objective protocols that are distanced from the subjective behavior of individual practitioners.

Dee seeks immunity from charges of transgressive learning (conjuration) by emphasizing his contribution to philosophy, mathematics and mechanics; Bacon seeks to develop methods and fields of learning–such as the mechanical arts–that are not constantly discredited.

According to Bacon, the abused and misunderstood category of natural magic is a crucial component of the "operative" aspect of natural philosophy. He finds that "vanity and superstition" corrupts the wisdom and prudence of magic. He is virulent in his attack on the practices of natural magic in his day.

> ...as for Natural Magic whereof now there is mention in books, containing certain credulous and superstitious conceits and observations of sympathies and antipathies, hidden properties, and some frivolous experiment, strange rather by disguisement than in themselves, it is far differing in the truths of nature from such a knowledge as we acquire. (96)

The "vanity and superstition" of magic comes from a language of "conceits" and "hidden properties" so that magical "observations" and "experiments" confound the truths of nature. But the pivot of the passage is not his sound dismissal of magic but the non-restrictive clause–"strange rather by disguisement than in themselves". It indicates that Bacon does not see magic as inherently estranged from truth but made enigmatic by its practitioners. He attributes the "error and vanity" to "...the great professors themselves [who] have sought to veil over and conceal by enigmatical writings, and referring to auricular traditions and such other devices, to save the credit of impostures" (29). He concludes that "true Natural Magic, which is the great liberty and latitude of operation" can be useful if we "incline not to vanities" (97). Bacon abstracts the concept of the "liberty and latitude of operations" from the disciplines of Natural Magic and recasts it as systematized "experiment", and makes it central to his own method for producing knowledge about nature from nature.[18]

Experiments, according to Bacon, are the "trials and vexations of art" that force nature to reveal its true characteristics. Natural philosophers engaged in the mechanical arts employ such experiments to create a systematized body of knowledge that is transparent, transferable and a bridge between the "speculative" and "operative" aspects of Natural philosophy:

> But if my judgment be of any weight, the use of history mechanical is of all others the most radical and fundamental towards natural philosophy ... [It will be effective] by a connection and transferring observation from one art to the use of another ...[And] it will give more true and real illumination concerning causes and axioms that is hitherto attained. For like a man's disposition is never well known till be crossed...; so the passages and variation of nature cannot appear so fully in the liberty of nature as in the trials and vexations of art. (71-72)

Exceptional circumstances reveal the truths about nature and experiments are a contrived production of those exceptional circumstances. Bacon is condescending towards the natural magicians such as the alchemists because their discoveries are accidental.[19] But as Michael Witmore points out, the accidental nature of discovery is the basis of the Baconian experiment.

> The Baconian program of experimentally vexing and artificially constraining nature, [...] can be understood as an appropriation or imitation of what nature does spontaneously with the Forms in unusual circumstances. Such a relationship to chance and accident that is significantly more complex than the one suggested by the metaphor of mastering Fortune through audacious action. (113-4)[20]

Witmore demonstrates that despite the rhetoric of dominating Fortune, Bacon's method imitates and is therefore indebted to the method of chance and Fortune's operations as the "real tutors of discovery" (129). This argument could also be extended to Bacon's overt critique of the methods of natural magic that are subtly belied by Bacon's own contribution of a rhetoric that allowed for the work of natural magic to be continued in a space that did not invite accusations of spiritual transgression and damnation.

By co-opting magic in mechanics, Bacon is able to disambiguate the tangled discourse of magical and spiritual learning better than

John Dee. He stresses the need for explanations that are consistent and drawn from processes that are standard and transparent. Bacon's method draws attention away from the practitioner to the practice of science itself. Dee's apologies are geared towards a personal vindication that depends on the vindication of his work as aspects of natural philosophy; Bacon's treatise vindicates natural philosophy by seeking to make it an impersonal, methodical and systematic field of knowledge. It would be a misrepresentation of Bacon's works to claim that his stated project is in any way a conscious recuperation of natural magic, but that is certainly the default. Bacon is able to depersonalize and distance the practice from the practitioner; whereas, Dee in his self-referential apologies could only make himself and the calumny against his person the locus of his arguments. As discussed earlier, Dee inverts the *ad hominem* by claiming the innocence of his work by his willingness to stand the trial reserved for witches to prove the innocence of his person. Bacon's polemics on learning could be read as unpacking Dee's strategy to seek refuge in the labels of "philosopher", "mathematician" and "mechanicien".

Elizabeth Spiller sees the Baconian new science, mediated by the knowledge making practical arts, as crucial to the early modern epistemology of knowledge that challenged the older Aristotelian paradigm of knowledge.[21] She emphasizes the Baconian use of the deliberate and artificial creation of accidents to simulate reality as an important method in the production of new knowledge. What scholasticism declared monstrous or miraculous, early modern epistemology saw as an occasion to gain insight about the nature. In her reading of *The Tempest*, Spiller sees knowledge as the end of Prospero's art; while his contrivances provide the mechanism by which characters reveal their true purpose and nature, his "ultimate concern is to educate the second generation into better forms of knowledge" (26). She reads Prospero's changing relation to knowledge traditions as enacting *The Tempest*'s break with scholasticism. According to Spiller, as a scholar in the tradition of the liberal arts in Milan, Prospero did not see his knowledge as practice even to the extent that he neglected his Ducal responsibilities. On the island, he learns that "knowledge must be used if it is to exist because knowledge cannot be abstracted from the human world" (35).

My reading of the play is indebted to Spiller's positioning of Baconian practical epistemology in the play. But Spiller does not quite identify Prospero's magic that is neither entirely Aristotelian nor quite fully Baconian as the historical Dr. Dee's situation also demonstrates. My reading of the play does not assume a clear narrative split between magic and science that Prospero strides confidently and easily. I hope to dwell instead on Prospero's recognition of the constraints that magic puts on him and demonstrates his attempt to reinvent himself, like John Dee but perhaps with a better possibility of success in his appropriation of the Baconian language. In my reading, Prospero is plagued with doubts and ambiguities and is less in charge of educating the other characters than he is invested in the process of inventing a coherent narrative about himself and his work.

The Tempest is a narrative of Prospero's self-justification that reflects Dee's discomfiting situation of being forced into a place where he has to explain his work. The form of that explanation is influenced by the Baconian reinvention of knowledge. The crisis of Prospero's situation is apparent in the concluding section of the play. Act 5 is usually read for the fruition of Prospero's "project". But the final act also consolidates and foregrounds the growing unease about magic that had begun with Miranda's reproachful lament after the opening tempest and had continued to be mutedly voiced by Ariel and Caliban through the play. Here is what Alonso has to say to Prospero once he is freed of the magic spell:

> This is as strange a maze as e'er men trod;
> And there is in this business more than nature
> Was ever conduct of: some oracle
> Must rectify our knowledge. (5.1.241-244)[22]

Prospero has, in the course of the play, "charmed", "justled", "enchanted" and otherwise wreaked havoc with the reason and sanity of a group of people who are his enemies. Among them is

Alonso, the King of Naples, whose wishes will enable or jeopardize Prospero's return to Milan. Once Prospero is satisfied with the extent of his enemies' torment, he frees them from his charms. His befuddled visitors know that they have suffered but are unaware of how it came about or who is responsible for it. Here Alonso wants to know what happened but is already sure that it could not have been anything natural. He seeks more than an explanation; he asks for a rectification of knowledge that Prospero cannot afford to take lightly. In Act 5, it appears that Prospero succeeds in exacting his revenge by inflicting severe psychological trauma on his enemies. He also regains his dukedom and arranges his daughter's marriage with the Prince of Naples, except that there is at least one potential roadblock in the plan. Could he tell the King and his crew that his magic was responsible for the tempest that shipwrecked them and for their every other suffering on the island since? Would not such an admission jeopardize his return to Milan as the rightful Duke?

As John Dee's historical precedent suggests, Prospero finds himself in the difficult but perhaps not entirely un-anticipated position of providing a convincing narrative that deflects witchcraft accusations. After all, even Gonzalo who is completely sympathetic to Prospero is frightened of everything that has happened: "All torment, trouble, wonder, and amazement/Inhabits here: some heavenly power guide us/Out of this fearful country!" (5.1.104-6). Prospero can only be aware that it would be rare to find a forgiving and receptive audience for his magic, much less in those who have just experienced its rough end. To soothe the gullible Gonzalo, Prospero puts the blame on the island itself: "You do yet taste/Some subtleties o' the isle, that will not let you/Believe things certain" (5.1.123-25). However, he knows that this explanation is not enough to shake Alonso's measured and un-conciliatory stand.

With Alonso, Prospero tries a different tack since it is important that the King of Naples "think[s] well". Prospero's project in Act 5 is to ensure the King's good cheer:

> Sir, my liege,
> Do not infest your mind with beating on
> The strangeness of this business: at picked leisure,

Which will be shortly, single I'll resolve you
(which to you shall seem probable) of every
These happened accidents; till when be cheerful
And think of each thing well. (5.1.245-51)

The parenthetic clause in this speech, perhaps spoken as an aside, immediately draws attention and serves the opposite rhetorical function of highlighting the very thing that Prospero wished to bury in the rest of the sentence. Prospero needs to deliver a narrative that will "seem probable" and allay the King's repeated suspicion that "These are not natural events; they strengthen from strange to stranger" (5.1.228-9). In the next few remaining lines before the epilogue, Prospero forgives his unrepentant, silent brother; the "strangeness" of the events is re-emphasized by Alonso, and Prospero repeats his promise to "deliver all". The ending of *The Tempest* leads the audience to a cliff hanger and leaves them there.

The ending is a cliff hanger because there is evidence of enough skepticism and discomfort amongst Prospero's erstwhile enemies that it could be possible to imagine a harsh judgment against him. The probable explanations are worthy of speculation, if we consider the wider context of King James's England where there was little clemency for those suspected of witchcraft.[23] What could Prospero say about his magic that could earn him amnesty where Faustus could only ask for a finite limit on his suffering? The suggestion of an extra-dramatic moment of Prospero presenting his probable explanation to his audience in the cave strategically manipulates the playgoer's response to the play. It implicates the audience in the choice of their response in terms of what they choose to find credible and frees the playwright from presenting a conclusion. The epilogue of the play puts the onus of judging Prospero squarely on the audience.

Epilogues in Renaissance drama are usually an extra-dramatic moment that reach out to the audience to court approval for the production and preempt criticism by a rhetorical gesture of seeking forgiveness. It is a commonplace in *The Tempest* criticism to read Prospero as a dramatist who stands in for Shakespeare to bid farewell to his audience, via the epilogue, after a long and successful career. Prospero is indeed a dramatist but instead of pressing his identification with Shakespeare, I would like to emphasize that the epilogue clinches his very conscious and strategic use of dramatic conventions and devices through the play. Critics have noted that it is odd that Prospero delivers the epilogue in character, but this oddity only indicates that the play is not over at the point that it ends. The epilogue could be read to serve two significant functions. First, it keeps the audience from assuming that once the visitors have heard Prospero's story all will be well and that he will return home as planned; second, it suggests itself to be a prologue to the apology that he is about to deliver to his audience in the cave.[24]

Although, this is not how the epilogue to the play is usually performed, it could be played as being delivered to two sets of audiences: the visitors on the isle, who were also the unwary actors in his play, and the playgoers. The epilogue acquires a darker resonance if Act 5 is read for the undertones of witchcraft accusation and Prospero's defensiveness apparent beneath a very routine gesture: "Now 'tis true/I must be here confined by you./Or sent to Naples" (3-5). His admission of weakness: "what strength I have's mine own,/Which is most faint" (2-3) is reminiscent of the tone in Dee's letters of apology. Prospero's anxiety seeps into the images of manacles and imprisonment: "Let me not,... dwell/in this bare island by your spell;/But release me from my bands/with the help of your good hands" (5-10). The trope of "bands", conventional enough in Renaissance poetry, suggests a threatening literality in Prospero's use. The pun in the use of "spell" as speech refers to any unfavorable judgment against him while playfully neutralizing the potency of magic by locating it in the verbal response of audience.

The epilogue is evidence for Prospero's parallel plans: he claims to have abjured his magic, and he submits himself to the mercy of his audience. It is crucial that he appears non-threatening if wishes to return to Milan.

> Now I want
> Spirits to enforce, art to enchant;
> And my ending is despair
> Unless I be relieved by prayer,

Which pierces so, that it assaults
Mercy itself, and frees all faults. (13-18)

Prospero's abjuration of magic is not enacted on stage; the audience can only take his word that he is no longer the powerful magician that he was even in the last scene of the play. His epilogue exceeds both rhetoric and convention when he uses it as a bargaining device. It has been argued that Act 3 marks a pivotal shift in Prospero's character and "project" when he realizes the virtue of forgiveness over vengeance. His penitence is routinely read as evidence for the humanization of a hard-hearted magician. But it is possible that for Prospero forgiveness is as much a strategy in the play as sending Ariel as Harpy to remind his enemies of their betrayal that would make the shipwreck seem like a just retribution. The strategic use forgiveness unfolds in the play and is driven home in the epilogue. His appeal for forgiveness comes from a *quid pro quo* logic: he has forgiven his deceivers hence he deserves to be forgiven for using magic to torment his deceivers. Prospero makes the forgiveness *ad hominem* "As you from crimes would pardoned be,/Let your indulgence set me free." (19-20). However, his absolute last word in the Epilogue, in case all logic and rhetoric were to fail, is an appeal to "indulgence"–a relaxation of rules that can only be based on "mercy"–a basis of forgiveness located in the generosity of the judge when the innocence of the supplicant cannot be proved.

Act 5 and the strategic but inconclusive epilogue recreate a scenario that recalls the misfortunes of John Dee. In his defense, John Dee had sought to represent himself in terms of his engagement with the production of knowledge. Similarly *The Tempest*, as Elizabeth Spiller reminds us, foregrounds its concern not just with different hierarchies of knowledge–Sycorax's versus Prospero's, for instance–but also with the ways in which knowledge is produced and apprehended. The desire to know, attempts to interpret or classify information, the inability to make sense of phenomena underlie the experiences of all the characters in the play. In Act 5 the King demands that his knowledge be rectified, but earlier Gonzalo had offered ways to interpret strange shapes that populate the isle; Stephano and Trinculo had attempted to categorize Caliban as fish or monster; Ferdinand had found himself unable to make sense of Ariel's disembodied songs. These are only a few instances of the play's preoccupation with the mechanism employed to apprehend one's surroundings that Prospero anticipates and manipulates. In a play that is curiously without any obvious twists in the plot or any kind of suspense at all, except perhaps at the end, the characters find themselves in inexplicable situations and constantly want to know what is happening and how it is happening. For a play that is set up to unfurl a master plan, the master of the plan is found constantly manipulating, re-reading, re-presenting events on stage and having to explain himself again and again. If Prospero's project is to explain himself out of a situation that even Dee did not manage to do successfully, then I contend that Prospero's vocabulary reigns in concepts from outside the domain of Neoplatonic magic and gestures towards the new mechanical philosophy that was gaining favor as an acceptable epistemology. Specifically, I argue that he expands his discourse to include two key Baconian ideas: there are mechanical explanations for natural phenomenon and the explanations are probable and hypothetical rather than the truth claims that both theology and magical-spiritual scholarship aspire towards and assert.

The Baconian language of fortune's accidental aid in the planned vexation of nature is echoed by Prospero when he gives in to Miranda's insistent questioning about the nature of his art in Act 1. It is telling that in revealing his art he juxtaposes magical methods with mechanical explanations that is the heart of this play. The reason for the double talk can easily be contextualized by recognizing that a straightforward confession of tempest-raising magic is potentially quiet damning. The ability to raise tempests is listed in contemporary demonologies as a sure sign of malevolent witchcraft and is used as such by Shakespeare in another play. The three witches in *Macbeth* perform a revengeful tempest akin to Prospero's own: "He shall live a man forbid. [...] Though his bark cannot be lost/Yet it shall be tempest-tossed" (1.3.22-25).[25] The audience is not meant to forget this affinity, later reinforced in the play via Sycorax, even as they register the difference between the witches and Prospero. The difference between them is indicated by the larger narrative thrust in each play. In *Macbeth* the witches uphold the inscrutable forces of Fortune that Macbeth disdains. But the narrative of *The Tempest* is invested in drawing out the complexity of the early modern scholar-magician in the character of Prospero who is seeking to join Fortune with skill.

While the witches in *Macbeth* pool their malice to create a tempest, Prospero talks about the same sort of work in a language that recalls not the demonologies but something new–a Baconian natural philosopher. In response to Miranda, Prospero explains his reasons for raising the tempest in a language that collapses reason and method, explanation and action, narrative and representation:

> By accident most strange, bountiful Fortune,
> (Now my dear lady) hath mine enemies
> Brought to this shore; and by my prescience
> I find my zenith doth depend upon
> A most auspicious star, whose influence
> If now I court not, but omit, my fortunes
> Will ever after droop. Here cease more questions:
> Thou art inclin'd to sleep; 'tis a good dullness,
> And give it way: I know thou canst not choose.
> Come Away, servant, come. I am ready now. (1.2.178-86)

Prospero claims to have joined his efforts with that of Fortune's, accident with skill ("astrological prescience"), and the arbitrary ripeness of time with his own readiness for action. In this speech Prospero shifts attention from Fortune's bounty to his own endeavor by naming his skill and by seamlessly transitioning his speech as narrative to speech as spell that charms Miranda to sleep and summons his familiar spirit Ariel. Prospero follows the Baconian explanation of combining accident and skill but he also adds angel calling to it, more seamlessly than John Dee had managed. In his speech Prospero draws attention to the strangeness of the accidental nearness of his enemies, invites us to consider it as an artifice of Fortune that he has only imitated by contriving an artifice of his own–the magical tempest that appears to have accidentally washed his enemies ashore. Even as he makes his method sound the language of a Baconian experiment, where individual skill imitates fortune to contrive artificial events that make new knowledge possible. Prospero performs exactly the kind of magic on stage that Bacon was hard pressed to explain and had overtly dismissed in *The Advancement of Learning*. Prospero's art thus brings together two different and not altogether compatible performative traditions: Dee's Neoplatonic magic and the mechanical arts re-categorized by Francis Bacon.

It should be noted that Prospero's agenda parts ways from the natural philosopher's in a significant way–Prospero is less engaged with the accuracy of the Baconian method than with its implications. The upshot of the Baconian method that is useful for Prospero is that it plays up the significance of artifice, natural or simulated, in the study of nature. The "trial and vexation" allows space for experiments–the space where usual judgment for the treatment of things is suspended. However, *The Tempest* also represents the misappropriation of the Baconian method, and leaves it susceptible to criticism as a means of apprehending knowledge as Dee was enduring for his methods and calling. The play presents a satiric take on Bacon's idea that the *mirabilaries* or curious artifacts produced by erring nature–such as monsters–are windows into the truths of nature (70). Trinculo's perception of Caliban's strangeness, monstrosity and commercial value as an exhibition curio in England is an instance where a moment crucial to the Baconian discovery of truth is confounded right from the moment of perception.

> What have we here? a man or a fish? dead or alive? A fish: he smells like a fish; a very ancient and fish-like smell; a kind of, not the newest Poor-john. A strange fish! Were I in England now, as I once was, and had but this fish painted, not a holy fool there but would give a piece of silver: there would this monster make a man... (2.2.24-30)

The obvious brunt of this comic-satiric piece is the English appetite for exotic curiosities. But the satire is also turned on Trinculo who goes through a specious piece of Baconian inductive reasoning to reach a misguided conclusion that Caliban is a fish. Not satisfied with Caliban's status as nature's artifice, Trinculo imagines adding his own coat of paint. Instead of discovering truth he disguises it twice over. Trinculo's example can be used to comment on Prospero's method too for Trinculo unveils truth to be an artifice biased in its presentation and dependent on communal approval. In fact, Prospero's own goals in the play are not to discover truth but to magically contrive events to prove what he already believes to be true as he hopes to win approval for his version of truth.

The yoking of Neoplatonic magic and mechanical philosophy in the play is made possible by the strategic dis-location of the island where the action of the play unfolds. To the nascent colonial imagination of early modern England, a hypothetical space between Africa and Europe would be relatively free of *a priori* signification making it both a legitimate location for wonder, whether pleasing or disturbing, and an acceptable location from where critiques and correctives to established norms, even if reluctantly acknowledged, may emerge. We see Prospero play up the magical otherness of the island (as in the speech to Gonzalo) but we also see him use this space as a theatrical laboratory where he routinely vexes nature (for instance of his enemies or even Ariel and Caliban's) to stage the production of knowledge. The geographical dis-location of this magical experiment is nonetheless made materially manifest onstage at Blackfriars and in James's court to celebrate the betrothal of his daughter to the Elector Palatine in 1611. The alternative to reading the staging of *The Tempest* as a colonial or celebratory fantasy is to view the stage performance as a practical epistemology that challenges normative knowledge. Prospero hopes to use the defense of theater as his own because theater as a mechanical art creates and preserves both knowledge and its illusion.

Prospero's Theatrical Experiment: Or the Makingness of Knowledge

Re-reading *The Tempest* from the beginning in the light of its very ambiguous ending can profoundly change the emphasis of the play.

Prospero's use of a rhetorical theatrical device, such as the epilogue, for a purpose that is not rhetorical alerts us to his particular use of theatrical devices. In the light of the ending, it is easier to see why and how Prospero uses theater to deflect attention away from magic. He performs his magic by staging, what the playgoer will recognize instantly and the audience in the play will come to see belatedly as, theatrical shows–a spectacle, a morality play and a wedding masque. As a closer look at the play text shows, Prospero emphasizes the enabling fiction of role play, draws attention to costumes and apparel that allow for the shift in roles, presents a stylized version of the backstage mechanics of theatrical spectacles and hopes in the end to take recourse in the reassuring fiction of theater. In the section that follows, I will examine the ways in which Prospero presents his magic by building on the idea of theater.

The Tempest begins with a "the direful spectacle of [a] wrack". The action opens onboard a drowning ship that the sailors are fighting furiously to keep from splitting. In this flurry of desperate activity the first issue that the play raises is one of conflicting authority. Antonio and Sebastian want the sailors to "play the men" or act as the social inferiors that they are to the political authority of the king and his retinue when the boatswain assumes authority on the ship on the basis of his mechanical knowledge of navigation. That mechanical knowledge should supersede the mystique of kingship in a crisis such as this would be obvious but for the fact that the boatswain needs to belabor the point and that the storm undermines both these forms of authority; the baleful ship cracks and drowns amidst the piteous cries of its royal cargo. The opening of *The Tempest* sets the tone for the rest of the play where authority and the forms of knowledge from which authority derives will be constantly performed, questioned and reconstituted.[26] Like the epilogue, Prospero's use of spectacle through the course of the play exceeds the purpose of this dramatic device and highlights, in the process, the ways in which theater as a mechanical art is invested in maintaining the enchantment of magical effect.

The spectacle of the opening tempest so moves Miranda that she approaches her father with a reproachful lament: "If by your art my dearest father, you have/Put the wild waters in this roar, allay them" (1.2-2-3). If the point of the first scene was a sobering reminder of the limitations of human enterprise, Miranda's reaction to it immediately adds a different, if not entirely unexpected, dimension to it. The Boatswain and the sailors were not battling the elements; they were battling Prospero's art. Human enterprise is pitted in opposition not against nature but against another human enterprise. The tempest of the first scene is less about the vagaries of nature and all about conflicting knowledge systems. The conditional syntax of Miranda's reproach could give Prospero the benefit of the doubt but it could also be read as implicating Prospero in the gravity of the suffering he has caused. She continues with a litany of her own suffering as a spectator, a reaction that the playgoer is likely to have shared: "O I have suffered/With those that I saw suffer!...O, the cry did knock/Against my heart! Poor souls, they perish'd!" (1.2.5-9). Miranda emphasizes the destructive use of her father's art. Prospero reacts to this accusation with his characteristic terseness: "Be collected:/No more amazement: tell your piteous heart/There's no harm done" (1.2.14-16).

Miranda's amazed reaction is precisely the effect that Prospero's spectacles are designed to achieve, if they have to be effective. However, in early modern England amazement was a dangerous reaction to provoke. As a reaction of bewilderment and unreason, amazement was what the devil was known to induce in the otherwise reasonable orderliness of God's world. This sense of amazement will be echoed again and again in the play and each successive repetition will narrow down Prospero's chances of explaining himself out of it. But in this very first scene, Prospero is in control and he commands Miranda and the playgoer to shake off the amazement and re-view the spectacle for exactly what it is—a dramatic device.

The effectiveness and indeed the enjoyment of a theatrical spectacle lie in its approximation of reality with a reassuring recourse to the caveat of fiction; it is something Prospero is hoping will work in his favor. While he needs the suffering of his enemies to be real enough, he needs to be able to dispel its effect as something fictitious without any really damaging consequences. In the scene following the tempest, Prospero attempts to neutralize the effects of his magic by playing up the fiction of spectacle. To do so he sets the stage a second time and this time with a change of costume:

> 'Tis time I should inform thee farther. Lend thy hand,
> And pluck my magic garment from me, - So:
> [*Lays down his mantle.*]
> Lie there, my Art. (1.2.23-5)

Through the play Prospero often prefaces a switch in role play by a change in costume; he has Miranda help him take off his magic robe as if to enable him shift from playing the magician to the attentive father. The purely symbolic value of this gesture–laying down the robe and addressing it as his art–will be evident towards the end of the scene when he not only manages to charm Miranda to sleep but he also summons his familiar spirit, his magic mantle folded away by his side. Whether or not Prospero actually needs his magic robe to perform magic there are two crucial points evident in this gesture. The first point is that in his self-representation as a magician Prospero locates his magic in his equipment–robe, books and wand–objects he can distance from himself if he needs to, as he will once he decides to abjure his magic in Act 3. The second point is that Prospero consciously performs his self-presentation and carefully regulates how he is perceived whether by his daughter or by his unwary enemies. In his critique of his usurping brother's behavior, Prospero notes that Antonio dropped the "screen between this part he play'd/and him he play'd it for" (1.2.106-7). To Prospero's own design this screen between his different roles is as crucial as it is necessary to maintain the social hierarchies.

Having set the scene for a performance, he proceeds to lessen the impact of the particularly successful spectacle of the tempest and the shipwreck. Prospero denies Miranda's accusation that the "brave vessel" is destroyed and the "noble creatures" in it have "perish'd":

> The direful spectacle of the wrack, which touch'd
> The very virtue of compassion in thee,

I have with such provision in mine Art
So safely ordered, that there is no soul–
No, not so much perdition as an hair
Betid to any creature in the vessel. (1.2.25-30)

Prospero speaks of the safety of the enterprise; he assures her that despite what it looked like no one in the shipwreck actually perished–it is, after all, only a spectacle. Thus the use of theatrical language and theatrical devices is not symbolic of Prospero's magic but a clever deflection away from his magic. He is expansively vague about the exact *techne* or the material status of the equipments which he just calls the "provisions" in his "Art". Prospero is keen to establish that he has not used his art for any harm by drawing a dubious distinction between suffering and harm. According to him the fictional nature of the suffering keeps it from being real harm. But it becomes clear in a later exchange with Ariel that the fictional suffering is meant to be psychologically real. In 1.2 he specifically asks for ways in which the tempest had infected the reason of the men caught in it. Ariel describes the effects as "fever of the mad", and such "trick of desperation" that the seamen plunged into the sea. The epitome of the torment is verbalized by Ferdinand who with "hair up-staring,–cried, "Hell is empty, All the devils are here" (210-215). On the ship it is really only the King of Naples and his own brother who wronged him but the suffering is inflicted on everyone else who is onboard and is innocent. To Miranda he stresses the fictional nature of the suffering precisely because, as mentioned earlier, early modern Europe was particularly suspicious of vengeance seeking, hurtful malevolent magic. Prospero's intent to inflict severe distress is evident both in the opening tempest and in the banquet scene of 3.3 where make believe suffering is meant to be psychologically real.

The opening tempest and the banquet scene work together not only as the products of Prospero's magic for wreaking vengeance on his enemies but also as companion pieces wrought and executed in explicitly theatrical terms. It is crucial for Prospero's design that the theatrical elements of these two scenes are foremost in the playgoer's mind. He adds a notch to the meta-theatricality of

3.3 by using the recognizable dramatic genre of a morality play and by drawing attention to his revenge with the convention of a banquet.[27] The scene is set and punctuated with stage directions that are quite elaborate by Shakespearean standards.[28] Solemn and strange music ushers in strange shapes carrying a banquet. The shapes dance and invite the weary and lost castaways to eat. The stage directions point out that Prospero overlooks the scene as visible to the audience but remaining invisible to his enemies. Like the spectacle of the storm, the strange shapes are designed to try the nature of the courtiers. Accordingly, Alonso and his company react with varying degrees of credulity to a banquet set in the wilderness. Led by Gonzalo, they fall back on the mythologies of travel tales to help them rationalize a scenario that would justify eating a meal under very strange circumstances. Gonzalo reassures Alonso, "Faith, sir, you need not fear..." (3.3.42) but Alonso reacts with a characteristic fatalism: "I will stand to, and feed,/Although my last, no matter, since I feel the best is past" (3.3.49-50). As the company approaches the table, a dramatic thunder and lightning replaces the solemn music; Ariel appears as a Harpy and makes the food disappear with a clap. He hovers menacingly mid-air and arraigns Prospero's enemies till they are driven to despair by the guilt of a crime they had thought was forgotten. Ariel's clap that makes the food disappear is supplemented with an additional direction that a "quaint device" does the job that Ariel appears to accomplish magically. The mythical, magical Harpy and a quaint theatrical device are two different narrative devices that are available for Prospero to deploy as he casts himself in a story that could either damn or redeem him.

In an article devoted entirely to the staging of 3.3, John C. Adams elaborates on the stage directions following what is known about the Elizabethan playhouses, especially Blackfriars where it was staged, and the resources in terms of costumes, props and machinery that were available for such a production.[29] He reads the direction for a "quaint device" as clue that the machinery used for the vanishing banquet was more ingenious and designed especially for the scene and was unlike anything used in the playhouses. Adams goes on to recreate the ingenuity of this device with available devices. He concludes that a table with a reversible tabletop is placed directly above a trap door by the strange shapes that bring the table in. A stagehand gets under the table through the trap and makes the banquet disappear at the sound of Ariel's clap. He even points to the technical necessity of an invisible Prospero standing at a vantage point on top to aid the system of signals so that the traps could be operated at precisely the right times. Adams bares the magician's trick; the magical set up of the scene is explained with its complete technical set up. In his book on the Jacobean private theaters, Keith Sturgess argues that this scene, and especially the disappearance of the banquet, is a "conjuror's trick, real magic to the courtiers and a stage illusion to the audience...The staging of the play is both device and meaning" (73).[30] Adams' article assumes that the playgoer sees exactly what the courtiers see and he unravels the trick behind an effect that could only be equally magical to the playgoer. But Sturgess reminds us that Shakespeare' audience and Prospero's audience don't experience 3.3 in the same way. What the courtiers experience as real magic the playgoers view as stage illusion. He further alerts us that the play stages both "device" and "meaning", a crucial distinction to appreciate the meta-theatricality of the play. In a move that is bound to leave some readers unsatisfied, Sturgess' reading of the meta-theatricality ultimately serves an apolitical aesthetic vision which makes the play into a self-contained and romanticized artifact like Keats' Grecian urn; he calls the play a "quaint device defeated by our clumsy handling" (96).[31] While I disagree with Sturgess' conclusion about the purpose of the play's meta-theatricality, his suggestion that "the play stages device" is useful to see Prospero make a distinction between magic as device and meaning.

I would like to argue that the magic in 3.3 is staged as a device, and this is necessary because otherwise Ariel and the meaner spirits would make the supernatural hazing of the enemies reflect very poorly on Prospero. I suggest that the stage directions in 3.3 are meant to allegorize Ariel and his spirits as stage machinery. The antics of the spirits as the strange shapes draw attention to them as handlers of the stage props. At the end of the scene Prospero commends Ariel and his "meaner ministers" for doing the job well. That Prospero commands a familiar spirit of uncertain nature, he calls Ariel both "delicate" and "malignant", for purposes that are meant to inflict suffering, puts Prospero in great proximity to a witch like Sycorax. If Prospero's project is to both get the vengeance he wants and a reconciliation leading to his return to Milan, his challenge is to save himself from the accusations of malevolent magic that is clearly on display in 3.3. What Prospero does with Ariel and the other nondescript spirits on stage unfolds after the staging of each theatrical event when Prospero seeks a report, commends the performance or reflects on the impact of the scene.

After the opening tempest, once Prospero has finished chastising Miranda for her amazement, Prospero seeks a detailed report on exactly the kind of fearful amazement that Ariel caused on the drowning ship:

> Pros: Hast thou, spirit,
> Perform'd to point the tempest that I bade thee?
> Ariel: To every article.
> I boarded the king's ship; now on the beak,
> Now in the waist, the deck, in every cabin,
> I flam'd amazement: Sometimes I'd divide,
> And burn in many places; on the topmast,
> The yards and bore spirit, would I flame distinctly,
> Then meet and join. Jove's lightnings, the precursors
> O' th' the dreadful thunderclaps, more momentary
> And sight-outrunning were not: the fire and the cracks
> Of sulphurous roaring the most mighty Neptune
> Seem to besiege, and make his bold waves tremble,
> Yea his trident shake. (1.2.193-206)

Prospero begins by asking Ariel if he "performed" the tempest exactly as ordered. The focus here is on Ariel as the performer and the executer of the task. Ariel is the agent enabling a performance, but as it turns out, he also embodies the performance. The invisible

Ariel inhabits the spectacle–"I flamed amazement: Sometimes I'd divide and burn in many places... would I flame distinctly"–that he is in charge of producing, not unlike the stage machinery that was used to pull off grand spectacles on stage. Ariel plays a special role in Prospero's plan of making action on stage appear like a stage-play; the serving spirit becomes the mechanical art of theater.

Prospero's plan for staging his magic as a theatrical performance becomes ever more apparent when he asks Ariel to return disguised as a water nymph and

> Be subject to
> No sight but thine and mine; invisible
> To every eyeball else. (1.2.302-4)

This act of rendering Ariel invisible and the representation of Ariel's invisibility from this point onwards is complex and invites further attention. Prospero hides Ariel from his audience on stage but Ariel continues to be visible to the playgoers. It is easy to see why Prospero would want to hide his *modus operandi* from the people he is manipulating with its help. But how is the playgoer or a reader of the play to interpret this visible invisibility? Ariel's invisibility is packaged to make the magical mechanics of theater explicit. When Ariel returns in the costume of a water-nymph, Prospero gives him a carefully worded approval: "Fine apparition! My quaint Ariel" (1.2.318). Ariel's apparel or costume makes him an apparition or gives him the illusion of being invisible. It is obvious that the playgoer is meant to note Ariel's invisibility as a theatrical illusion wrought with a change of costume. However, it is a word in the second sentence that reveals the complexity of the plan. Prospero endearingly describes Ariel as "quaint"–a word, used in 3.3 and corroborated by the OED, used to describe elaborate, ingenious or cunning device or machinery. It is a connection that the text itself strengthens in 3.3 when the stage directions call for a "quaint device" to make the banquet disappear. Ariel is rendered invisible to the audience in the play but is made visible to the playgoer as a normally invisible part of theater. Ariel's representation is the embodiment of the mechanical arts.

While the audience onstage experiences the effects of Prospero's magic charms, the audience offstage is invited to it as a theatrical experience from the vantage point of those who know the trick behind the trick. Prospero's plays within the play are a theatrical experiment. He uses the space of the stage, the mechanics of theatrical machinery, and the wonder of theatrical production as the explicable trick behind his magic. Theater becomes a cover for his magic just as mechanical devices cover his non-human spirits. If Shakespeare's audience finds this ingenious layering of theater and magic plausible, chances are that Prospero's audience might too. The relationship between magic, mechanics and theater is then set in terms of the relationship between the varying and coinciding perceptions of the stage audience and the playgoer. It goes on to show that Prospero puts up for the stage audience the play that Shakespeare presents to the playgoer, except that Prospero's persona is split in a way that Shakespeare's play and Prospero's play within it do not seem seamless.[32]

"Sir, I Am Vex'd": The Disenchantment of Prospero

Prospero overwhelms the play with his presence as he is undoubtedly meant to. As a magician who consciously makes use of dramatic devices to manipulate action on stage, Prospero's subjective vision has been linked to Shakespeare's own.[33] As Francis Baker and Peter Hulme point out, it is easy to miss Prospero's status as a character on the stage, like the others, playing out a dramatic vision that is not his own.[34] The playwright affords the playgoer a far more privileged position vis-à-vis Prospero than is available to the characters on stage. On stage Prospero is the controlling patriarch, the European colonizer with superior knowledge and skills, and the scholar-magician who expertly uses the status of theater, as a practical art, to forge a narrative of explanation in the language of mechanics. But the playgoer sees the process of Prospero's making and unmaking which is not entirely in Prospero's control. For instance, the playgoer witnesses the anxious self-appraisal that underlies Prospero's controlling and emphatic self-presentation.

By promoting himself as the ethical, scholar magician he

inadvertently makes visible the narrative that he wants to suppress. Part of Prospero's project of self-justification involves making very clear distinctions between his magic and malevolent magic by pressing his difference from Sycorax. But Prospero is unable to check the escalating similarities between them beginning with the fact that he was washed ashore the same island where Sycorax was exiled in punishment. He notes that Ariel was an unhappy servant to Sycorax but Ariel does not want to work for him either. Ariel only complies because Prospero threatens him with the same punishment that he suffered at the hands of Sycorax. Prospero assumes the stance of the good magician who freed Ariel from Sycorax's captivity but he enslaves Caliban and keeps him captive. Perhaps Prospero is not entirely convinced of the theatrical, mechanical narrative for magic that he is shoring up in his defense. Or perhaps he is convinced that his return to Europe is contingent on his disenchantment. In Act 4, Prospero both enacts and calls to doubt the basis of his narrative strategy invested in the spectacular materiality of theater.

Prospero's involvement in the opening tempest and in the banquet scene is invisible though he emphasizes his role as the mastermind behind the dramatic action. But in the spectacle that he produces to celebrate Miranda and Ferdinand's betrothal, he holds a visible disdain for the merely spectacular. He calls the betrothal masque "another such trick", as the banquet scene in 3.3, but calls the masque a "vanity of [his] art" (4.1.40).[35] He calls attention to the setting of the stage by commanding: "no tongue! All eyes! be silent" (4.1.59). Enchantment is literally magic that charms visually, for instance, in the mythical powers of the basilisk (that even Bacon recalls in the *Advancement*). Theatrical illusions are visual enchantments; sound is employed by theater to aid and advance the visual action on stage. Prospero's most candid admission to demonic magic comes in the guise of a theatrical production of a masque which was known for involving the supernatural realm.[36]

> Ferdinand: This is a most majestic vision, and
> Harmoniously charming. May I be bold
> To think these spirits?

Prospero: Spirits, which by mine Art
I have from their confines call'd to enact
my present fancies. (4.1.118-21)

It is at this point that the interconnectedness of the discourses of magic and theater become most obvious. Theater stands to gain much from the charm of magic, and sustaining a sense of wonder is crucial for the success of spectacle. Here Prospero is like Faustus vowing his audience by parading Alexander and Cleopatra. After the spectacle of the tempest, Ferdinand had uttered what would suffice for a conjuration charge and a witchcraft trial in early modern England: "All hell is empty, all the devils live here". The masque of Juno invokes an equally amazed reaction from him but this time it comes from being harmoniously charmed not frightened. The same Ferdinand is willing to entertain a different understanding of the magic and spirits once it packaged in the language and logic of theatre. The literalness of invoking spirits to enact fantasies is perfectly disguised by the theatrical metaphor.

Critics have stressed the note of benediction and harmony that the masque strikes as the center piece of the play. But the masque is also important for the insight it allows on Prospero as a magician and dramatist. If as I have argued so far, Prospero's defense of magic rests on its elaboration by theatrical machinery and the banquet scene is its best illustration, then in the wedding masque he comes very close to exposing the vulnerabilities of his method and narrative. Prospero is counting on the indulgence of his audience; indulgence can be requested, earned or courted but it cannot be coerced. In the banquet scene Prospero had made the immaterial spirits manifest as theatrical machinery, but in the masque which traditionally calls for "quaint devices" he is faced with the immateriality of theatrical productions instead. Prospero's abrupt dismissal of the masque is followed by an elegiac meditation on the ontology of theater and what it means for it to be the only way to produce his magical masque of spirits. In "Our revels have now ended" he delves into the fundamental categories of materiality and immateriality common to magic, mechanics and theater:

> Our revels now are ended. These our actors
> As I foretold you, were all spirits, and
> Are melted into air, into thin air:
> And, like the baseless fabric of this vision.
> The cloud-capp'd towers, the gorgeous palaces,
> The solemn temples, the great globe itself,
> Yea all which it inherit shall dissolve,
> And like the insubstantial pageant faded,
> Leave not a rack behind. We are such stuff
> As dreams are made on; and our little life
> Is rounded with sleep. (4.1.148-57)

Prospero begins by describing the betrothal masque as a revel, the sort of merry making that is typically associated with riotous, noisy mirth and celebration. The OED locates the etymology of the word revel in a sense of rebellion and disturbance that one would expect in an anti-masque such as the drunken revelries of Stephano, Trinculo and Caliban. The stateliness of Prospero's masque contrarily described as a revel connects it formally to Caliban's rebellious anti-masque, essential to the form of the masque, but more importantly it suggests that Prospero's masque is a revel because it is a rebellion against nature. He has disturbed the spirits and called them for a performance that even Prospero knows is "vanity". This elegiac meditation on the ontology of theater grows out of his need to justify the specific magical masque of the spirits. In this speech Prospero is invested in the relationship between the material and immaterial nature of reality as mediated both by magic and theater.

One approach to grapple with the concept of the immaterial or the abstract is by way of symbolic material representations, as for instance in mathematics or theater. John Dee had called attention to the fertile category of immateriality that lies between the absolute and perfect state of the supernatural and the base and gross state of the natural in his "Preface to Euclid":

> thinges immateriall are nevertheless, by material things hable to be somewhat signified. And though their particular Images, by Art, are agg[...]egable and divisible: yet the general

> *Formes*, notwithstandyng, are constant and unchaungeable, untransformable and incorruptible.

For Dee mathematics occupies the immaterial middle ground which does not seek "probability and sensible proof" that things natural require but "only a perfect demonstration, of truthes certaine, necessary and invincible". The perfect demonstration of truths can come in the form of marvels that challenge ones' experience of nature's law: "you will finde Mervailes upon Mervailes: And esteme one Drop of Truth more worth,...then whole libraries undemonstrated: or not answering to Natures Law, and your experience". For Dee mathematics is not only confined to its demonstrable uses in the many practical and mechanical ways he lists but ultimately it provides the possibility of reconciling the natural with the supernatural, the immaterial with the material. Dee's emphasis on mathematics as being able to visualize and signify an abstract thought that relies on "demonstration" rather than "conjecture" and "probabilitie" makes it possible to see theatrical representation, as visual and mechanical representation of abstractions, working on some of the same principles such that theater is a practical epistemology.

Prospero relies on theatre as practical epistemology to paradoxically spin an ontological uncertainty into the status of all theatre so that he can accommodate the dubious ontology of his masque of spirits. Because *his* actors are spirits, all actors become spirits who melt into thin air. He creates an elaborate simile by collapsing the differences between his spirit-masque and the nature of all theater to continue to build on the idea that actors are like spirits. He claims that "like the baseless fabric of this vision" the more solid and material things in the world are also transient.

The OED denotes the use of the word "fabric" specifically as "a product of skilled workmanship" such as "buildings or edifices" or a "contrivance of an engine or appliance" during the renaissance. So Prospero imagines theatrical spectacle–"this vision" as a mechanical contrivance or an edifice without a foundation. The very materiality of created contrivances and structures are undermined as vision; though they are visible, they are, according to Prospero, unreal visions. The undermined materiality of theater becomes an argument for the immateriality of all things that are usually considered more enduring than dream visions: "towers", "palaces", "temples" and "the great globe itself". These created edifices too are like his "insubstantial pageant" that fades without leaving a "rack" behind. He collapses different levels of immateriality and transience and imagines things to end in nothingness. All human life seems like a dream, which in the Renaissance representations was usually troubled and nightmarish, that is relieved by death. For Prospero the insubstantial masque of the spirits contains the substance of materialized immateriality that human life is all about and that theater encapsulates.

Prospero's nihilistic vision of nothingness is not just a function of his theatrical aesthetics; it is a bleakness that informs his politics on the island, reflects in his odd acknowledgment of Caliban as his "thing of darkness", and carries through to the epilogue where he imagines an ending in despair. Prospero's disenchantment runs deeper than the melancholia attributed to the scholarly temperament.[37] Prospero's disenchantment makes him abjure his magic. In his representation of magic there is none of Dee's sense of awe for a discipline that might, in the end, reveal the truths that he seeks. His abjuration speech recounts the powers reminiscent of Ovid's Medea, thus giving him a genealogy of the darkest of magic that abounds in literature that is further substantiated by Prospero's list of magical accomplishments–solar eclipse, tempests at sea, destructive lighting, sky shaking chaos with uprooted trees, and raising the dead, that he attributes to his "potent Art". The tempest of the opening scene and the magical masque testify Prospero's claims. His list grows progressively more powerful and spectacular but the rendition of the list betrays neither pride nor regret and could easily be performed as an even toned litany that culminates in a very long statement of abjuration:

> But this rough magic
> I here abjure; and, when I have requir'd
> Some heavenly music, - which even now I do, -
> To work my end upon, their senses, that

> This airy charm is for, I'll break my staff,
> And bury it certain fadoms in the earth,
> And deeper than did even plummet sound
> I'll drown my book. (5.1.50-57)

The abjuration speech raises more questions than it answers. He gives no reasons for why he needs to abjure magic, or if he abjures it at all since it is not enacted on stage. It is unclear what the adjective "rough" exactly means; if it refers to his list of destructive spectacular achievements, it does not account for it as a source of "heavenly music". It is equally mystifying to think of whether he abjures it in part or whole since we have seen him cast spells without the above mentioned tools of his trade. The abjuration of magic literalizes Prospero's disenchantment.

As Prospero's own narrative of theatrical mechanics takes over as the coherent explanation of his art, his growing disenchantment reflects his failure to account for magic from within the discourse of magic. In a way Prospero contributes to the historic failure of magic. Prospero is unable to stretch his magic to occupy the ideological registers that shifted between Dee's practice of magic as knowledge and Bacon's theorization of knowledge without magic. Denise Albanese locates the break as between Prospero's book owning theoretical magic and instrumental magic that exerts control on the material world:

> If magic "fails" historically as a discourse, it is in taking on a task for which it is not suited. We may almost say that the impossibility of magic, its historical untenability, lies in its attempt to bring together a written legacy with a desire for instrumentality over the phenomenal world. By aiming both at socio-discursive and material control, magic becomes an attempt to occupy two increasingly different ideological registers. (68)[38]

Producing the theatrical materiality of magic brings Prospero to recognize that the narrative of mechanics compromises the socio-discursive value of magic drawn paradoxically from its location of non-conformity and alienation. Prospero abjures his magic to return to the fold.

Prospero's disenchantment would take the magic right out of the play except that the excess magic, uncontainable in his narrative is relocated. As Prospero prepares to submit himself to a freedom where he needs to surrender his access to excess, Ariel prepares for his freedom and exceeds the heavy handed signification that he is burdened with through the length of the play.

The Burden of Sweet Sprites

One of the first things we learn about Ariel is that he wants to be free. The colonial context provides a framework within which to understand Caliban's desire to be free of Prospero's control. It is harder to understand what Ariel's freedom means since freedom is usually not absolute; it is usually about the freedom to choose constraints. Every character who seeks some form of freedom simultaneously chooses a constraint, all except Ariel. Prospero chooses the constraints of governance over the freedom to be "rapt in secret studies"; Caliban's bid for freedom involves a revolt where he subjects himself to a different master. Similarly Miranda and Ferdinand speak the language of willing servitude that the freedom to love brings. Ariel, on the other hand, is not human and presents an instance of alterity that is absolute, making Prospero's attempts and our attempts to anthropomorphize him or mechanize him ultimately inadequate.

I have been using the masculine gender to refer to Ariel, but even that only betrays an attempt to pin down a reference to a character who defies it. As critics and performances have argued and shown, the play bears out the performance of an Ariel who is neither male or nor female or both at once. If magic is the excess that remains inexplicable to reason and is best expressed in the experience of wonder then, I would like to read Ariel for the ways in which he escapes Prospero's strict and regimented categories. Earlier in the chapter I talked about the ways in which Ariel fulfils the dual function of spirit and mechanical art which would explain his role in the play, but now I would like to return to the question of Ariel's freedom and his songs to read the ways in which he becomes the locus of wonder and enchantment even as Prospero becomes more and more disenchanted.

Ariel operates as spectacle and as songs. Michael Neill has stressed the superiority of sounds over spectacle in the play which bears out in the two entirely different kinds of effects achieved from Ariel as sight and Ariel as sound.[39] Prospero's insistent questioning of Ariel after each spectacle makes Ariel's performance seem scripted and controlled such as in the opening tempest:

> Pros: Hast thou, spirit,
> Perform'd to point the tempest that I bade thee?
> Ariel: To every article. (1.2.93-5)

Later, after the banquet scene, Prospero commends Ariel's performance of the Harpy: "Of my instruction hast thou nothing bated" (3.3.85). While Prospero controls Ariel's visual aspect and his spectacles to the extent that he can make Ariel invisible, he has little control over Ariel's songs. Ariel's songs and songs in general in the play counterpoint the explicability of magic and in the process call to doubt the narrative of explanations that the play builds on. Ariel's songs have been read within the paradigms of Neoplatonic theories of music where they are a source of curative magic which Prospero clearly uses to his advantage.[40] In his abjuration speech he asks for "heavenly music" to break the spell that binds his enemies. But it is also worth pursuing the ways in which Ariel's songs exceed Prospero's control and use.

David Lindley is one of the few critics to note that even when the critical consensus on *The Tempest* changed to emphasize "inconclusiveness, ambiguity and doubt the music has consistently been accepted as imaging and enacting ideals of harmony and concord, whether or not those ideals are finally attained" (47).[41] Lindley's reading of music in the play suggests that Prospero's use compromises the symbolic significance of music and creates a pattern of uncertainty in audience response. For instance, Ariel's most famous song, the elegy "Full fadom five" is a lie because Alonso is alive. Lindley locates the disquiet in the play's music within the larger disquiet surrounding the form of the masque which is the primary focus of his work. Lindley's readings of the songs, showing that they only partially fulfill the Neoplatonic symbolisms attached to them, support my claim that Ariel's songs articulate excess. The excess often takes the form of a disparity between, what Lindley calls, "song and dramatic action" (48). Ariel's very first song is meant to soothe the troubled Ferdinand, lure him into the island and keep him in a state of mind that is conducive to love-at-first-sight. To that extent the song does its job but it does something more. What is striking about "Come into these yellow sands" is the "burden" or chorus of the "sweet sprites":

> Foot it featly here and there,
> *And sweet sprite bear*
> *The burthen. Hark, Hark*
> Burthen dispersedly. *Bow-wow*
> The watchdogs bark
> Burden dispersedly. *Bow wow*
> *Hark, Hark! I hear*
> *The strain of strutting chanticleer*. (2.1.381-5)

The dispersed chorus of the barking is jarring and has no connection with the first few lines of the song. It gets even more disorienting when Ariel sings a response to the chorus that says that he heard the bark as a cock's crowing. While the playgoer might register the comic note of the song, Ferdinand registers it as heavenly music. Ariel strikes a chord with the playgoer that is outside and in spite of Prospero's control.

Ariel's appeal to the playgoer mimics Prospero's attempts to establish an extra-dramatic connection and share a unique subject position. If Ariel's songs are excessive in their meaning, they are an indication that they bear a bigger burden than Prospero's bidding requires. "Full fadom five" comes close at the heels of the barking spirits and alters the mood of the previous song entirely. It has no jarring edges or dramatic disparity; but as it reaches out to the audience, it articulates the most important alternative to Prospero's experience of magic in the play.

> *Full fadom five thy father lies;*
> *Of his bones coral are made;*
> *Those are pearls that were his eyes;*

Nothing of him that doth fade.
But doth suffer a sea change
Into something rich and strange, (1.2. 399-404)

Despite the fact that the premise of the song is false, this dirge is a very effective song about continuity and transformation. It is a subtle revision of the idea from *Genesis* 3:19 adapted into the English burial service in *Cranmer's Book of Common Prayers* to denote death and burial as a return to the elements that created the body: "Ashes to ashes and dust to dust". It reminds the mortals that the body disintegrates and is devalued as it returns to its constituting elements. Ariel's song turns death into transformation and the body into riches. There is no "ending in despair" only sea-change and transformation. However, Ariel and his songs are not easily romanticized or domesticated; the transformations are rich but they are also strange. The concept of strangeness recurs through the play and is invoked in every other set of speeches in Act 5. In this chapter I have argued that Prospero's desire to be rehabilitated in Europe requires him to present what appears as strange in a narrative that normalizes the events. Ariel presents and maintains the opposite point of view that strangeness can be enriching. Magic is strange but the minute it becomes familiar and is explained it becomes mechanical. There is no way to render magic in a normative narrative without losing the magic to a system of explanations. And that is perhaps why Prospero must be disenchanted and Ariel ultimately must make no sense.

In Act 5, after his somewhat strange transformation to the virtues of forgiveness, Prospero calls for "solemn music" to uncharm his enemies when he also tells Ariel that he will soon be free. To David Lindley the song that follows is the best example of disparity between song and dramatic action: "...to accompany the gesture that signals the triumphant conclusion we are not offered a ceremonious fanfare but a song about lying in cowslips" (48). He reads Ariel's final song, "Where the bee sucks", as Ariel's "fugitive fantasy" where he "slips into solipsism" (57). Lindley's reading expresses frustration with the pastoral inanity of Ariel's last song. When at last he is moments away from freedom, Ariel bursts into spontaneous song and represents himself in a way that is unique to this particular song. But that representation seems anti-climactic.

For everything that Ariel seems to have said and done in the play, in the end he is no different from a common garden butterfly which does not square with the powerful with his three simultaneous roles as a Neoplatonic spirit, witch's familiar and as embodiment of theatrical mechanics that was visibly at work through the play. If Ariel is indeed where the magic of the play is located then Ariel presents the problem of representing magic as magic. If magic is located in the leftover inexplicabilities, after all explanations have been given, then Ariel's final representation is a stroke of genius. Shakespeare uses the most accessible pastoral imagery in the tritest of verse forms to make Ariel completely inaccessible. Ariel among the cowslips makes no sense, but suddenly his desire for freedom makes complete sense at the very moment that he escapes both Prospero's and the reader or playgoer's normalizing narratives about him.

Conclusion

Prospero's narrative of magic as mechanics, especially theatrical mechanics that allowed an acceptable space for wonder, could be a probable explanation that Prospero holds out to his auditors. But Ariel escapes Prospero's explanation of magic as theatrical mechanics and the burden of magic shifts from Prospero to Ariel. As Prospero prepares for the prospect of his return to Europe, the magic stays behind in the figure of Ariel and in the island itself.

Prospero's disenchantment is a version of the progressive distancing of magic from the magician. The explanation of magic as mechanics might deflect the risks of transgression associated with the study of magic but it does so by changing the terms of magic to fit the narrative of normalizing explanations about it. However, the attraction of magic lies in its being mostly inexplicable and somewhat out of reach. The inexplicability of Ariel and the magical island stand for the space of suggestive *not knowing* and uncertainty as a reservoir of untapped power and possibility that allow for the possibility of re-imagining whatever is socially and material real and present. Gonzalo's first response to the island was to mentally populate it with his possible utopia, as perhaps Prospero himself did when he first arrived on the island and took on the responsibility to educate Miranda and Caliban according to his vision. These imaginary utopias reflect the constraints of the world from which it is supposed to be free and far away.

The next chapter turns to the social realities shaped by witchcraft and vagrancy legislations and the imaginary hiatus of utopia that the transaction of magic makes possible, even if only briefly. Prospero's theatrical alibi for magic returns in Jonson's *The Alchemist* as a tongue-in-cheek excuse; it suggests that the credibility of magic, like the credibility of theater, relies on the customer/audience's ability to accord reality making powers to magic and to theater. In this chapter the Baconian method of experimental and mechanical knowledge emerges as a bid to standardize and make credible the disciplines of knowledge that were susceptible to charges of dis-ingenuity, but the next chapter examines the process of producing credibility as a measure against which dis-ingenuity is judged.

NOTES

1. Following Curry, Sisson, Kermode, and Yates Prospero's magic has traditionally been read as the power of a Renaissance philosopher magus. In his Introduction to the Arden edition Frank Kermode calls Prospero a theurgist who "exercises the supernatural powers of the holy adept". There have been a few scholars, such as D' Orsay Pearson, who take the contrary view that Prospero is "a damned sorcerer and a malevolent magician". Robert West is one of the earliest critics to have promoted the middle ground, suggesting that making Prospero belong exclusively to either one of the traditions is necessarily limiting. In the 1980s when interest in the nature of Prospero's magic was replaced by the new historicist excitement over the play's colonial context, Barbara Traister, Barbara Mowat and John Mebane continued to write about magic. Both Traister and Mebane took consider take the literary and philosophic

view of magic and Prospero but Mowat suggests a less unified source for magic and Prospero's representation in the play. Her essay "Prospero, Agrippa and Hocus Pocus" (1981) argues that Prospero is a reflection of multiple traditions of magic including wizardry and sleight of hand jugglery.

2. The "triumphalist whig narrative" of progress, where science prevails over the irrationality of magic, was challenged by historians writing after the two world wars. Peter Elmer surveys this literature in "Science Medicine and Witchcraft". Historians of science and magic have since attempted to study magic on its own terms.
3. Most Dee scholars recount this incident; Benjamin Woolley recreates it in detail and with great relish in *The Queen's Conjuror* (12-15). Dee's scarab is also mentioned by Orgel and Strong in *Inigo Jones* with reference to the use of machinery in classical drama. (7)
4. Paolo Rossi discusses the heritage of magic in the Bacon corpus in the chapter "The Mechanical Arts, Magic, and Science" in his book *Francis Bacon from Magic to Science.* (1968). Rossi suggests, "If Bacon had reservations about magic and alchemy they were not concerned with the experimental nature of their enquiries, for the idea of an active, inventive science was basic to his own method" (22).
5. The classification of theater as a mechanical art dates back at least to Hugo St. *Victor's Didascalion* (1120). He categorizes "theatrics" under the "mechanical sciences" along with fabric making, armament, commerce, agriculture, hunting and medicine.
6. Henry Turner. *The English Renaissance Stage: Geometry, Poetics, and the Practical Spatial Arts 1580-1630.*
7. Elizabeth Spiller. "Shakespeare and the Making of Early Modern Science".
8. In *Magic and Technology* (2005) Anthony Grafton discusses the use of automata and mechanical contraptions that performed magical effects. See also Steven Shapin's *The Scientific Revolution* (1996) where he argues that there was no single coherent cultural entity as "science" in the seventeenth century to undergo a revolutionary change. He also provides a useful survey of early modern mechanical philosophy (30-57). Brian Vickers'

Introduction to *Occult and Scientific Mentalities in the Renaissance* (1984) surveys the intermingling of the occult and non-occult mentalities of seventeenth century.

9. Francis Yates. *The Occult Philosophy of the Elizabethan Age*. London, Boston: Routledge and Kegan Paul, 1979.
10. Peter J. French recounts this story in *The World of an Elizabethan Magus*, 8.
11. EEBO Accessed on August 4, 2011 http://name.umdl.umich.edu.proxy.libraries.rutgers.edu/A20021.0001.001.
12. EEBO Accessed on August 4, 2011.
ttp://quod.lib.umich.edu.proxy.libraries.rutgers.edu/cgi/t/text/text-idx?c=eebo;cc=eebo;rgn=div1;view=trgt;lvl=1;idno=A20027.0001.001;id=DLPS1;note=inline#DLPS1.
13. To quote from Dee's letter: "to cause your High|nesse sayd Seruant, to be tryed and cleared of that horrible and damnable, and to him, most grieuous and dammageable Sclaunder: generally, and for these many yeeres last past, in this Kingdome raysed, and continued, by report, and Print, against him: Namely, That he is, or hath bin a Coniurer, or Caller, or Invocator of diuels: Vpon which most vngodly, and false report, so boldly, constantly, and impudently auouched: yea, and vncontrolled, and hitherto vnpunished, for so many yeeres, continuing: (Albeit, your Maiesties said Suppliant, hath published in Print, diuers his earnest Apologies, against it)... [O]r any o|ther,) to haue your Highnesse said Suppliant, to be tryed, in the premisses: Who offereth himselfe willingly, to the punishment of Death: (yea, eyther to be stoned to death: or to be buried quicke: or to be burned vnmercifully)".
14. "The Mathematicall Praeface to Elements of Geometrie of Euclid of Megara, by John Dee". The Project Gutenberg ebook. Accessed on August 4, 2011 http://www.gutenberg.org/files/22062/22062-h/main.html.
15. William Sherman, *John Dee: The Politics of Reading and Writing in the English Renaissance*, 19.
16. Ronald Levao. "Bacon and the Mobility of Science".
17. All quote from Francis Bacon's *The Advancement of Learning* is from G.W. Kitchin's edition.

18. We see the beginning of this idea in the *Advancement* but it is fully developed in his later work *Novum Organum* 1620.
19. Bacon likens the work of the alchemists to the fable of the father who tricked his sons to dig the land for gold. Once the land is plowed it yields a good harvest and brings riches, but not quite in the way the sons had imagined: "So assuredly the search and stir to make gold hath brought to light a great number of good and fruitful inventions and experiments, as well for the disclosing of nature as for the use of man's life" (29).
20. Michael Witmore. *Culture of Accidents: Unexpected Knowledges in Early Modern England.*
21. Spiller, pp. 24-25, 27.
22. All quotations from the play are cited by act, scene and line numbers and are from *The Tempest* The Arden Shakespeare. Eds. Virginia Mason Vaughan and Alden T. Vaughan. Surrey: Thomas Nelson and Sons Ltd., 1999.
23. King James and Queen Anne's wedding voyages were marred by tempests. King James' subsequent interest in witch hunts and demonologies is attributed to those journeys.
24. In "Miraculous Harp: A Reading of Shakespeare's *Tempest*", Harry Berger Jr. also reads the epilogue as a prologue, but unlike my reading, he sees it as the beginning of Prospero's life outside the magic circle. Interestingly, Berger also sees the Prospero's renunciation of magic as tentative and finds Prospero unwilling to leave the island (276-277).
25. *Macbeth* Edited by Stephen Orgel.
26. In "What Cares these Roarers for the Name of King": Language and Utopia in *The* Tempest", David Norbrook sees this initial social transgression and undermining of authority as a pervasive concern of a utopian play where the vision of society transcends existing codes and signs" (21).
27. In *Banquets Set Forth* (2001) Chris Meads argues that the Elizabethan stage established an "enduring link between banquets and consummated revenge, a link that gains from and develops both visually and figuratively the metaphorical appetite for revenge..." (70).
28. In his Introduction to the Arden Edition (1954) Frank Kermode describes the inconclusive theories that suggest that the stage

directions are Shakespeare's own, written at Stratford during his retirement, or that they might belong to the "incompetent coadjutor" who also allegedly inserted the dream masque in *Cymbeline.* Since the stage directions are borne out by the action in the text, I treat them as an essential part of the text and its performance history.

29. "The Staging of *The Tempest*, III.iii".
30. "A Quaint Device": *The Tempest* at Blackfriars" in *Jacobean Private Theater* (1987) .
31. "*The Tempest* is insistently an art object...[it] reduces the story to the unified and elegant form of Keats' urn... If we cannot play it now, it is because it is a "quaint device" that defeats our clumsy handling. We would turn it into our own–as cruel theater, or psychological theatre or political theater. Shakespeare tells us what it is–an insubstantial pageant..." (96).
32. Robin Headlam-Wells is also of the view that meaning in the play is generated by a dialogue between the play and its audience. She also suggests that "the view of art that *The Tempest* ultimately takes is one of exposing the fictionality of theatrical spectacle" (63). Headlam-Wells prises apart the player-audience dynamics in the play to re-establish Prospero as the musician king who uses art to create political order.
33. See for instance, George Slover's essay "Magic, Mystery and Make-Believe: An Analogical Reading of *The Tempest*" where Slover identifies Prospero's magic with Shakespeare's playwriting (187).
34. Baker and Hulme suggest that distinguishing Prospero's play from Shakespeare's makes it possible to see the lengths to which the play goes to problematize its own narrative, for instance in the narratives of multiple beginnings that Prospero rehearses in the play (203). "Nymphs and Reapers Heavily Vanish: The Discursive Con-Texts of *The Tempest*" in *Alternative Shakespeares.* Ed. John Drakakis.
35. Nora Jonson's essay "Spectacle and the Fantasy of Immateriality: Authorship and Magic in *John a Kent and John a Cumber*" in *Spectacle and Public Performance in the Late Middle Ages and the Renaissance* (2006) compares Ben Jonson's stance of asserting theatrical authorship through anti-theatricality in his famous

falling out with Inigo Jones. She goes on to see Prospero playing out Jonson's stand and in that she finds both Jonson and Prospero disingenuous in being dismissive of spectacle.

36. Stephen Orgel was one of the first critics to see the masque as an essential part of the play, thus dispelling the debates about whether the masque is a later inclusion. More recently David Bevington and David Lindley have shown that the politics of masquing is closely connected to Stuart court politics. John Demarary's book length study, on the spectacles and theatrical forms in *The Tempest*, stops short of claiming that the play is a masque. Ernest B. Gillman sees the masque as an inversion of the Jonsonian masque.
37. Noel L. Brann. *The Debate Over the Origin of Genius During The Italian Renaissance: The Theories of Supernatural Frenzy and Natural Melancholy in Accord and in Conflict on the Threshold of the Scientific Revolution.* Brann elaborates the theory that magicians/scholars were meant to be melancholic which gave them a bleak view of the world and made them vulnerable to the devil.
38. See Denise Albanese's *New Science, New World.*
39. Michael Neill. "Noise, Sound and Sweet Airs: The Burden of Shakespeare's *The Tempest*". Neill also unpacks the multiple musical and non-musical puns built into the word "burden" (44-45).
40. See for instance D.P. Walker's outline of Ficino's "music-spirit" theory in *Spiritual and Demonic Magic.*
41. "Music, Masque, and Meaning in *The Tempest*".

Chapter 3

Fraudulent Magic in Jonson's *The Alchemist*

Ben Jonson's *The Alchemist* (1610) was produced at the Blackfriars theater around the same time as Shakespeare's *The Tempest.* Though both plays are about magic each play takes a remarkably different approach to represent it.[1] *The Tempest* like most other magical plays assumes that the audience, even if ambivalent about the moral status and uses of magic, believes in or suspends other kinds of knowledge in favor of Prospero's wonder working. Jonson's play, on the other hand, courts, coerces and capitalizes on the audience's skepticism about magic. The two plays are also different because of the different kinds of magic that they represent. *The Tempest* takes on scholarly, esoteric magic and *The Alchemist* represents the popular magic of cunning men and women. Where *The Tempest* imagines the practice of magic only in isolation from civic responsibility and requires Prospero to "abjure" his "rough magic" before he can return to his ducal responsibilities, *The Alchemist* places magic squarely in London to explore the circumstances of less dramatic, more routine transactions of magic.

Underlying the differences of the two plays is the commonality of changing seventeenth century discourses of magic that reflect a gradual severance of magic from diabolism. This change is evident when Prospero invokes the language of proto-mechanics as he prepares to give a "probable explanation" of his art in the last act of *The Tempest. The Alchemist* reflects the changing legal interpretation of popular practitioners of magic, the cunning men and women, as fraudulent rather than damned. *The Alchemist* plays on the associations of the word cunning–defined by the OED as the magic of cunning-folks, the knowledge of skilled craft, wisdom and wit but also deceit, underhand craftiness and artifice. Where Marlowe's *Faustus* and Shakespeare's *Tempest* were about scholarly magic and its spectacular theatrical dimension, Jonson's *Alchemist* is about popular magic and its association with fraudulence. The play uses fraudulent magic to suggest that the legitimizing politics of class is crucial in determining the difference between craft and craftiness, knowledge and mis-conception, scholarly magic and popular magic.

The Alchemist declares in the Argument that there is no magic in it, there are, however, three rogues–Subtle, a cheater, Dol, a punk, and Face, a defaulting manservant, who sell fake magic to gullible gentlefolk of the Blackfriars. Led on by Jonson, scholars of *The Alchemist* have seen the magic in the play as no more than a con of the kind that cony-catching pamphlets of the period made their business to expose and the vagrancy laws aimed to punish. Consequently, fraudulence in the play has been examined primarily in the context of early modern vagrancy in the newly emerging proto-capitalist economy.[2] However, as the title of the play suggests, the context of magic, specifically popular magic, is equally important to appreciate the full scope of Jonson's use of fraudulence in the play. This essay argues that *The Alchemist* draws attention to an overlap between Tudor-Jacobean vagrancy and witchcraft laws for its significant bearing on the construction of popular magic.[3] The overlap indicates the ambiguities that accompanied the perception of popular magic as fraudulent. Jonson uses popular magic to satirize the processes called upon to discern fraudulence and establish credibility. The play strategically promotes an off-stage skepticism for what the gulls believe to be credible magic in order to examine the social, material, and metaphysical moorings of credulity. This chapter argues that ultimately Jonson directs the spectator's skepticism from the fraudulent magic on stage to the certainty of knowing the difference between credible and fraudulent magic. In the process, the play offers magic as a tool in the hands of the social outcasts to scrutinize the sublimated desires of the socially privileged.

Confuting with a Cudgel: The Overlapping Semantics of Vagrancy and Witchcraft

The Alchemist opens with a quarrel between Subtle and Face. Each threatens the other in escalating verbal violence,–until Face lays the trump card on Subtle: "I'll bring thee rogue, within/The statute of sorcery, *tricesimo tertio* of Harry the eighth" (1.1.111-112).[4] It is curious that having exposed Subtle as a rogue, who is vulnerable to the vagrancy statue, Face threatens to have Subtle indicted under the witchcraft law. That Jonson's rogues are fashioned in response to the discourses of early modern vagrancy barely needs restating, but this allusion to an overlap with the discourses of witchcraft merits attention because it substantially complicates the objective of Jonson's satire. If the gulls are unable to see through the fraudulence of the rouges, it is because in its functioning popular magic had acquired a deceptively close association with fraudulence.

Face threatens Subtle with Henry VIII's witchcraft statute of 1541/2 *An Acte Against Conjurations, Witchcrafts, Sorcery and Enchantments* devoted to persecute practitioners of magic. It is worth noticing that the genesis of this witchcraft Act was in Henry VIII's vagrancy statute from a decade earlier: *An Acte Concernyng Punysshement of Beggers & Vagabondes* (1530). This statute was legally innovative not only because it criminalized the idle, unemployed vagrant but even more significantly, for the purpose of this essay, because it included a group of people who:

> ...usyng dyvers & subtyle & unlawfull games & playes & some of them feynyng themselfes to have knowledge in Physyke, Physnamye, Plamystrye, or other craftye scyence whereby they beare to the people in hande, that they can tell theire destenyes deceases & fortunes & suche other lyke fantasticall ymaginaciouns to the greate decepyte of the kynge's subjects...".[5]

For the first time in English legal history practitioners of popular magic are identified as vagrant even as vagrancy is declared illegal.[6] This aspect of the statute, left out by Edward VI, is reinstated, almost word for word, by Elizabeth I in 1572 in *An Acte for the Punishement of Vacabondes, and for Releif of the Poore and Impotent.* In addition, the 1572 Act makes the term "roges" synonymous with "vacaboundes" and "Sturdye Beggers" and uses these categories to identify and classify practitioners of popular magic, especially if they were itinerant. Travelling practical wizards were among the hordes of the unemployed migrants that flocked London in the seventeenth century.[7]

The magic clause of the vagrancy statutes has gone mostly unremarked by scholars of either vagrancy or witchcraft studies.[8] While the vagrancy statutes might be read as aiming to punish rogues like Subtle scamming to sell fake magic, these statues applied in letter if not spirit to just about every practitioner of popular magic since only a dissatisfied customer could tell the difference between an authentic popular magician and one that was only pretending. The role of the customer in deciding the nature of magical practice is especially significant since early modern law depended on neighborly surveillance for criminals being turned in as rogues or witches.[9] The customer's perception of magic was thus a crucial measure of its credibility as either helpful or harmful magic. Sorcery and witchcraft were seen as harmful magic owing to the *maleficium* of the practitioner derived directly from the devil as discussed in Chapters 1 and 2. But *The Alchemist* draws attention to the legal and cognitive elisions and amplifications necessary to the differences between helpful and harmful magic distinct. Henry VIII's *Acte against Conjurations, Witchcrafts, Sorcery and Enchantments,* meant to persecute witches and sorcerers, but the Act is also directed against such magic as "use, devise" or "practice" to "get or fynd money or treasure" or to "provoke any persons to un-lawfull love" or have "taken upon them to declare where things lost or stolen should become".[10] These magical activities refer to the practice of popular magic. The severity of the laws acknowledges both the widespread belief in magic and the slipperiness of distinctions between helpful and harmful aspects of popular magic.[11]

Although Jonson's play is called *The Alchemist,* alchemy being one of the most learned forms of magic, the play locates the fascination with alchemy and the fantasy of gold within a rubric of popular appeal and dramatizes the assumptions and practices of popular magic. While alchemy recalls the esoteric practice of select adepts and refers to scholarly magic, the seventeenth century saw a growing traffic between practitioners of practical trades–distillery, metallurgy, mining and medicine and the practice of alchemy.[12] The increased popularity of alchemy, and its directly proportional notoriety, intersected richly with the practical aspect of popular magic especially in an urban context that Jonson exploits in his play by calling it *The Alchemist.* Jonson calls attention to the popular and practical aspect of alchemy as the defining feature of his stage magician instead of astrology that was regarded as the foundation of all magical thought and practice including alchemy. Popular magic is practical. Its beliefs and practices are aimed towards solving problems by manipulating supernatural forces that the common people resorted to in consultation with local magic specialists.[13] The largely illiterate specialists of popular magic denoted as the cunning-folk or village wizards were practical magicians. They were not solitary dwellers of theoretical abstractions in the discipline of magic; they divined, prescribed, concocted, conjured, found, spelled and reversed the magic of other practical magicians.

Keith Thomas suggests that "the work of the practicing wizard was sustained by the parallel activities of many contemporary intellectuals" but he also emphasizes the need to resist the temptation to explain the practice of popular magic as a reflection of the interests of the scholarly magicians (215).[14] Thomas argues that despite a material and metaphysical milieu that was sympathetic to all kinds of magical activity, there were clear distinctions between popular magic–a continuation of classical and Anglo-Saxon folk and fairy inherited from the Middle Ages and Neoplatonic revivals such as Ficino's magic, studied in England by John Dee.[15] It is important to note the difference between popular and scholarly magic because not only does the provenance and practice of each point to a different social strata of early English society but also because it makes it possible to appreciate instances that bridge or defy the boundaries between the two. *The Alchemist* is one such example where the boundaries between popular and scholarly magic are meant to reveal and play the class politics.

The cunning-folk performed a range of practical magical tasks—these included healing, which often took the form of reversing enchantments, and finding lost goods, which needed divination which made for their easy collusion with witchcraft.[16] Owen Davies suggests that the cunning-folk escaped the enforcement of the witchcraft laws that targeted both cunning-folk and witches.[17] The charge of not being magic at all but "subtle game and play" deflected the malice of witchcraft by associating popular magic with the deception of petty fraudulence. By the end of the seventeenth century public opinion would turn "to an overwhelming view that the cunning-folk were pernicious tricksters rather than the servants of Satan".[18] For popular magic, the distancing from diabolism came with the simultaneous association with fraudulence.

The conundrum that presents itself is that legal acknowledgement of magic resulted in the persecution of witches; those practitioners of magic that were not persecuted were exempt because they were regarded as fraudulent for professing fake magic. The overlap of fraudulence between witchcraft and vagrancy laws served a fortuitous turn to the practitioners of popular magic. While vagrancy legislation used fraudulence to criminalize vagrants, fraudulence became an unwitting guise that protected practitioners of popular magic from the witchcraft laws. Ironically, fraudulence became a protective mechanism for popular magic that any consumer or producer of magic in the seventeenth century would have to have known. It is commonplace to read Jonson for his jabs at the cupidity and naiveté of the gulls for their failing to discern the fraudulence; consequently, scholarly attention continues to bring out the enterprising smartness of the rogues.[19] But a wider perspective on popular magic, especially in the way that it emerges from a tangled legal discourse and cuts across the class and calling of its users, shows that Jonson's gulls may be greedy but are not naïve; they have, what Ann Barton calls "cunningly enlarged aspirations".[20] The overt transaction of obviously fraudulent magic in *The Alchemist* is only the beginning of a deeper examination of what the spectator assumes to be obvious about fraudulence and magic.

Making Matters Subtle: Fraudulent Magic

The Alchemist's Argument promises a play where popular conceptions of vagrancy and magic converge into a heady mix "Till they and all in fume are gone" (11). The Argument claims that an "idle servant", whose master is out of town, gets to know a "cheater and his punk" who have given up their "narrow practice" to become "cozeners at large". While Face, temporarily masterless and Dol, a prostitute, recall archetypes from the rogue literature, Subtle is a less easy fit. How his new practice of cozening is different from his earlier cheating is unclear till the Argument also tells us that they "contract" a venture to sell magical goods and services in Face's absent master's house. It could be assumed that Subtle's contribution makes it so that "Much company they draw, and much abuse,/in casting figures, telling fortunes, news/Selling of flies, flat bawdry with the stone:.." (8-10). The charge of fraudulence was common to both vagabonds and magicians; however, the fraudulence of each group was constructed and regarded differently.

Face reflects the rhetoric of the rogue literatures in his accusations when Subtle, assuming his contribution to be the substance of the "venture tripartite", demands "primacy in the division" (1.2.131) which leads to the quarrel with Face. Before Face stumps Subtle with his legal knowledge, his mounting allegations help locate Subtle in the social spectrum of seventeenth-century London. Face's opening salvo is: "Rogue, rogue! Out of all your sleights"(1.1.4). As indicated earlier, Elizabeth I's 1572 statute had made the "rogue" synonymous with being a vagrant or a beggar. And indeed Face paints Subtle to be exactly a homeless beggar, inhaling steam at Pie-Corner for his meals: "Where, like the father of hunger, you did walk/Piteously costive, with your pinched-horn-nose,/And you complexion of the Roman wash,/Stuck full of black melancholic worms" (1.1.26-30). Richard Harp glosses Subtle's constipation, sallow complexion and blackheads as the signs of a starving melancholic scholar.[21] Rogue literature was instrumental in forging the automatic connection of homeless scholars with vagrant beggars and both as fraudulent.

Rogue literatures produced the figure of the rogue by ascribing an existential illegitimacy to the vagrants who were unmoored from their manorial ties and traditional trappings of social legitimacy.[22] Pamphleteers like Awdeley, Harman, Greene, Dekker and Rid saw the mobile population of dispossessed workers as choosing a life of idleness, deception and disguising.[23] Consider, for instance, Thomas Harman from *A Caveat for Common Cursitors, Vulgarly Called Vagabonds* (1566): "I have been accustomed [to] talk and confer daily with many of these wily wanderers...by whom I have gathered and understand their deep dissimulation and detestable dealing, being marvelous subtle and crafty in their kind, for not one amongst twenty will discover, either declare their scelerous secrets".[24] The adjectives "subtle" and "crafty" to describe vagrants are repeated in every cony-catching pamphlet since Harman's. These adjectives are a semantic link to vagrancy statutes of Henry VIII and Elizabeth I which identified cunning-folk as "subtyle" and feigning knowledge of "craftye syence". This reminder brings into context the second part of Face's accusation: "out of all your sleights". He considers Subtle's magic to be sleight-of-hand, feigned knowledge not worthy of a bigger share in the profits.

In naming his vagrant magician "Subtle," Jonson creates a character out of the overlapping semantics of vagrancy and magic. In Jonson's Subtle, the subtlety of the cunning-folk, mined for the tenuousness of their social and legal position, is mingled with the subtle rarefaction and exaltation of matter that marked the work of alchemists in the laboratory.[25] Alchemical subtlety is to see the tentativeness of matter in the context of its possible perfection. However such tentativeness, especially as embodied by the mobile vagrants and cunning-folk, swayed the balance of subtlety from needful nuance to artful equivocation that finally tilted in favor of epic imposture in Milton's serpent.[26] But in Jonson, the achievement of subtlety over inertness and the positive ambivalence of fluid social categories constitute Subtle as much as the imposture inherent in his name. Subtle is made of the social and moral illegitimacy of vagrants and beggars, but he also invokes the subtlety and craft of magic which thrived in spite of its association with fraudulence and sometimes even because of it.

Face, himself the master of disguise, carefully produces Subtle, for the "venture tripartite", as a man of magic by combining the fraudulence of alchemists, cunning-folk and rogues. His first full description of Subtle prominently includes alchemy:

> When all your alchemy and your algebra,
> Your minerals, vegetals, and animals,
> Your conjuring, cozening, and your dozen trades
> Could not relieve your corpse with so much linen
> ...
> I gave you countenance, credit for your coals
> Your stills, your glasses, your materials,
> Built you a furnace, drew you customers.
> Advanced all your black arts; lent you, beside,
> A house to practice in- (1.1.40-9)

Face argues that Subtle's magic did not earn him a living till Face scoped him as a partner.

Although he throws "cozening" in the list with other "dozen trades" that he doesn't yet elaborate, he establishes Subtle's primary identity as an alchemist which indicates Face's interest in teaming up with him. Subtle's scholarly demeanor would be attractive to the gentry of London and give the "venture tripartite" an air of credibility. Face's investment makes him, in a way, Subtle's first patron and a disgruntled one at that.

Egged on by Subtle's insulting insinuations, Face elaborates on the other "dozen trades" in a speech that will be closely echoed in Act 4.4 by Surly, the play's dubious rogue-catcher.

> I'll write thee up bawd in Paul's; have all thy tricks
> Of cozening with a hollow coal, dust scrapings;
> Searching for things lost, with a sieve and shears,
> Erecting figures in your rows of houses,
> And taking in of shadows with a glass,

Told in red letters; and a face cut for thee
Worse than Gamaliel Ratsey's. (1.1.94-100)

This list describes some prominent activities of the cunning-folk: searching for lost things with sieve and shears, casting astrological charts, divination by reading fortunes in a glass. Elsewhere Dapper calls Subtle a cunning-man, Mammon confirms that Subtle has the reputation of a rare healer, and Subtle himself admits to fortune telling through metoposcopy (1.3. 44). The plot to divine and enable love for Dame Pliant only adds to the list of things that Subtle does as a cunning-man. But Face finds that Subtle's association with popular magic as cunning-man undermines him as the scholarly alchemist and a necromancer magician. As a cunning-man, Subtle is more easily classed with the homeless vagrants who are charged with bawdry and robbery both of which involved deception but not magic. But letting Subtle slip away for a common rogue would hardly be a triumph for Face; hence, he goes for the jugular: "I'll bring thee rogue, within/The statute of sorcery, *tricesimo tertio* of Harry the eighth". Face knows that although Subtle fits the bill of a rogue, the accusation of sorcery holds a mightier spectacle of punishment.

Although Face uses the rhetoric of rogue literatures to discredit Subtle, as a member of the "venture tripartite" he contributes to a greater ambivalence about who Subtle is and what he is capable of doing. Such ambivalence is in clear contrast to how the play's actual rogue-catcher Surly, views Subtle. Surly arrives with Mammon, the chief financier of Subtle's alchemical experiment, who wants ostensibly for Surly to be convinced of the legitimacy of alchemy. Surly declares that "alchemy is a pretty kind of game,/Somewhat like tricks o' the cards, to cheat a man/With charming" (2.3.180-82). Surly, as is expected of a rogue-catcher, is already convinced that Subtle, Face and Dol are "household-rogues" incapable of doing anything that is not fraudulent. When Mammon pits Surly and Subtle in a debate, Subtle accurately recounts the basic premises of alchemy, the principles of transmutation and the properties of elements as it informed the alchemists of his day.[27] To Surly it is "Next to canting" of rogues (2.3.43).[28] Surly's insistence that alchemy is only the trick of rogues points to the figure of the false-alchemist and the numerous fraudulent alchemical ventures attributed to them in the period.[29] However, Jonson appears uninterested in the rogue-catcher's narrow understanding of rogues or magic. If his name were not indication enough, Surly is also beaten and run off-stage in Act 4.7 at a moment when he thinks that he has all but triumphed in exposing the rogues.

In playing up the overlapping semantics of vagrancy and magic, *The Alchemist* privileges the confusion of social categories and magical practices and, though brief, its empowering effect on the socially dispossessed. The ambiguities in Face's characterization show that Subtle's magic is more complex than Surly's reasons for seeing Subtle only as fraud. Because Surly's views are rejected, it could be argued that Jonson encourages the play to be read for the process of fabricating credible magic rather than its obvious dismissal as fraud. Surly's insistence on fraudulence makes Mammon keen to know the genuine alchemist from the fraudulent one. Tara Nummedal emphasizes the importance of understanding early modern alchemical frauds within the context of a widespread belief in the transmutation of metals rather than the *a priori* position of assuming alchemists to be deceiving and the patron as foolish.[30] Subtle and Mammon have been read in the tradition of the false alchemist and the deceived patron as Surly sees them, but even critics who read the play as profoundly engaged with the scientific practices of its time, and who have fruitfully extended the play's interpretation beyond its grinding satire, do so by riding the debunking of alchemy.[31] Since the audience does not see the alchemical experiment as happening or not happening, an alternative to reading the alchemical talk only as evidence of overwhelming and obvious fraud, is to read it for what it does achieve. For instance, beneath Mammon's extravagant fantasies lies a careful pragmatism.

Mammon is well educated in the vocabulary and methods of alchemy and he finds that Subtle matches, in piety and knowledge, *his* expectations of a credible alchemist. Where Surly only sees the fraudulence of rogues, Mammon sees the possibility of magic along with the risk of fraudulence. To have the alchemist himself debate the ignorance out of Surly serves Mammon's purpose of reassuring himself of Subtle's credibility. It could be argued that Mammon is the greater fool for being duped despite his knowledge or indeed that he is duped because of it. Such an objection directs the reading of the play towards a bigger design where greed of the gulls is but a paltry matter. The play's satire questions the assumed basis of credibility of which knowledge, such as Mammon possesses, is one. The few opening scenes of the play make it apparent that its real investment, unlike the visible front put up by the Argument, is in discrediting the certain apprehension of fraudulence as fraudulence.

It would seem necessary that a reading of the play as a comic satire requires the rogues to be cheating thieves which they are. However, the play in the quarrel scene, in the discrediting of Surly, in the gulling of the dupes puts their fraudulence in a complex social context of class inequality and repressive social laws. Instead the play insists attention to why they appear credible to the gulls, since the category of popular magic especially disallows any guaranteed distinctions between fraudulence and credibility. It is possible then to claim that in the early modern mind popular magic had to have existed in negotiation with fraudulence and malevolence to be an experience of credible magic.

By Your Fac': Credible Magic

Declaring the lack of magic in the Argument is an ingenious ploy that reverses the call for a willing suspension of disbelief. The setup of magic as fraudulent baits the playgoer's skepticism to draw attention to the way that magic works and why the gulls think that the magic is credible. The working of popular magic seems not to be about its ultimate efficacy but about the systems that it engages–social, metaphysical, material, and the consciousness with which its users negotiate its credibility. The negotiation of magical credibility between the gulls and the rogues indicates that the discerning of fraudulence relies on the processes that produce credibility. The gullings demonstrate that the gulls calculate the odds as they risk being gulled. The measures to establish credibility that the rogues and gulls employ are no more outlandish than what the spectators employ to discern and judge the fraudulence. The gulling of Able Drugger and Dapper demonstrates the provisional nature of credulity by exposing its shifting material and semantic grounds.

Able Drugger's sign making brings together a talismanic assemblage of resemblances that is the hallmark of early modern magic.[32] Drugger wants an astrological sign to hang outside his shop to attract more business. The obvious comic parody of the scene is written over with a curious bid for its credibility:

> He shall have *a bell*, that's A*bel*;
> And by it standing one whose name is Dee
> In a *rug* gown, there's D, and Rug that's *drug*;
> And right anenst him a dog snarling Er;
> There's *Drugger*, Abel Drugger. That's his sign. (2.6.19-23)

This sign is layered with references to vagrancy and magic. Eric Wilson made a correlation between this sign and the woodcut that appeared on the title page of one very popular text from the rogue literature of the period: *The Bellman of London* "bringing to light the most notorious villanies that are now practiced in the kingdome" that was serialized and printed more than ten times between 1608 and 1610.[33] The woodcut features a bellman, a man in a gown holding a bell and a dog snarling at his heels. However, the signification runs even deeper since the figure of John Dee, the one "in a rug gown" is superimposed on the figure of the rogue catcher. If the rogue-catcher stands for the imperative of legitimacy gained by hunting frauds and villains, John Dee also stands to legitimize the magic that Drugger is paying for. Dee's notoriety was not based in accusations of fraud but rather in the fear that his angel calling was all too effective. The Bellman and Dee together make up a doubly legitimate sign for Drugger.

The success of the rogues' venture is attributed to the rapid and dexterous manipulation of the hapless gulls by the rogues. But the gulls, even the most hapless of them all as Dapper seems to be, are conscious users of magic and the rogues can be seen as responding to *their* cues. Dapper's gulling is easily read for the extra ridiculousness heaped on him by Subtle, Face and Dol. No other character is stripped nearly naked, gagged with gingerbread and locked up in a smelly bathroom for the better part of the play; his gullibility must mark the lowest point for any measure of credulity. And yet, Dapper's gulling from his own points-of-view re-redirects attention from his inability to see the fraudulence of magic to the rapidly transforming ties of belief and credit in the seventeenth century. As Dapper sets about making his expectations clear, he highlights the suggestive space of dissembling that even customers expected popular magic to occupy.

The gulling of Dapper does not in fact begin with Face finding himself an easy dupe, but with a subtle calculation on Dapper's part evident from his very first question: "Is this the Cunning-man?" (1.2.9). Reassured by Face that he is, Dapper asks, "Is he a doctor"? (1.2.11). Dapper seeks a fly for gambling. Face mediates Dapper's request to Subtle for a "rifling fly, none of your great familiars" (1.2.85). A fly, although a diminution, serves Satan, known as the Lord of the Flies asking for a fly instead of a familiar is just about the difference in the visible size of the magical agents not in its quality.[34] It is important to remember that Dapper is the source of all of Face's knowledge of the witchcraft statutes (1.2.20); inherent in his two questions is *his* plan to work around the danger of his request. It is telling that Dapper should first ascertain that Subtle is a cunning-man. Cunning-folk were expected to have commerce with the countryside fairies, hobgoblins, imps and elves that urbane doctors of magic would not condescend. The evolving ambiguities in the witchcraft statutes ensured that dealings with a cunning-man were safer than to approach a witch or doctor of necromancy. Thus, the significance of Dapper's second question, if Subtle isn't also a doctor he cannot get Dapper the demonic fly.

Dapper's logic represents the requirement to synthesize folk and learned, fairy and demonic magic that Regina Buccola sees as the play's defining achievement.[35] Although Buccola remarks on Jonsons' impressive synthesis of different magical traditions with religion via the rouge's interpretation of fairy magic, she reads the play for Jonson's skepticism of folk and fairy belief. For her the satire works because neither Jonson nor the audience believes in fairies. While Buccola's careful contextualization of fairy belief is very useful, I would like to argue differently about its use by Jonson. The satire is successful precisely because people believed in fairy magic. That belief is certainly challenged by the fairy cons but the challenge lies in recognizing a false mediator rather than in discrediting all fairy belief. The preponderance and success of cons implies belief in a system that is understood to be complicated enough to be left to the wisdom of the experts. In that early modern fairy or alchemical scams are no different from financial or scientific scams in our own times. Dapper not only approaches the rogues as experts but as ones who can cater to his whimsical understanding of what magic is and how it might be negotiated or accessed.

Dapper's gulling plays up the close connection of monetary credit and credibility in its various iterations in the early modern proto-capitalist market. Like the concept of fraudulence, early modern credibility has an interesting social and etymological history. Peter Stallybrass argues that before creeds and credit were put into different realms–religio-cultural and economic, they belonged together as the Latin *credere* suggests: to believe is where you put your credit.[36] This overlap between creed and credit, monetary and metaphysical belief is made explicit in this exchange between Drugger and the rogues.

> Face: Come
> You know well enough, though you dissemble it
> Dapper: I'fac, I do not: you are mistaken
> Face: How!
> Swear by your fac, and in a thing so known
> Unto the Doctor? How shall we Sir trust you
> In other matter? Can we ever think,
> When you have won five or six thousand pound.
> That you will send us share in't, by this rate? (1.2.127-133)

Face and Subtle are trying to convince Dapper that he is related to the queen of fairies. Such a belief is a matter of faith, that Dapper calls on to say that he had no such inkling. Face asserts Dapper's fairy lineage as a matter of fact and faith that would make him a credible business partner except, they claim, that Dapper kept such vital information from them. Face's indignation over the breach of faith translating to a lack of credibility goes right to the heart of Dapper's own convictions.

Dapper uses monetary credit to negotiate the danger that credible magic involved. He demands that the rogues present magic as both convincingly material and metaphysical. When he makes Face negotiate with Subtle on his behalf, Face pleads his request with increasing numbers of "angels":

> Face: Four Angels here.
> Subtle: You do me wrong, good sir
> Face: Doctor, wherein? To tempt you with these spirits?
> Subtle: Fore heaven, I scarce can think you are my friend,
> That so would draw me to apparent danger. (1.2.39-42)

The punch in this exchange is the pun on angels, the English gold coin which had acquired the superstitious significance in the magical ritual of "the king's touch" to cure scrofula.[37] At the same time, Face alludes to angels as "spirits" that tempt one to damnation–once again recalling John Dee's recent public fall from grace for angel calling. Subtle emphasizes the "apparent danger" in such an exchange. In the very first step towards establishing the credibility of the practitioner, this exchange, where magic is couched in money, establishes the monetary and material moorings of credibility. However, the magic itself lies in the "apparent danger" that demonologists and theologians from all the splintered sides of the Reformation outdid each other in spelling out. To Dapper money appears to reduce the "apparent danger" of the enterprise to manageable pinch sized portions that Face happily delivers to him in the fairy scene.

From Dapper's perspective the humiliation that the rogues heap on him in the name of ritual ceremony is a transformed experience of danger that exceeds what money can buy. The purification rites function like Drugger's sign to the consumer of magic the act of its performance overrides the appearance of overwhelming parody to an outside perspective.[38] The apparently nonsensical ceremonies actually result in his meeting the fairy queen. She gives him an invisible fly in a touching benediction that he receives in a speechless rapture: *"Much nephew shalt thou win, much shalt thou spend;/Much shalt thou give away, much shalt thou lend*" (5.4.29-30). Dol dressed as fairy queen blesses Dapper with unending credit and credibility; she blesses him with an increased ability to spend money which, in the logic of the emerging capitalist economy, ensured wealth in the form of further credit.[39]

Monetary credit shaped the idea of credit as belief. Since the system of monetary credit was in a state of flux in the seventeenth century, it unsettled the connection between reputation and credibility. It also gave a wide berth to new entrepreneurial ventures in the early modern market. The play draws on the interaction between the newly emerging contractual credit system and the established but increasingly defaulting system of household credit that was testing the tight knit of belief and credit in the early modern period.[40] The contractual credit system was shifting the weight of belief from the reputation of people to the contract of the venture itself. The "venture tripartite" is a contractual credit agreement between Face, Subtle and Dol to dissemble a household credibility in the 'friars with the proper "words and fashion". However, the dissembling magic takes the form of contractual credit between each customer and the rogues. Therefore so long as Mammon himself does not doubt the profitability of the venture, it is of little value that it appears to be a scam to Surly or even the spectator. So long as Dapper is a satisfied customer, not even the spectator can call his experience of magic fraudulent. Dapper is Face, Subtle and Dol's only satisfied customer who does not return to seek vengeance at the end of the play.

The appeal of popular magic lay in its practical materialization of things to do, say, or keep and it could be argued, as is evident in the case of Dapper and Drugger, that the process, the language, the things evoked to represent magic actually *constitute* magic. Why are Dapper and Drugger's experiences of magic inauthentic while Prospero's shipwrecked enemies are considered to have truly been gripped by powerful magic? Is invisible Ariel necessarily more magical than Dapper's invisible fly? The work of magic is not ultimately only about efficacy but about the systems it engages—social, metaphysical, material, epistemological—that shape the conscious and unconscious assumptions about everything else as well. Popular magic was not sought, articulated, experienced or derided in isolation from everything else that made real life real; it was there with everything else underlying or overwhelming all kinds of transactions that made up the dailiness of daily life. The gulling of Dapper and Drugger foregrounds the precariousness of the established standards of credibility against which the certain fraudulences of the rogues is meant to be measured. The "judging spectator" is invited to laugh at the gulls, but to laugh at them is to also acknowledge the loopholes of the very systems of producing credibility that are used to judge them. Knowing the true from the false and developing better means to approximate and perpetuate what is held to be true could be said to be the basis of most human endeavors. *The Alchemist,* as a satire, is not as interested in the inability of the gulls to tell the true from the false as much as in highlighting the fraught processes that are used to construct the true and the false. This cognitive breakdown from certain knowing to not knowing anything for sure is in preparation for an even deeper unraveling of certainties that the expansive potential of alchemy enables.

To argue that popular magic was only seen as capable of small scale enhancements of ordinary life would be to inadvertently miss its full potential. The cunning-folk remained at the center of witchcraft and vagrancy laws because of their protean versatility in providing different kinds of services across social classes. They mediated desires for access to things or experiences that could very easily exceed expressions of ordinariness. Popular magic posed a constant threat to institutions that propagated normative order not because of what the cunning-folk actually did but what they were feared to be capable of doing. Dapper and Drugger's attempts to bolster their wealth are meant to overtake not challenge the imperatives of the socio-economic credibility within which they find themselves. But the imagination and desire for a philosopher's stone brings socio-economic discrepancies into sharp contrast and with it a version of utopia that briefly stands the central imaginative space of the play on its head.

Magic, with its promise of extraordinary wealth or power, occasions obvious self-aggrandizement for which there could be no better literary example than Sir Epicure Mammon. Mammon's expression of self-centeredness is so superlative that it requires him to re-imagine the value of things around him and with that the socio-economics of the world that would have to change to accommodate him. Similarly, the Anabaptists also re-envision the logic of the world in which they are marginalized. Though it does not bear any motive of altruism, magic makes the individual imagination at the height of its self-centeredness become, oddly, most sociable.

"Extracting the Soul of Things": The Real Value of Magic

With its promise of absolute wealth and immortality, alchemy is probably where the ceaseless imaginings to improve the human condition finally comes to rest. Unlike Dapper's fly and Drugger's sign, the magic of the philosopher's stone is so expansive in its scope that existing systems of value or expressions of consumption are inadequate to even express it. Alchemy is the ultimate magic. The philosopher's stone can produce gold and elixir which could, in effect, erase material scarcity and mortal suffering: the two things that underlie and undermine human effort. The philosopher's stone thus also mandates a radical re-imagining of the world in which it is realized. Jonson explores the nature of the default utopia that that Mammon and the Anabaptists might establish with the philosopher's stone.

Wayne Shumaker suggests that in its earliest known histories, alchemy developed from two distinct traditions of laboratory experimentation and philosophical meditations.[41] Peggy Knapp's succinctly summarizes the popular perception of alchemy as a blend of technology and spirituality:

> The [philosopher's] stone was seen as a scientific/technological artifact and a pious penetration of God's secrets and these two faces of alchemical work co-existed through its long history with varying emphasis on one or another...Alchemy offered a utopian promise that knowledge, some blend of technological expertise and spiritual insight, would enhance human happiness. (576)

Although they were not always distinct, by and large, practical alchemy was pursued by the proto-chemists and mystics developed its spiritual aspects.[42] Accordingly, Jonson splits the experience of alchemy along the lines of technology and piety as Epicure Mammon and the Anabaptists–Ananias and Tribulation Wholesome–approach the stone with their particular bent of mind to transform the world into to two very different places.

It is important that for Mammon especially, but certainly the others as well, the quest for magic is not fueled by necessity. Mammon is a rich nobleman "a grave sir, a rich, that has no need" (2.3.279), as Surly puts it. Mammon and the Anabaptists, a beleaguered, radical sect of puritans are the two financiers of the philosopher's stone. Mammon and the Anabaptists have very little in common. Mammon seeks the philosopher's stone in order to fulfill his desire for every form of physical appetite that he can imagine and the Anabaptists, working on behalf of the their exiled brethren, want to re-instate their faith by making up their lack of popularity with gold and elixir. It is a part of Jonson's larger satiric scheme that these differences meld into a shocking recognition of similarity by the end of the play. In the final act, Mammon is ready to "mount the turnip cart and preach/the end of the world" (5.5.81-82), while Ananias stakes a claim on Mammon's material possessions. But the beginning of the play finds Mammon confident that the artifact stone can be bought along with the piety that needs to be invested in it and the Anabaptist brethren see no problem with becoming "temporal lords" (3.2.53) in their spiritual quest. While Mammon and the Anabaptists are obvious targets of Jonson's satire, the absurdity of their imaginative excess is a mock-serious comment on the values and moral standards that are taken for granted outside the confines of the play world.

Mammon is able to re-imagine the world around him partly because his apprehension of the world is already de-contextualized and less strictly temporal:

> Come on, Sir, Now, you set your foot on shore
> In Novo Orbe, here's the rich Peru
> And there within, sir, are the golden mines
> Great Solomon's Ophir! He was sailing to't
> Three years but we have reached it in ten months...
> This is the happy day, wherein, to all my
> Friends I will pronounce the happy word, "Be rich". (2.1. 1-7)

Mammon conflates actual sources of wealth for colonial Europe such as the New World and Peru with mythical cities of richness such as King Solomon's city of Ophir. Gold in its preciousness, rarity and power over Mammon's imagination is already magical and he imagines magic to be the best way to derive it. He disassociates gold from the realities of colonization by mythologizing it and investing instead in the technology of alchemy which even speeds up the process to a mere ten months.[43] For Mammon, gold is at once mythical, transcendental and a marketable commodity produced in a laboratory. Mammon's evaluation of gold invites a comparison to Marx's critique of commodities produced in industrialized economies which Marx made with a backward glance to colonialism.[44]

A commodity is magical because its value is measured not in terms of its utility but by its exchange value which is above all an expression of the social value of the commodity. The materialism of industrial capitalism, its ability to turn every human experience into a marketable product, ironically, involves a kind of magic–the kind that comes from seeing the value of a thing as an experience so transcendental that it can barely be described in words and hardly contained in things.[45] This critique was Marx's *tour de force* because he was able to reproduce in the heart of rational European materialism the very thing, magic, that the nineteenth-century colonizing Europeans used to distinguish themselves from the primitive fetishisms of the colonized natives.[46] So Mammon, it would appear, is an early financier of industrial production attracted, not surprisingly then, to a set of enterprising entrepreneurs in a market that is beginning to heave and create spaces for such exchanges. As he tells Surly, "I buy it/My venture brings it me" (2.1.100). However, Mammon commodifies magic to find that he needs to articulate the magic of magic, its distilled essence, or value that the philosopher's stone must have in spite of its easy commodification and the money that he pays for Subtle's piety and Face's labor. Mammon finds that he risks compromising the magic of alchemy so he resorts to articulating its magic in terms of what it will enable him to do. He begins by "pronouncing" to his friends the words "be rich".

Mammon's fantasy for great wealth, predicated by his second name, is complimented by his first name, Epicure, which compels him to express his desire in terms of great aesthetic taste and pleasure. Aesthetics becomes his means of expressing the abstract value of things and rendering ordinary things extra-ordinary. That Mammon is so ready to make his friends (and cooks and entire cities) rich is less an indication of his generosity and more a pathology where poverty and ill-health are a matter of bad taste. Mammon best expresses his desire in terms of his various appetites and the aesthetic standards of its fulfillment. He imagines luxurious clothing of "taffeta-sarsnet, soft and light like cobwebs" and "gloves of fishes and bird skins perfumed/with gums of paradise and eastern air" (2.2.89,92). Down is too hard a bed for him, and his sexual appetite is to be met either by "succubae" or by sublime pure wives of wealthy men who are pimped by their parents. He describes with great flourish what he would eat: beards of barbells, oiled mushrooms and the swelling unctuous paps/ Of a fat pregnant sow newly cut off/Dressed with an exquisite and poignant sauce (2.2.82-5). Mammon's detailed and expansive imagination, that surpasses Faustus' imaginative appetite, rarifies his desires. It is evidence of such ardor in his pursuit for material excess as can only come from a need made poignant by the fact that it cannot ordinarily be even expressed as a need. Mammon's attempt to decontextualize and aestheticized the use of wealth is his way to give it a value that is extraordinary. Mammon desires and articulates such a conspicuous consumption and expression of wealth with such poetic hyperbole that it can be fulfilled only by either imagining its use in ways not yet explored or by going against the norms that contribute to the making a thing or experience ordinary. His choice of alchemy as a way to fulfill his desire for the extraordinary is aptly met in alchemy because alchemy makes the impossible sound probable it is the art of "nature naturized" (2.1.63). The secrecy and obscurity of alchemy supplements the impetus of maintaining Mammon's taste for the extraordinary so he chooses Subtle who he believes "is a rare man/An excellent artist" who "can extract/The soul of all things by his art" (4.1.81-2, 85-6). Mammon feels Subtle can render the value of things not by its use but by its subtle ineffable essence.

The politics of extravagant consumption and the apparent power of sociability inherent in the value of gold draws attention to the ways in which magic complicates the value of things and the relationship between things and people. A magical thing such as Drugger's sign or the philosopher's stone is said to exert more power than the logical sum of its material parts. A philosopher's stone with its alleged power to transform things of less value and easy availability, such as iron, into gold, the thing of ultimate value against which the value of other things are measured, threatens the imagined stability of the social structures and relationships of exchange that are based on the power derived precisely from the difference in the value of gold and the prosaic materiality and easy availability of iron. For instance, while preparing himself to meet with the lady, that he thinks Dol is, Mammon rehearses how he will "heighten his talk" such that "she shall feel gold, taste gold, hear gold, sleep gold;/Nay we will *concumbere* gold" (4.1.29-30). He hopes to have enhanced the value of feeling, tasting, hearing, sleeping and having sex by substituting it with gold. The love that he expresses for Dol sounds like the love for gold. Gold is the extraction of the essence or the soul of all things pleasurable to him because it stands in contrasting value to iron. But he inadvertently erases this difference in value when he imagines suffering the opposite problem of running out of iron: "My only care is/Where to get stuff enough now to project on;/This town will not half serve me" (2.2.11-13) to which Face makes a sly dig: "No, Sir? Buy/The covering off o' the churches" (14). Unaware that the rogues are planning to sell his household goods to the exiled church of the Anabaptists, Mammon agrees that it is a good idea.

Quite in spite of himself, Mammon re-imagines the community around him on the basis of gold and elixir. Any form of authority, temporal or spiritual, becomes meaningless to him as he imagines erasing sickness, poverty and suffering from his field of vision as he allows his expansive excess to spread from the satisfaction of his appetites to that of everyone around him, "My foot-boy" he says, "shall eat pheasants, calvered salmons,/Knots, godwits, lampreys" (2.2.79-80). While Mammon erases all social and class differences in his utopia of consumption and consummation, the Anabaptists who are the other financiers of the alchemical experiment, set about revising the basis of sin and evil in their self-justifying version of the perfect republic.

The Anabaptists are unlike all the other customers of Subtle, Face and Dol because they do not want the riches for personal material gain but for the purpose of their faith, and unlike Dapper, Mammon and Able Drugger, the Anabaptists don't represent the privileged mainstays of gentle society. In early modern England the Anabaptists occupied a category of derision not unlike the one that the rogues and witches occupied. The Anabaptists were the Dutch separatists, followers of Melchiore Hoffman, whose presence in England was first felt prominently in England during Edward VI's reign after Henry VIII's anti-heresy laws were repealed. The Anabaptists were identified as radical and seditious evangelists and declared as heretics because they denied Christ's humanity, questioned the doctrine of free will and predestination and rejected secular governments. However, as Carrie Euler argues, the reformers felt compelled to preach against them, although their presence in England was relatively small and unorganized; and there is little evidence of their actual rebellion against secular authority.[47] The scapegoating of the Anabaptists was also turned on a particular class of Anabaptist prophets and followers, as Peter Lake suggests in his reading of *The Alchemist*: box makers, bakers, butchers (such as Ananias); in other words, low class artisans who hoped to have a voice in church and state. While Jonson's attack on the Puritans for the charge of hypocrisy and casuistry is a reflection of the mainstream opinion of the time, his choice of the Anabaptists to represent the Puritans is intriguing. His use for the Anabaptists becomes clearer in the figure of Pastor Tribulation Wholesome precisely for the kind of hypocrisy and casuistry that he produces to convince Ananias that financing alchemy is a godly enterprise.

Peter Lake calls Ananias Jonson's comic/polemical invention, not a reflection but a design (606). Ananias is designed to take on the burden of satire aimed at both mainstream and underground Puritans of Jonson's day.[48] In their berating of Ananias, Dol, Subtle and Face leave little to the imagination. Ananias is introduced, after the gulling of Mammon is set in full swing, by Dol who thinks he looks like a "gold-end-man"–a merchant who buys odds and ends of metal. Subtle puts on "a new tune and a new gesture [in the] old language" (2.4.26) to make the posturing of the godly more obvious. Subtle frames the Anabaptists' desires in terms of an appetite, not unlike Mammon's even as he recognizes the difference of their verbal and social discourse in the new tune and the new gesture.

Ananias's "pure zeal" sets the stage for Tribulation Wholesome's wholesome casuistry. Ananias expresses his conscientious objection to Subtle and his project that seems clearly contrary to their mission. "In pure zeal,/I do not like the man; he is a heathen/ And speaks the language of Canaan, truly" (3.1.4-6), Ananias says and Tribulation agrees, "I think him a profane person indeed" (3.1.7). Mammon had resorted to overplaying the mysterious inaccessibility of alchemy to couch his easy commodification of it and the Anabaptists resort to revisiting the basis of profanity and its relation to the sanctified. Ananias objects to Subtle not because he is able to see the fraud, like Surly, but in terms of evil which is the sharpest contrast to the experience of God's goodness:

He bears
The visible mark of the beast in his forehead.
And for his stone, it is the work of darkness,
And with philosophy blinds the eyes of man (3.1.8-11)

Recognition of fraud would make magic impotent and useless but recognition of evil accords magic a power that can potentially serve the ends that Anabaptists desire. In Marlowe's *Doctor Faustus* for instance, there is no question that magic is evil and that evil is damned; and even if there is a promise of redemption it is not really viable as it is not for Faustus. It is Pastor Tribulation Wholesome's job to work out a logic where he both contextualizes evil and argues a viable possibility of its alleviation. "We must bend unto all means/That may give furtherance to a holy cause" (3.1.10-11), he begins with but counters Ananias' objection, that the means should be as holy as the end, with a very interesting and radical re-reading of evil.

Tribulation locates evil in its social and environmental context. "What makes the devil so devilish, I would ask you, Satan our common enemy, but his being perpetually about the fire, and boiling brimstone and arsenic" (3.1.25-27), he asks, Ananias rhetorically. It is an interesting reversal of logic where damning behavior is a result of being in hell and not the other way around. From the devil, Tribulation moves to people who seem devilish for the same reasons, like cooks, he says, or bellfounders whose human nature is transformed by the character of their workplace: "Besides, we should give somewhat to a man's nature./The place he lives in, still about the fire/And fume of metals, that intoxicate the brain of man and make him prone to passion" (3.1.17-18). Evil is not endemic but contextual which leaves open the possibility for transformation and redemption: "It may be so,/when the work is done, the stone is made,/This heat of his may turn into zeal,/ And stand up for the beauteous discipline/Against the monstrous cloth and rag of Rome" (3.1.29-33). This logic-chopping casuistry contains a satiric recuperation of magic by radical Protestantism against Catholicism and a revision of the idea of evil. Though the audience is not encouraged to take him seriously, Pastor

Wholesome's magical reimagining is much more through going than Mammon's utopia of consumption. Mammon forgets that in a utopia where the cooks are knights of his own making, he is likely not to have any cooks left at all. For Mammon's excessive desire to work, the difference between cooks and knights, gold and iron is a crucial one, one that is immured in the social process of value making. The magic of the philosopher's stone is that it is advantageous in a system of unrequited needs but the irony is that its realization it will eradicate inequity and suffering thus completely devaluing a device that turns iron to gold or sickness to immortality.

Fundamentally Mammon stands for a paradoxical position: he desires things that are impossible, precious, or difficult to get but to attain them he has to make them accessible and available to be bought which would render them ordinary commodities of trade. He embraces the "abstract riddles of the stone" (2.1.104) deliberately to preserve an aura of un-attainability in the very thing that he is making available in the market "Because the simple idiot should not learn it,/And make it vulgar" (2.3.201-2). Mammon's desire to preserve the exclusivity of alchemy from "simple idiots" and Surly's assumption that alchemy is "humbug" and like the canting of thieves ultimately lands them both on the same side of the argument: knowledge in the hands of the socially dispossessed and unprivileged is not knowledge at all. On Dol Common's prompting Mammon also retreats from his very sociable vision of his use of magic to imagining isolation and private consumption of rarities, "T'is no idle fear./We'll therefore go withall, my girl, and live/In a free state..." (4.1.155-7).

Mammon's retreat is hastier than Pastor Wholesome's whose ideas resonate further and longer in this odd and morally ambiguous play. Pastor Wholesome's name hearkens back to a promise in the Prologue:

> However, the age he lives in doth endure
> The vices that she breeds, above their cure
> But when the wholesome remedies are sweet
> And in their workings gain and profit meet. (12-15)

The play notoriously does not bear out the sweet wholesome remedy of gain and profit in terms of conventional morality. Instead Tribulation Wholesome suggests that evil is not an absolute lapse in morality; it is relative. Evil may be nurtured in a context of deprivation waiting for an opportunity for redemption and transformation. Social displacement and lack of work at the foreground of the problem of vagrancy and disenchantment at the helm of witch hunts points to crisis in the system of evaluation, such as those that fueled rogue-catching and witch-hunting, saw deprivation not as the cause but the consequence of moral failure. Instead Tribulation asks the play's audience to reconsider the relationship between poverty and crime. He adds that "the children of perdition are oft-times/Made instruments even of the greatest works" (3.1.15-16). Couched in this casuistical defense of alchemy are two profound insights: that the "greatest works" are not necessarily tied to the social processes that legitimize or dismiss knowledge as authentic or fraudulent and that knowledge needs means or "instruments" to be constituted as such. In Jonson's vision, the conjunction of the "workings of gain and profit" and the "instruments ...of the greatest works" is neither straightforward nor simple. But for the moment, Ananias is moved by Tribulation's explanation: "I have not edified more, truly, by man/Not since the beautiful light first shone in me" (3.1.45-6).

The magic of alchemy appears to transform the world and some of its founding premises as Mammon and the Anabaptists and the audiences of the play know it. The world of *The Alchemist* is a world of poverty not plenty. Mammon's imaginings of wealth could potentially change it completely. Similarly, Tribulation Wholesome's re-definition of evil could radically redefine the connection between crime and poverty. The play uses alchemy to tease out the possibility of such an alternative. However, neither Mammon nor the Anabaptists see the full potential of their vision as Mammon steps back into a fantasy of private consumption and the Anabaptists focus on the service of pure zeal. The audience is not encouraged to take either of these characters seriously. Jonson, in other words, rejects the idealistic, romantic solution to the problems that he unravels. He takes instead a pragmatic, if somewhat opportunistic, approach to winding down his play.

Conclusion: "Stretching Ages' Truth and Cracking it Too"

The crisis of the play's plot consists of a combination of ways in which the rogues can no longer sustain the illusion of magic. The alchemical experiment explodes, Surly very nearly exposes their tricks and at the end of Act 4, Dol Common spots Face's master–returned unannounced, surrounded by forty complaining neighbors. The internal tensions between the rogues also bubble back to the surface of their "venture tripartite". There is very little to save them from the joint testimony of the neighbors and the disillusioned avenging gulls who return with the Marshalls to have the Subtle, Face and Dol committed and punished for a morally satisfying conclusion to the play. Lovewit's departure had allowed his house to become a temporary experiment in social re-imagination. Familiar hierarchies, economies, exchanges, services and identities had been temporarily put away. Lovewit's return comes with the possibility of returning the play world to what it was before. But, to borrow Surly's words, "there is no such thing intended". At the end, the play has the option of retreating from the complexities it unraveled or allowing the complexities to influence its concluding stand. I suggest that the play ends with the latter by placing a bid on legitimizing fraudulent magic in the figure of Lovewit.

The ending of *The Alchemist* is superbly morally ambiguous. Subtle and Dol decide that it is not deception but justice to deceive the deceiver as they the plot to cut Face out of his share of the loot. However, they fail to trick Face and are tricked instead by Face–"the precious king of present wits"–by a turn of the very same logic (5.4.13). The rogues' seemingly well functioning republic collapses as Face formally ends the "indenture tripartite". The play's lack of investment in reinforcing a conventional morality is made explicit in the figure of Lovewit who presumably arrives to set the moral balance right. But Lovewit loves wit and is nourished by new devices; as he helps himself to the rogues' loot and a young wealthy widow, he admits that he has helped "his fortune, though with some small strain/Of his own candor" (5.5.151-2). Lovewit's return does not bring moral censure for fraudulence, the construction and experience of magic is not banished from the stage either, instead it is recast in a language of truth telling.

Having returned home unannounced, Lovewit finds his neighbors reporting that "all sorts of rag-tag" had flocked his house in his absence and reduced the neighborhood to another Pimlico. Lovewit's initial response is of curiosity mixed with disbelief about what his butler Jeremy could possibly have done: "What device should he bring forth now?" (5.1.15) Before investigating the matter further, Lovewit also admits: "I love a teeming wit as I love my nourishment" (5.1.16). Lovewit's value of wit is absolute and quite divorced from morality. Although his arrival is accompanied by a need to investigate and establish the truth, his investigation and conclusion err on the side of full disclosure rather than on the need to uphold what would be conventionally moral. Lovewit's neighbors had played the ungainly role of neighborly surveillance which was given much weight in the context of turning in witches and rogues. Accordingly, Lovewit accords due respect to his neighbors and admits to "wonder" and "amazement" at the reports of the goings on that his neighbors make, but he is not completely impressed: "These be miracles, or you make 'em so" (5.1.39). When Lovewit finds no evidence for their claims and sees no signs of the visitation of the throngs that the neighbors claim to have seen, he discredits the neighbors' claim by discrediting the basis of their testimony: "Fine rogues to have your testimonies built on" (5.2.40). It is significant that Lovewit ultimately disarms and dismisses his neighbors not for the lack of evidence, for that soon appears on stage in the form of the beleaguered gulls themselves, but in the face of truth as he securely corners the slippery Jeremy/Face:

> Lovewit: No more tricks, good Jeremy,
> The truth, the shortest way.
> Face: Dismiss this rabble, sir.–
> [aside] What shall I do? I am catched.
> Lovewit: Good neighbors,
> I thank you all. You may depart. (5.4.74-77)

The difference between Surly's failed attempt to expose Face's exploits to the law and Lovewit's success in getting Face to admit that he is "catched" perhaps lies in the difference of their approach. Surly was attempting to expose a fraudulent scam in order to have the rogues punished; whereas, Lovewit delights in and indulges the ingenuity of wit and makes indulgence not punishment the consequence for confessing the truth. Accordingly, Face recasts his magical fraudulence in terms of wit and mirth "Sir, you were wont to affect mirth and wit:/(But here's no place to talk on't in the street)" (5.4.79-80). Lovewit's wit re-appropriates the space for popular magic that had been overwhelmed by the discourse of fraudulence.

Lovewit extracts a full confession from Face but he does not relinquish Face to the law; instead, he draws Face into a new alliance. What Face doesn't have but Lovewit does have is the legitimating power of social position.[49] In Act 5, Lovewit re-directs the performance of knowledge from the framework of fraudulent magic to public performance of acknowledging truth in a situation where the outcome is exactly what the rogues had plotted, which was to keep the goods that belong to others. He tells Mammon: "Sir, I can take no knowledge/... but by public means" (5.5.67-68). He refuses to let Mammon take his own goods back because Mammon is not prepared to admit to having been cozened. Lovewit keeps Mammon's goods for himself along with the rest of the rogues' loot. Lovewit could represent the moral and practical opposite of the rogues' fraudulent magic since he clearly bears the onus of truth telling at the end of the play but Lovewit's exercise in truth telling, though public, is not moral. Between the rogues' venture tripartite and Lovewit's intervention, truth becomes a provisional experience.

The Alchemist allows for the scrutiny of credibility in the enactment of fraudulent magic. In the end, the satire of the play is trained on the "judging spectator" that the Prologue had respectfully allowed immunity from any kind of complicity with the follies on stage.[50] Dol Common's republic forged out of a quarrel is decidedly tenuous and it gives way to a new venture tripartite between Lovewit,

Jeremy a "good brain" and the audience of the play. The spectator is drawn right back into the play in Face's Epilogue. Face points to the "pelf"–alternatively the rogues' loot or the admission price for the play–and asks the audience to let slide the misdemeanors they paid to witness in return for continued theatrical collaboration. He asks the spectators to choose, like his master did, "some small strain/ Of...candor" (5.5.150-1). The experience of theater as fraudulence reinforces the play's engagement with the idea of fraudulent magic and its complex relationship to authentic magic.[51]

Popular magic lays bare the shaping power of desire in formulating conviction out of the very fabric of fraudulence. The privileged double perspective of the spectator set up to judge fraudulence by an absence of credibility ceases to be effective by the end of the play. Magic is deemed impossible to categorize in any absolute terms of authenticity or imposture without committing to exactly the kind of social and semantic tangle of fraudulence and credibility that the gulls find themselves in. The play makes apparent the legal, social, and economic subtleties in the constructions of fraudulent magic. Its triumph also lies in recognizing further that the candor, presumed to judge the gulls, is also constructed and out of the same subtle matter.

Unlike *The Tempest, The Alchemist* flirts with the sociability of magic; it throws the value of things into disarray along with the social relations attendant on it. The semblance of order that emerges to contain the chaos shuffles the usual hierarchies of power and credibility. Milton's *A Masque at Ludlow Castle* materializes the sociability of magic more fully which is the subject of the next and final chapter.

NOTES

1. For the similarities in theme and motifs that run through the two plays see David Lucking's "Carrying Tempest in Hand and Voice: The Figure of the Magician in Jonson and Shakespeare". Lucking argues that Jonson had *The Tempest* in mind as he wrote *The Alchemist.*

2. The most detailed treatment of vagrancy and criminality in the play is by Jonathan Haynes in "Representing the Underworld: *The Alchemist*". William W.E. Sleights reads the three rogues as Jacobean con artists in *Ben Jonson and the Art of Secrecy* In "The Game of Wits in *The Alchemist,*" and Joyce Van Dyke makes distinctions in the knavery of each rogue. Cheryl Lynn Ross sees the plague as a metaphor for socially dispossessed in "The Plague in *The Alchemist*" in *Ben Jonson* Ed. Richard Dutton. Peggy Knapp makes a case for the early capitalism as a tenor for the overarching metaphor of fraudulent magic in "The Work of Alchemy" *Journal of Medieval and Early Modern Studies.*
3. For Jonson's interest in laws and his complex representations of the judicial system see Lisa Klotz's "Ben Jonson's legal imagination in *Volpone*" 385-408.
4. Jonson. *Plays and Masques*, ed. Richard Harp (200-313). All quotations from the play are from this edition and are noted parenthetically by act, scene and the line numbers.
5. 22 H. 8.c.12 *Statutes of the Realms.* Accessed on June 13, 2011 http://home.heinonline.org.
6. For a comparative study of the early modern English vagrancy laws see "A Sociological Analysis of the Law of Vagrancy" by William J. Chambliss in *Social Problems Law and Society* ed. A Kathryn Stout, Richard A. Dello Buono and William J. Chambliss pp. 87-99.
7. For statistics regarding the number of cunning men and women in the English country side and in London see Owen Davies's *Cunning-Folk: Popular Magic in English History* Also see A.L Bier's *Masterless Men: The Vagrancy Problem in England* .
8. The notable exceptions are C.J. Ribton–Turner's early study *A History of Vagrants and Vagrancy*, A.L. Bier, W.J. Chambliss and Paola Pugliatti's *Beggary and Theater in Early Modern England.* Ribton-Turner reads the magic clause as superstitions of the time. Bier notes that the law targets "travelling wizards" p. 103, and Chambliss reads these practitioners of magic as engaged in criminal activities. Pugliatti sees them as "deceptive myth makers" (41), and Chambliss reads these practitioners of magic as engaged in criminal activities.

9. Davies 7 and Richard Kieckhefer, *European Witch Trials*, 28.
10. Davies 4.
11. Chapters 6 and 7 in Bernadette Filotas' *Pagan Survivals, Superstitions and Popular Cultures in Early Medieval Pastoral Culture* document the "beneficent" and "ambivalent" magic practiced by the cunning-folk. Filotas demonstrates why the distinction between witches and cunning-folks was precarious.
12. See Bruce T. Moran, *Distilling Knowledge: Alchemy, Chemistry and the Scientific Revolution* and Tara E. Nummedal, *Alchemy and Authority in the Holy Roman Empire*, 33-39. Both Moran and Nummedal emphasize the appeal of alchemy to practical crafts. Jonson makes a similar suggestion in the play when Subtle predicts that Abel Drugger, a tobacconist who also sells some chemicals, will one day attempt the philosopher's stone himself. (1.3.75-80).
13. See Keith Thomas, *Religion and the Decline of Magic*, Stuart Clark, *Thinking with Demons: The Idea of Witchcraft in Early Modern Europe*, Karen Jolly, "Medieval Magic: Definitions, Beliefs and Practices" in *Witchcraft and Magic in Europe: The Middle Ages*, and Owen Davies.
14. "By this period popular magic and intellectual magic were essentially two different activities, overlapping at certain points, but to a large extent carried on in virtual independence of each other. Most of the magical techniques of the village wizard had been inherited from the Middle Ages and had direct links with the Anglo Saxon and the classical practice... they were only slightly affected by the Renaissance revival of magical enquiry or by the learned volumes which were its most characteristic product" (228).
15. Thomas 228.
16. See notes 9 and 12.
17. Davies 4-7.
18. Davies 37.
19. Derek B. Alwes is the most recent champion of the rogues in "Service as Mastery in *The Alchemist*". In my view, Jonson does not trade in absolutes and the nuanced representation of the rogues calls for an equally nuanced understanding of the gulls.

20. Anne Barton sees an oblique triumph in the dupes who have large and complex fantasies and longing. I follow her recuperation of the dupes from the position of utter and entire stupidity. Ben Jonson, The Dramatist, 139.
21. Harp 203 n. 1.
22. See A.L. Bier, "Vagrants and Social Order in Elizabethan England", Linda Woodbridge, *Vagrancy Homelessness and English Renaissance Literature*, Craig Dionne and Steve Mentz, ed. *Rogues and Early Modern English Culture.* Patricia Fumerton *Unsettled: The Culture of Mobility and the Working Poor in Early Modern London.*
23. These pamphlets are anthologized in A.V. Judges, *The Elizabethan Underworld* and in Arthur F. Kinney's , *Rogues, Vagabonds and Sturdy Beggars.*
24. Kinney 110.
25. In an alchemical poem, George Ripley (d.1490) describes subtlety as a cleansing process: "Take Heavy, Soft, Cold, and Drye; / Clense him, and to Calx grind him subtily:.." (from *Theatrum Chemicum Britannicum*, 1652). Accessed June 13, 2011 http://lion.chadwyck.com/. Gareth Roberts signals the significance of making matter subtle: "All alchemical processes were governed by the idea of improving or making matter more refined or subtle. Concepts such as "exaltation,", "making noble" appear in the definitions of many processes such as sublimation and distillation..." (59). *The Mirror of Alchemy.*
26. In *Humanism, Machinery and Renaissance Literature*, Jessica Wolfe reads the subtlety of machinery as instrumental in "altering the early modern culture's conflicts between force and fraud" (10-11).
27. Edgar Hill Ducan carefully correlates alchemical descriptions in the play to alchemical texts to show that they are accurate. However he reads it like Surly to argue that Jonson did not have to make up jargon to show that alchemy was nonsense.
28. There are no alchemical rogues in the detailed typology of rogues in the rogue literature. The only exception is Sam Rid's brief description of jugglers and alchemists that he lifted straight out of a demonology–Scot's *The Discovery of Witchcraft* (1584). Surly's objections to alchemy echo Scot's.

29. Nummedal describes the figure of the false-alchemist appearing in the critique of alchemy by prominent humanists such as Petrarch, Brant and Erasmus (48). This fictional character was produced along the lines of vagrant rogues and sturdy beggars (60). Fraudulent alchemists, reduced to poverty and led to a life of crime, became the whipping horse for non-alchemists as well as alchemists who took the practice seriously. In the seventeenth century there was a burgeoning of alchemical treatises aimed at the differentiation between true and false alchemists (62-72).
30. Tara E. Nummedal, "The problem of fraud in early modern alchemy". In *Shell Games: Studies in Scams, Frauds and Deceits 1300-1630*. Bruce T. Moran, among others, changed the perception of alchemy from an accidental branch of knowledge to highlight its systematic and methodical practice.
31. Katherine Eggert, "The Alchemist and Science" in *Early Modern English Drama: A Critical Companion*, 200-212. Also see John Shanahan "Ben Jonson's *Alchemist* and Early Modern Laboratory space,"35-65.
32. Thomas. M. Greene describes the significance of talismanic magic in court spectacles in "Magic and Festivity in the Renaissance Court" 646-647.
33. Eric Wilson, "Abel Drugger's Sign and the Fetishes of Material Culture" in *Historicism, Psychoanalysis and Early Modern Culture* 110-135.
34. Edward Partridge traces the history of the "fly" to draw out its demonic provenance in *The Broken Compass: A Study of the Major Comedies of Ben Jonson* 130-31.
35. In *Fairies, Fractious Women, and the Old Faith: Fairy Lore in the Early Modern British Drama and Culture*, Regina Buccola addresses Jonson's use of fairy magic and locates it at the intersection of rural fairylore and the condescending urban attitude towards it. Fairy scams, such as the rogue literatures exposed, and Puritan railings lumped all fairies of the English countryside with the demons associated with witchcraft. She remarks on the comic economy in *The Alchemist* which invokes such a complex set of social practices in its use of fairy lore and argues, along with Rosalind Miles in *Ben Jonson: His Craft and Art*, that Jonson's satire validates the belief of the "educated and intelligent

people", who had "stopped crediting something which had been unquestioningly accepted as true earlier in their lives" (116).

36. In "The Value of Culture and the Disavowal of Things" in *The Culture of Capital* 275-292.
37. Donald C. Baker, "The 'Angel' of English Renaissance Literature" 85-93.
38. For rituals of purification recorded in magic books, see Barbara Mowatt "Prospero's Book" 1-33.
39. Stallybrass 284.
40. In *The Economy of Obligation: The Culture of Credit and Social Relations in Early Modern Europe,* Craig Muldrew addresses the tight knit of belief and credit the seventeenth century credit culture in England. He suggests that the credit system then was predominantly inter-personal where the reputation of a household was closely tied to its creditworthiness, but he also documents the increased defaults in credit and the fledgling new system of contractual credit that was gradually becoming an alternative in the changing marketplace.
41. Wayne Shumaker's chapter on alchemy in the *The Occult Sciences in the Renaissance* (1972) remains one of the most helpful introductions to the subject.
42. In *Secrets of Nature* (2001) Lawrence Principe and William R. Newman's chapter "Some Problems with the Historiography of Alchemy" summarizes the popular perceptions of alchemy. They also suggest that it was only in the eighteenth-century that alchemy fell into disrepute as wholly fraudulent.
43. Mammon's colonialist imagination is quite disconnected for the realities of the colonialist trade of his time. The New World and Peru yielded the colonialists with silver not gold. The gold standard in Europe, through the Middle Ages and the Renaissance, came from Africa.
44. In *The Capital* Marx finds fetishism at the heart of commodity making. He argues that commodities are magical things "...the analysis [of a commodity] brings out that it is a very strange thing, abounding in metaphysical subtleties and theological niceties"(163). Commodities are fetishes because the social relations between men assume the fantastic form of relationship between things (165). He goes on to suggest that the "whole

magic and necromancy that surrounds the products of labor disappears in other forms of production" (169).

45. In a chapter entitled "Love and Gold" in *The Commercialization of Intimate Life* (2003), Arlie Russell Hochschild demonstrates the twin process of commodifying love and care-giving, things that are not considered commodities, while commodities, for example an SUV, are fetishized to an extent that they seem to no longer be objects or things among things.
46. William Pietz makes this argument in *Fetishism and Cultural Discourse* (1993).
47. It is very illuminating, therefore, to find that the Anabaptists were seen as a threat to the stability of England and their rejection of secular authority was connected to the peasant rebellions of 1549, even though the real reasons for the uprisings were in the economic oppression of the peasants. Euler provides a detailed reading of Jean Vernon's introduction and translation of Heinrich Bullingers' *A Most Necessary and Fruitful Dialogue, betzveen ye Seditious Libertin or Rebel Anabaptist and the True Obedient Christian* (1551), to show how the connection between Anabaptism and social unrest was drawn (50-51).
48. For example, in "Jonson's Satire of Puritanism in *The Alchemist*", Ferreira-Ross argues for the historical accuracy with which Jonson portrays the separatist Puritans of his day. She finds the satire to be an accurate reflection of the popular perceptions of the Puritan stereotypes.
49. In *A Social History of Truth* (1994), Shapin argues that early modern regime of veracity was closely connected to the social construction of civility. I see Lovewit as a parody of the gentlemanly enterprise of producing truth. *A Social History of Truth*.
50. Alexander Legatt notes the disconcerting implication of the spectators in the con game of the play in *Ben Jonson: His Vision and His Art*, 35.
51. Mary Thomas Crane parses the fraudulence of theatrical performance in the play to argue that the act of performance constitutes an "exercise" that effects material change in the world. I argue that popular magic worked in the same way. "What was Performance" (184).

Chapter 4

The Virtue of Magic in Milton's *A Masque at Ludlow Castle*

In the court masque magic found a home. Neoplatonic magic was the basis of the English court masque as developed by Ben Jonson and Inigo Jones. Wonder evoking, lavish spectacles, so central to the production of the court masque, were only just the most obvious manifestation of the genre's close connection to magic. The masque was perfected as a genre of entertainment in the Jacobean and Stuart court culture, but it also came to be associated with the excesses of the royal culture that it was meant to flatter.[1] Ben Jonson's quarrel with Inigo Jones over the relative merit of mechanical spectacles in these royal entertainments had already begun a scrutiny of this genre already made susceptible of falling from its function of praise to flattery.[2] When the young John Milton was invited to write a masque to celebrate the appointment of the Earl of Bridgewater to the Presidentship of Wales and the Marches he wrote *A Masque at Ludlow Castle* performed in 1634 that, some scholars have argued, reformed the genre.

Milton's reformation of the masque is seen in terms of his implicit critique of the spectacular excesses and an explicit move towards Christianizing the genre. Scholars who are sympathetic to the Puritan cause discount the significance of magic in the masque. Barbara Lewalski, Maryann Cale McGuire, and Cedric Brown have re-read *A Masque* as a Puritan masque of chastity in which the Platonic ideas merely reference the vestiges of masque conventions.

These readings are aimed to counter the Platonic readings of the masque. John Arthos and Sears Jayne have written convincingly of the masques' philosophic basis in Platonic thought by locating the central conceits of the masque–"virtue" and "chastity" in Platonic texts. Platonic and Neoplatonic thought deriving from Plotinus was instrumental in the way that Ficino, Pico, Agrippa of Netteshiem and Paracelus developed the concept of early modern magic. Thomas Greene reads the masque unambiguously for its magic and insists that there is no Christian allegory intended in it. Greene's position is exactly the opposite of the Puritan readers of the masque. Instead of joining the argument about whether the masque is magical or Christian, I would like to ask instead what it means for this dramatic poem to be able to sustain both magical and religious readings. Georgia B. Christopher calls the masque a "syllepsis of traditions".[3] She reads Faith as a reformation conceit that resolves the conundrums in the masque; but to do so she draws on the agreements between Platonic and Reformation doctrine. Following Christopher's lead, this chapter considers the ways in which religion and magic converge in Milton's masque, and not quite as disruptively as it did in Marlowe's *Faustus* as discussed in Chapter 1.

In the evolving narrative of magic in the early modern period, Milton's masque is remarkably syncretic. Magical thought, as developed by its practitioners–Ficino, Agrippa, and Paracelus, and channeled in the masque through the figure of Sabrina, enables a resolution for the central impasse in the plot brought about by the locking of powers between religion and magic as embodied by the Lady and Comus. To summarize, the plot of the masque revolves around three children, a young girl called The Lady and her two brothers, who are to cross the drear woods by themselves where they are endangered by the presence of Comus, who traps weary travelers with a magical drink and adds them to his rag tag followers who terrorize the woods and trap other travelers. Jove sends down an Attendant spirit to protect them, who nonetheless fails his charge. Comus traps The Lady, though she steadfastly debates him against his arguments to taste the drink and counters him with her ability to stay true to her chastity, she is ultimately trapped on the magic chair, frozen and unable to move. She is finally freed by the magic of Sabrina, a river nymph. In this story the antagonistic alterity of magic in relation to religion, such as was experienced by Marlowe's Faustus, is eased into a much larger context in Milton's masque that allows for the synthesis of religious and magical thought. The practitioners of magic not only derive their practice from the same fount of Platonic thought that informed the theology of the early Patristic fathers and the later reformers, but they also go to great lengths to embed their explication of the power of magic within the parameters of Christianity. Yet, magical thinking necessarily assumed such networks of occult power to exist in nature that made the post-Reformation Christian thinkers especially suspicious. Milton's masque draws its dramatic tension from the tantalizing assonance and dissonance of religious and magical discourse.

In this chapter, I argue that the masque form enables Milton to reflect on the nature of magic and the ways in which it intersects with Christian thought, particularly in the figuration of sympathy. Milton's re-forming moves make the masque more reflexive of its own form such that it transcends simple binaries between monarch and subject, virtue and vice, body and soul, heaven and earth, and most significantly between the pastoral and masque forms. He blurs the distinction between the main masque and the anti-masque, redoes the transformation scene and, finally, he departs from the usual adulation of power to confronting the basic assumptions *about* power. Central to *A Masque* is the concern about power, how it is derived and how it might be best exercised. The confrontation between the heroine and the villain of the masque is about the nature of power as each derives a sense of power and the privilege of its exercise from different sources. Milton resolves the confrontation not with an unambiguously triumphant unmasking or transformation scene but by introducing a third dimension of power–the power of sympathy. In what follows, my reading of the synthesis of religion and magic in the masque hinges on the sympathetic magic that not only informs the masque frame but becomes the healing release for the deadlocked oppositions in the masque.

Magic and the Masque

The court masque is about power–its production, negotiation, circulation and celebration. Stephen Orgel located the monarch at the center of the spectacle both as the subject of homage but also as the object whose presence controlled the fictions of power.[4] Such was the influence of the king's body that it controlled the action on the stage and transformed discord to harmony. Harmony is the aim of Renaissance court spectacles according to Thomas Greene:

> The tremendous ambition of the court entertainment during the mature Renaissance focused on the effort to recapture that celestial music and to realize its harmony in the setting of the palace. If magic by definition is the imitation through signs of that which the manipulator wants to bring about, then the recovery of cosmic harmony was persistent, supreme end of aristocratic magic. (645)[5]

What Greene calls the "aristocratic magic" of the masque form was devoted to enable harmony not only through music and dance but through the idealizing virtues of good governance. Magic came to play a crucial role in the masque form because the imagination and representation of power, as the motivation and occasion for the masques, is also the substance of magic. The influence of the sacred body of the divinely ordained king was assumed to work in much the same way as the astrological concept of the fluid influx of power from the celestial to the terrestrial bodies that it controls. The inventors of the masque devoted themselves to drawing out the occult power in the body of the king in the theatrical space of the masque and consequently formulated the spectacle of political power in the process of representing it. Magic found a home in the masque because both masque and magic are invested in the knowledge and manipulation of power.

The heart of the masque is composed of ritual power that could not be drawn from the rituals or rhetoric of the Church for fear of blasphemy. Instead, as Tom Bishop points out, masque inventors "borrowed from the great reservoir of Renaissance 'second culture', using the fragmentary record of pagan religious practices–mysteries, orgies, and so forth, to set their nonce imaginings implicitly alongside church ritual as a secular counterpart with yet a quasi religious ambience, and the dignity and prestige of antiquity"(94).[6] This "second culture" of pagan mysteries shot through with the principles of Neoplatonism formed the magical core crucial to the mounting of masques.

Ben Jonson famously theorized that the "high and hearty inventions" of the masques were "grounded upon antiquity and solid learnings" and meant to "lay hold on more removed mysteries"; the "outward action" of "magnificence" furnished the "inward parts" of the Princes who performed them."[7] The "removed mysteries" are first apprehended by the senses in the magnificence of the spectacle. As the visual representation of monarchical or courtly power, the spectacles made visible the Neoplatonic notions of numinous power. Following from the Florentine Neoplatononism of Ficino and Pico, court spectacles, especially in Italy, represented a universe quickened by the *anima mundi*, with daemons and living stars that could be drawn into a harmonious connection to the human soul to aid its progress. The figuration of the presiding figure of the masque as well as the music and dance were based on the idea of images and emblems, *impresa* or devices used to draw the influence of the stars to affect celestial harmony.[8] Jonson and other masque inventors of the period found a vehicle for the "removed mysteries" in traditions of Neoplatonic magic.

Although scholars have demystified the fiction of sovereign power, such as Jonathan Goldberg's deconstruction of the spectacular representation of James I's monarchy, the monarch continued to be seen as the spectral center of the masque.[9] But, Martin Butler staked out a post-New Historicist project for masque studies by suggesting that courtly power did not just circulate in the controlling orbit of the monarch's all engaging influence; rather it is a negotiation that marked the symbolic transactions between differently empowered participants in the courtly arena (26).[10] Tom Bishop, like Butler, sees several different foci for courtly authority that impacted the performance of masques. But ritual invocation and ceremonial representation of power, albeit differently focalized, remain the identifying features of the masque.

James I found use for the masque to encourage reverence for monarchical power even at significant court expense. It has been remarked that the idealizations of the masques clashed quite significantly with the disrepute of James I's court culture. After the coronation of Charles I in 1625, there was a concerted attempt by the royal household to reinvent the image of the court as pure and chaste. Queen Henrietta Maria initiated the cult of Platonic love, and both the king and queen participated in several masques that celebrated the chastity of their marital love. However, the masques become even more lavish and expensive than had been under James I. The masque form invited criticism most notably from among the Puritans. Since Milton wrote his masque in this milieu, and though it is in conversation with entertainments written by his contemporaries, it is markedly different in its tenor allowing scholars to read Milton's masque as specifically Puritan.

The Puritan reformation of the masque is seen as an express critique of the fashionable promotion of Neoplatonism in the court of Charles I and Henrietta Maria in the propaganda for royal absolutism. In this context, the Puritan readings of Milton's masque foreground the deepening rift between the royalists and Puritans in the 1630s over such controversies as the reissued *Declaration of Sports* (1633) and the Prynne affair.[11] To the Puritans, the court culture of Neoplatonism promoted by Henrietta Maria looked suspiciously Catholic and Laudian. Barbara Lewalski argues that "In form, theme and ethos, the *Masque*, reflects Puritan religious and political sensibilities...More importantly the Platonism in this masque is a far cry from that in the Caroline court, and evil is conceived in Protestant not Platonic terms" (308).[12] While it is possible to see Milton repudiate some form of misguided Neoplatonism appropriated by the court culture, there *is* an insistent "Platonism" that is a "far cry from the courts".[13] Similarly MaryAnn Cale Mcguire begins by conceding that in the reformation of the masque

> the most profound and encompassing change involve[d] Milton's handling of his Neoplatonic materials. Royal masques turned these materials to political ends. Milton rejected the politicized philosophy and instead integrated his Neoplatonic *données* into a larger Christian context developed in terms of Puritan concerns of the day. (76)[14]

However, she concludes that the masque's "similarities with Neoplatonism" are merely "superficial" (137) because even at the level of the plot Milton's *Comus* "transcends the simple Neoplatonic strivings" (76). McGuire's reluctance to accord any complexity to the Neoplatonism in the masque stems from the scholarly tendency to see intellectual consistency and homogeneity of thought in Milton's vast oeuvre. Milton does indeed integrate magical Neoplatonic thinking with his understanding of Christianity, but not by simplifying one to give traction to the other.

The Puritan reading of the masque turns, as Lewalski suggests, on its conception of evil. Cedric Brown argues that Milton's "vigilant Protestantism" is nowhere so clear as in his "dynamic, detailed presentation of deceptive evil" (59).[15] Evil is the perversion of God's works, and the masque's adversary Comus thrives on the diabolic perversion of truth. McGuire, Brown and Lewalski see the conventional court masque parodied and critiqued in Comus' anti-masque. They read he masque as a spiritual instruction that the Attendant Spirit, cast in the role of a teacher, facilitates for the three offspring of the new President of Wales. The children's journey through the woods is a spiritual journey in the tradition of the pilgrim's progress where their virtue is tested in a manner of a lesson for spiritual growth. And lastly, "while Milton's masque exalts virginity and chastity, it undermines claims for their magical power as developed in the court masques..."[16]

The Puritan reclamation of the masque downplays if not rejects magic altogether. It overlooks the significance of magic in the masque form and Milton's innovations with it. The modesty of spectacle in Milton's masque is seen to be commensurate with his Puritan leaning and that of his patron's. But John Creaser disagrees with this view and suggests that critics have missed the splendor inherent in the occasion and performance of the masque. The modest spectacle reflects the constraints of Milton's commission and was not wholly artistic choice.[17] Thus spectacle alone is hardly the measure of how much Milton reformed the masque. Ann Coiro suggests that Milton does not reform but outdoes the contemporary masque by pushing the genre's inherent tendencies to the new dramatic and social limits.[18] I argue that one of the inherent tendencies of the masque is its use of magic.

The discipline of early modern magic developed as a practical application of Platonic and Neoplatonic understanding of physical nature and its connection to the celestial bodies. In *The Three Books of Occult Philosophy*, Agrippa of Netteshiem defines the significance of astrology to magic as "so near joined to, and of much affinity with astrology, in so much that he that professeth magic without astrology, doth nothing , but altogether is in error" (689).[19] Practicing magicians were particularly interested in utilizing the celestial influence as gauged by astrology in healing the body. In *The Book of Life*, Marsilio Ficino documents recipes for the care of the human body that makes use of things in nature made efficacious by their alliance to particular stars and planets. A section of the book entitled "Making Your Life Agree with the Heavens" draws on the works of Plotinus to detail how terrestrial bodies, human and non-human, draw the favor of heavenly bodies, "gifts of the animate world and the living stars" (87).[20] Magical charms are materials prepared such that they become lures for the "world soul" drawn in from the stars. Such lures can be made in song or spell or found hidden in nature that can ultimately aid the fleshly body acquire the numinous essence of the soul. John Arthos and Sears Jayne have each argued for the platonic basis of Milton's masque which contributes to, what Angus Fletcher has called, the masque's "radically magical texture"(159).[21] If, as I argue, magic is the practical application of ideas deriving from Platonic thought then identifying Platonic thought is not enough to see how the masque is also invested in the idea of magic.

Magic, as I suggested earlier, depends on the ability to recognize occult powers and further in the skill and knowledge of putting it to use. But Milton does not simply assume the nature of power, magical or otherwise, instead his masque examines it. The context for such an examination of power lies within the spiritual aspiration of the mortal body that is embedded in nature. *A Masque* is structured around three agents of magic–the Attendant Spirit, Comus and Sabrina, who form the framework of interconnected powers within which its three mortal actors, the Lady and her two brothers will learn about power and its exercise.

Power in the Masque Frame

Magic is about the exercise of power. Thomas Greene claims that "the struggle for power at the core of the Comus narrative takes the form of a contest between different versions of magic" (298).[22] In Greene's analysis the struggle between each version of magic is not simply moral but semiotic "since the real action hinges on the efficacy of competing magical powers... and the participation of empowered signs with their referents" (298). My reading of the masque takes as its starting point the process of empowering the sign. In other words, Milton does not simply assign power to its magical agents but also locates them carefully in the contexts from which they derive their power.

Power is defined in the OED as the ability to affect change. It is a quality that is sensed only upon its impact. The impact of power felt as force results in either movement or transformation. The world of Milton's *Masque* is a mobile, animate world that directs attention to the movements and actions in the masque and the forces that enable it. The Attendant Spirit, Comus and Sabrina are three different loci of power in the paradigm that the masque sets up as a context in which chastity will be formulated as a power.

The first scene opens to a wild wood where an Attendant Spirit descends and describes the circumstances of his descent. A bright aerial spirit of immortal shape, he has arrived from the starry threshold of Jove's court. He makes a distinction between the "calm and serene air" of the region of his inhabitance above; and below it the "smoke and stir of this dim spot which men call earth". He characterizes life on earth as one of "low thoughted care" lived by people "pestered in a pinfold" and "unmindful of the crown that virtue gives/After this mortal change,.." (9-10). In the first few lines, the Attendant Spirit plots the masque world in a vertical space. Earth, rank and moldy with sin, its people frail and feverish, is inferior to the superiority of the heavenly world. He adds further that a few people on earth "with due steps aspire" upwards to be amongst "enthroned gods on sainted seats" (11). For such, Jove directs that he make "errands" on earth and so he risks soiling his "pure ambrosial weeds" (15-16).

The Attendant Spirit outlines the trajectory of power in this vertical heaven to earth space. Jove is the source of all power; though life on earth derives from him, people live in willful ignorance. For those who recognize Jove's power, virtue is a way to connect to Jove and escape the feverish, discordant life to experience the celestial harmony. Power flows outward from Jove and strengthens those who seek to be strengthened by it in their upward ascension and final transformation to be rewarded with a place in Jove's court; the Attendant Spirit aids this process. In the Attendant Spirit's introduction, the language of Neoplatonism is synthesized with the notion of redemption through a Christian God. This clear paradigm of power for the powerless that enables their ascent to heaven through the diligent pursuit of virtue is interrupted by Comus' preferred way to provide an escape from the same horrors of existence on earth.

The wild woods in which the Attendant spirit is discovered nods with horror because it is the haunt of Comus. The Attendant Spirit introduces Comus as the son of Bacchus and Circe who "Excels his mother at her mighty art" (63). Comus leads the routing anti-masque by manipulating the powers that come from the very opposite of everything that the Attendant Spirit had described. Comus and his band revel in darkness. He invokes "Dark-veiled Cotytto" the "mysterious dame" whose "ebony cloud chair" only stays when the "Stygian darkness spits her thickest gloom" (129-136). He calls the anti-masquers "the vowed priests" of Hecat. The rites or "the concealed solemnities" (143) that Comus refers to are the nightly orgies in the forest that "only daylight makes sin" (126).

Comus' band of routers is made up of people transformed to the likeness of beasts for having accepted Comus' "orient liquor in a crystal glass/to quench the drought of Phoebus... (For most do taste through fond intemperate thirst)" (165). People with intemperate thirst and appetite, living feverishly, are the most likely to fall for the further temptation that Comus presents. The "orient liquor" not only transforms their visage to that of beasts but takes away their ability to know the disfigurement; perfect in their misery, they "roll with pleasure in a sensual sty" (75). Comus' magical power concentrated in his cup of drink inherited from his mother perverts the idea of "mortal change" that the Attendant Spirit had introduced as the reward for virtuous living: "Whoever tasted, lost his upright shape,/And downward fell into a groveling swine" (52-53). In the schema of movement along a vertical axis, Comus presents the depth of fall.

At the beginning of the masque, power as a means to affect transformation is polarized between The Attendant Spirit and Comus. These two figures can be read for their obvious anti-thesis given their function in the masque. However, Comus as the enchanter and magical manipulator of nature, who is located on earth presents a relationship to it that deviates from the Attendant Spirit's paradigm of vertical transference of power. Comus' opening song of the anti-masque elaborates the Attendant Spirits' aerial vision of the earth as a smoky, dim spot. This song starts as a celebration of dusk turning slowly into night, "the slope sun his upward beam/Shoots against the dusky pole" (198-99) marks the time for the beginning of joyous feasting and revelry after the watchful and disciplining authorities have gone to bed. Comus leads the dance with an analogy to the movement of the stars: "We that are of purer fire/Imitate the starry quire" (111-112). The dance and festivities reveal things that are usually hidden. The sands and shelves revealed by the receding tide is where pert fairies and dapper elves dance. The dimness that the Attendant Spirits sees and the blot of darkness that Comus himself calls upon reveals as much as it conceals. The first half of Comus' song carries the sheer joy of his surroundings that echoes Milton's ode to mirth in "L'Allegro".

It is not till the second half of the song that Comus brings up the darker implications of his complete investment in the bodily experience of nature that Milton backs up with a specially crafted genealogy for him.

In the Greco-Roman traditions, that Comus comes from, he is a minor pot bellied God whose dominant vice is gluttony. Jonson's use of Comus in his masque *Pleasure Reconciled to Virtue* is meant precisely to allegorize desire and appetite. However, Milton makes Comus the son of Bacchus and Circe; this invented kinship gives Comus added degeneracy, vice and the compelling prowess of enchantment. The lineage from his father associates Comus with the cults of Dionysus as is evident from his first song which is as much about communal festivity as about orgiastic revelry. He inherits from his mother the "charmed cup" as well as the "mighty art" of enchantment. His power then consists of creating participatory spaces of revelry with the use of magic. The bodily revelry of the orgies that he produces in the forest are however not entirely volitional on the part of his followers. Though Comus' victims already have a "fond intemperate thirst", it takes deception and forgetfulness induced by the charmed drink that darkens the revelry that Comus promotes.

Critics who read this as a Puritan masque, call up Comus' revelry as Milton's anti-theatrical critique of the Royalist masque. Cedric Brown, for instance, finds Comus to be an apt adversary in the masque because

> He engaged in the chief delights of the masque festivities with his infectious evil...Calling upon the figure of Comus enabled Milton to frame an action in distant Ludlow which debated the nature of the princely festivity itself, though with finer discrimination than Prynne had used against the stage. No masque ever examined the moral basis of its own rituals more directly than this. (72-73)[23]

Comus is twice the adversary. As the anti-masque he blears the distinction with the main masque of the genre but he is also the magician who makes the magic of the masque suspect. The participatory space of the masque that is essential for the energized universe of Neoplatonic magic as well as the court masque is compromised by Comus. The villainy of Comus is scripted both as occupying the bottom rung of the Plotinian ladder, where the body is bound up in matter, and as the arch-deceiver conceived in Christian terms.[24] Comus embodies the kind of magic that was seen as a perversion of Christianity. His role as the Lady's tempter allies him with Satan and any power that emanates from him. The repudiation of Comus both in terms of the nature of his villainous power and his compromise of the participatory space in the masque leaves Milton to re-imagine the nature of the participation and a force that can productively negate and replace Comus' power.

Sabrina, the river goddess, forms the third site of power. She is not a part of the vertical axis of power that the Attendant Spirit and Comus embody. As the nymph of the Severn river, she flows through the landscape of the earth and creates a much more effective horizontal axis of power. The Attendant Spirit invokes her in song, and she emerges from the same landscape of nodding horrors that Comus has so terrorized. Like Comus, she too emerges from the Attendant Spirit's, and Milton's, genealogical frame as a figure of English myth, as Erin Murphy has recently argued.[25] As the illegitimate child of King Locrine, in her attempt to fly from the pursuit of her stepmother Queen Gwendolen, she "commended her fair innocence to the flood that stayed her flight with his cross flowing course" (830-831). The water nymphs and King Nereus revived her: "...through the porch and inlet of each sense/Dropped in ambrosial oils till she revived, and underwent a quick immortal change/Made goddess of the river" (838-841). While the Attendant Spirit holds out the promise of an immortal change with a celestial reward, and Comus presents the threat of a beastly transformation, it is only Sabrina whose own mortal transformation makes her truly magically effective for the transformation scene at the end of the masque.

The Attendant Spirit, Comus and Sabrina can channel power into transformative influences. These three non-mortal, mythic characters form the structural paradigms of power within which the mortal actors learn the meaning of virtue not simply with an eye to the afterlife, on the vertical axis, but also in recognition of the horizontal diffusion of power through nature, and the court as they claim their space in the world and learn to live in it.

As in the masque tradition, the actors in the main masque are both the subject and object of the masque; it is with a view to their transformation that the masque employs its critical and tutelary functions. The three children of the Earl of Bridgewater are lost in the drear woods on their way to the Ludlow Castle for the celebration of their father's investiture. The two brothers are separated from their sister; their challenge is to find each other and find their way home. Being lost in the dread wood on one's way home is an allegory for the spiritual wandering that comes with the sage advice to follow the straight and narrow path of a virtuous life. The virtue, according to the masque, that would be particularly enabling in negotiating the spiritual wilderness is chastity. The masque grounds the abstract discussion of spiritual chastity in the context of an actual threat of rape.[26] In the grips of helplessness and fear, the Lady and her brother draw on what strength they can to literalize chastity as a palpable power that can withstand and repel the very material threats and temptations that their adversary will put in their way. Their exercise of power literally takes the shape of verbal debates. Words spoken, shape ideas and ideas, *A Masque* suggests, have a powerful reality that shapes the reality perceived by the senses.

Exercising the Power of Chastity

Milton replaces the magic of the king's body, parodied in the anti-masque, with the magic of chastity in the main masque. If Comus is the quintessential body bound up in matter then chastity, as it is figured both in Platonic and religious thought, is the virtue that keeps the body in a condition that can most closely resonate with the soul. Chastity is the main emblem in the masque; it implies a state of purity that comes from chastening the body. Chastity requires temperance or abstinence. In that the ideal chaste body also reflects a mechanism of control. As Kathryn Schwarz suggests: "Formulated in terms of self-control, chastity stands in an odd relation to the presumption of control by others; it is not a straightforward mechanism of hierarchical imposition by others but a complicated and always potentially contested interplay of constraint and will" (270).[27] The prescriptive chastity for the female body, especially in the language of idealization, turns on a fundamental paradox. At the same time that the virgin is seen as vulnerable, helpless and in need of protection, she is empowered by the concept of chastity so that the very virgin body that is helpless becomes its own source of militant defense. Feminist readings of the masque have emphasized Milton's choice of a heroine who speaks up and defends herself.[28] By wresting control of her body and making the abstract powers of chastity an act of will, the Lady becomes, as Comus acknowledges, a contesting site of magic. In *A Masque* chastity is a form of vigorous engagement with the discourse of magic.

But before they can learn about the magic of chastity, the Lady and her brothers must first experience the full extent of her helplessness. The Attendant Spirit's presence signals their helplessness and the imminent dangers of the woods: "And here their tender age may suffer peril/but that by quick command of sovran Jove/I was despatched for their defense and guard" (40-42)". He localizes the peril to the threat that Comus represents, an assault on chastity that is at once physical and spiritual that the Lady does not yet know. She becomes properly aware of the gravity of her situation when she follows what she thinks are the sounds of a rural mirth, but is actually the anti-masque abruptly halted, to encounter only more blinding darkness in place of the "tumult of loud mirth" (201). She learns of the unreliability of the senses and is momentarily truly lost, "O where else/Shall I inform my unacquainted feet/in the blind mazes of this tangled wood" (179-181).

As the Lady reckons her powerlessness, her unnamed fears are made worse by imagining. Her memory serves as the repository of socialized and primal fears of being beckoned into harm in language tellingly reminiscent of Shakespeare's Ariel when he lured Prospero's enemies by their guilty conscience into a trap of torment.

This resonance becomes more apt when she calls on "strong siding champion Conscience" to help herself out of her fear (211).[29]

> A thousand shaping fantasies
> Begin to throng into my memory
> Of calling shapes and beckoning shadows dire
> And Airy tongues and syllables of men's names. (204-207)

The "fantasies", "shadows" and "airy tongues" make the danger worse for not having a concrete shape or name. In another part of the woods her realistically worried younger brother names and gives concrete shape to her fears.

> O that hapless virgin, our lost sister
> ...What if in wild amazement or affright
> Or while we speak within the direful grasp
> Of savage hunger, or of savage heat? (349-57)

Although these lines make explicit the sexual nature of the danger, it leaves the subject of the hunger and heat tellingly ambiguous. It leaves open the possibility of reading the lines to imply that the sister is in the grasp of her own savage hunger and heat. It is an anxiety that bears out Schwarz's suggestion that chastity is a complicated interplay between constraint and will. That the younger brother might be worrying about their sister's weakening will is reinforced by the elder brother's rejoinder: "I do not think my sister so to seek/Or so unprincipled in virtue's book" (365-366). It brings into context the Attendant Spirit's early parenthetic information about the prior disposition of those that taste Comus's enchanted drink: "(for most do taste through fond intemperate thirst) (67). The threat of Comus' assault can be seen as the younger brother's protective patriarchal position pushed to its logical and opposite extreme.

The younger brother fears that the Lady needs to be protected from herself and from those that her preserved beauty lures: "Beauty, like the fair Hesperian tree/Laden with blooming gold,/ Had need the guard/Of dragon–watch with unenchanted eye./To save her blossoms,/and defend her fruit/From the rash hands of bold Incontinence" (392-396). He calls attention to her body as ultimately valued for the fruits that it will bear within the sanctioned marriage that the Attendant Spirit alludes to in the epilogue. The younger brother is anxious that their "unowned sister" would be vulnerable to "ill-greeting touch" (405). Comus completes the picture that the younger brother paints. His unrestrained desire and pleasure principle comes from the same sexual economy that represses desire. He assumes much the same of the Lady as the younger brother and finds her chaste presence quite alluring. He abruptly breaks off the rowdy measure of the anti-masque when he hears her footstep:

> Break off, break off, I feel the different pace
> of some chaste footing near about this ground
> Run to your shrouds, within these brakes and tress
> Our numbers may affright: some virgin sure
> (For so I can distinguish by mine art)
> Benighted in these woods. (145-50).

He not only senses the presence of a helpless virgin in the forest, he recognizes that chastity is a power with a radically different pace from his. The Lady's chastity is a subject of discussion between everyone around her. Chastity hems her into the curious system of patriarchal protection that makes her not just vulnerable but culpable to be outside of it. Her challenge in the masque is to be able to own the logic of her chastity over and beyond the assumptions of her aggressor and her protectors.

The power of chastity is the power of an idea over the visible body of the world. One clear articulation of the idea of chastity comes from the elder brother in response to the younger brother's apprehensions about their sister's safety. As a virtue, chastity is meant to achieve no less than the ascension of the body to the soul:

> So dear to heaven is saintly chastity
> That when a souls is found sincerely so,
> A thousand liveried angels lackey her.
> Driving far off each thing of sin and guilt.
> And in clear dream, and solemn vision

Tell her of things that no gross ear can hear
Till oft converse with heavenly habitants
Begin to cast a beam on the outward shape
The unpolluted temple of the mind,
And turns it by degrees to the soul's essence
Till all be made immortal: but when lust
By unchaste looks, loose gestures, and foul talk,
But most by lewd and lavish act of sin,
Lets in defilement of the inward parts.
The soul grows clotted by contagion
Embodies , and imbrutes, till she quite lose
The divine property of her first being. (452-468)

The elder brother explains chastity in terms of a basic Platonic principle: the chaste mind can by contemplation turn the body into soul's essence and its reverse that a corrupt body infects the soul. John Arthos traces the origin of Milton's particular use of the concept of chastity to the Greek *sophrosyne* as translated and interpreted by Ficino in his Epitome to the *Charmides.*[30] Arthos suggests that the reason Milton would embed a cardinal Christian virtue in a Platonic text is to "treat the magical power of virtue... to show how the key virtues of Christian theology have a parallel and support...particularly when that is supported by reasoning and philosophy. This would be an effort...to show the harmony and sometimes identity between right philosophy and Christianity" (274). As argued earlier, magic is the practical application of Platonic ideas as Ficino himself applied to practice. Accordingly, the elder brother moves on from the spiritual implication of chastity to its practical impact.

He describes chastity as the Lady's hidden power that will keep her safe from all harm. The very virginity that renders their sister more vulnerable in the forest than the brothers is turned into her source of strength. A virtuous mind, he says will stay stable even a situation of frightening deprivation because it is a "hidden strength".

My sister is not so defenseless left
As you imagine, she has a hidden strength

....
'Tis Chastity my brother Chastity
She that has that is clad in complete steel. (413-420)

He goes on to imagine chastity not only as a defensive armor but its possessor as a "quivered nymph with arrows keen" against those that would "dare soil her virgin purity" but also against "the blue meager hag", "unlaid ghosts that breaks his magic chains", "goblins" and "swart faery" (433-35). The elder describes chastity to be an occult power against sexual or magical assault. The Lady's power works like that of the herb Haemony's though the brothers are unaware of the analogy till the Attendant Spirit disguised as Thyrsis tells him.

The elder brother is not the only one who figures chastity as a magical power. When Comus hears the Lady sing out to Echo, he exclaims in spite of himself: "Can any mortal mixture of earth's mould,/Breathe such divine and enchanting ravishment. Sure something holy lodges in that breast (243-45). Comus the anti-masque, the enchanter with a reputation experiences the Lady's presence and song as an enchantment. As the villain of the piece, he also embodies the most disreputable form of magic. It is against Comus's "magic structures" that the magic of Milton's masque takes shape. Comus draws a set of founding distinctions between his magic and the magic of the Lady's chastity. He compares it to the songs that his mother and the Sirens sang that "pleasing slumber lulled the sense,/And in sweet madness robbed itself of itself" (259-260). But the Lady's song, the like of which he has never heard before, is "sacred", "a home-felt delight", with "the sober certainty of waking bliss" (261-262). He sees exactly that sobering, wakeful certainty that the pursuit of a virtuous life promises as opposed to the pleasurable though only in a slumbering, forgetful way that his own inheritance of magic represents. It is not just that Comus is a powerful adversary in the masque but that the lady is a fit protagonist to challenge Comus. Her sober and certain chastity is matched in a debate against the intemperate and lulling pleasures that Comus lives by.

The debate between the Lady and Comus is preceded by the Lady's attempt to take stock of her situation and rally what forces she thinks she has. Mistaking the anti-masque for the sounds of rural mirth, she finds herself deceived by what was "perfect in [her] listening ear" (202). Frightened by her own fantastical imaginings, she makes an effort to rouse herself from her fearful premonitions and calls upon the powers she thinks will stay her course from leading herself into danger. To counter the fearful fantasies, she conjures instead powers that will help defend herself, "These thoughts may startle well but not astound the virtuous mind" (210). The virtues that she calls upon are "Conscience", "pure eyed faith", "white-handed Hope" and the "unblemished form of Chastity" (211-214). In the darkness where nothing is visible at all she has a vision of chastity "as a hovering angel, girt with golden wings" (213) that reassures her in the face of visible adversity, "...now believe,/ That he, the Supreme Good,.../Would send a glistering guardian if need were to keep my life and honor unassailed" (215-219). The "glistering guardian" that the heavens send her is the Attendant Spirit but it also sends her Comus and his rout in his glistering apparels to try her.

It is worth noting that the Lady has not yet met Comus. In the absence of an explicit threat when her fears are still imaginary, being lost in the woods is frightening precisely because of the primal and spiritual fears of being lost. It explains why she turns to doctrine. What it is not evident yet is the implication of the substitution of "charity" with "chastity" in the doctrinal triad of "faith, hope and charity". Chastity was a familiar dramatic trope in court theatricals of Queen Henrietta Maria which popularized the cults of Platonic love in which chaste love was meant to help the lover transcend from the realm of physical to spiritual love. Since, in Platonic thought all life emanated from the Good or One in descending stages of Intellect, Soul and Body, chaste love helped the body unite with the Good.[31] However, the Lady is evoking chastity not as a means of loving engagement but, having substituted it for charity, as a means to preserve her virginity and life. Having rallied her forces, her first step towards self-preservation is hallowing to an unresponsive

Echo with a song for her brothers which falls instead on the ears of her aggressor. Comus disguised as a Shepherd, "with the power to cheat the eye with blear illusion" and "well placed words of glozing courtesy/baited with reason not unplausible" baits her with an offer of help (155,161-162). The Lady's eyes touched with the "virtues of [Comus'] magic dust" are unable to see through his disguise or his courtesy (165). Before long, she finds herself on an enchanted chair in Comus' palace of dainties being asked to accept a drink from his charmed cup that she steadily refuses.

The crux of the Lady's debate with Comus is on the nature of virtue and the virtues of nature. Comus confronts the Lady with a proposition of pleasure that links the body not to the heavenly virtues that the masque has so far expounded but to the virtues of nature. He reminds her that her body shares the "unexempt conditions/By which all mortal frailty must subsist" (684-685). His arguments, lush with the bounties of nature, seek to divert the Lady's attention to the appetites and desires of her body that the "vaunted name of virginity have kept her from knowing" (737). The Lady's first line of defense is exactly to claim the superiority of the mind over the body. She rebukes him, "Thou cans not touch the freedom of my mind/... although this corporal rind/Thou hast immanacled" (662-664). The Lady counters Comus' arguments point for point about the sanctioned and temperate use of her body against the indulgent licentiousness that he proposes. Against his charge that she has inverted the covenants of nature's trust, she argues that the virtues of "sober laws", "spare temperance" and "even proportion" are taught by nature. Besides, she argues that Comus has misunderstood and abused the virtue of nature. As she finally sees through his guise of a shepherd, she recognizes suddenly not the falleness but the innocence of nature: "Imposture do not charge most innocent Nature/As if she would intend her children to be riotous" (761-2). Her recognition of nature's innocence marks what John Rogers has called "the disjunctive moment in Milton's masque" (230).[32]

The Lady suddenly turns from her defense of married chastity to "the un-yielding, absolutist virtue of sexual abstinence" (231).[33]

Rogers outlines the "liberal" and "radical" formulation of virginal power in *A Masque.* He calls the liberal expression of virginity an imagined liberation of the virgin from the social constraints of marriage while "the radical assertion of virginal power posits the virgin's magical capacity to effect change in the world by virtue of nothing more than the static condition of moral and physical purity" (237). He draws attention to the self-enclosure of the virgin; "it was her literal self-enclosure, her protection, however tenuous, from forces outside of herself that could render the female virgin not only a pious participant in the private realm but a figurative embodiment of the private realm itself" (238). While Rogers only uses this instance of the discourse of virginity in Milton to argue for the larger political import of the idea of virginity in revolutionary England, it would be useful to examine the implication of his suggestion of the virgin's "self-enclosure" in the dramatic context of the masque itself.

To return to the "disjunctive moment", it is also sharply marked by the Lady's sudden disavowal of speech; not only does she mock Comus' "dear wit and gay rhetoric", she questions the use of her own continued speech in the defense of the "sun-clad power of chastity": "Fain would I something say, yet to what end"? (782). Speech becomes inadequate to express "The sublime notion and high-mystery/That must be uttered to unfold the sage/And serious doctrine of virginity" (784-786). The "high-mystery" of Milton's central device in *A Masque* recalls the significance of the function of "removed mysteries" in Jonson's vision of the masque form. Edgar Wind glosses mystery as a "ritual terminology to assist and incite the exercise of intelligence" in a process that "induced the soul to rise to a state of philosophic enthusiasm" (4, 5).[34] What follows, not surprisingly then, is a speech of vehement rapture before the Lady falls completely silent for the remainder of the action:

> Thou art not fit to hear thyself convinced;
> Yet should I try, the uncontrolled worth
> Of this pure cause would kindle my rapt spirit
> To such a flame of sacred vehemence,
> That dumb things would be moved to sympathize

And the brute Earth would lend her nerves a shake,
Till all the magic structures reared so high,
Were shattered into heaps o'er thy false head. (791-798)

The apocalyptic vehemence in this speech short-circuits the elaborate pattern of patriarchal expectation that both her brothers and Comus have set up for her. Comus breaks into a visible cold sweat upon hearing this speech. As Rogers points out, she tightens her boundaries and shrinks inside herself in an act of self-enclosure. The older brother had claimed a similar moment of vehemence while defending the abstract powers of chastity, "if this fail,/The pillared firmament is rottenness,/and earth's base built upon stubble" (596-598). But his vehemence is undercut, almost comically, by the Attendant Spirit's patronizing intervention that makes it sound like youthful enthusiasm instead. The silence that follows the speech of the sister's speech mutes the last word that her notion of chastity might have had in the masque, which scholars have nonetheless read as wresting control and staging rebellion that will be contained once she is restored to her father's home.

More than one scholar of the masque has noted the isolating and insular affect of chastity. As Thomas Greene points out, "chastity by nature *repels*". In response to the Second Brother's insistent skepticism, the Elder Brother calls up a list of chaste figures from Antiquity "to testify the arms of chastity" (439). He recalls Dian's "dread bow", Minerva's "Gorgon shield" that turned its foes to stone as the effect of the "rigid look of chaste austerity" (439-450). The irony is that the doctrine of chastity meant to divert the attention from the body to the soul emerges as a concentrated focus on the body. In its self-preservation the body becomes an insular system of self-protection. At the end of her powerful speech the Lady sits frozen on the enchanted chair, either manacled by Comus's spell as she had predicted she could be or stilled into herself in her moment of rapture. Kathryn Schwarz sees at least a contested version of the Lady's agency in her own paralysis, "Describing the Lady's simultaneous bondage and triumph, *A Masque* suffers a sympathetic paralysis, balanced between strongly conflicting versions of agency" (275). The Lady's paralysis on the chair brings the masque to a point of impasse. The resolution of the impasse takes the masque overtly into the realm of natural magic.

Touching Transformation: The Sympathetic Magic of Sabrina

One of the innovations of the masque is in its treatment of the transformation scene. A transformation scene is expected to separate the anti-masque from the main masque in a dramatic moment of discovery that overcomes vice and folly. Peter Walls has observed that the Elder brother's description of the effect of Minerva's Gorgon shield–which congeals her foes to stone in a way that "noble grace" dashes "brute violence/With sudden adoration and, blank awe (446-51)–is an almost perfect description of what happens at the transformation scene in a typical Jonsonian masque from which Milton departs (110).[35] Although the Lady's vehement rapture over the "sage and serious doctrine of virginity" is like "cold shuddering dew" to Comus, it does not overcome him. The brothers rush in and dash the magic cup but Comus manages to escape with his wand leaving the Lady fixed on the chair. Instead of a clear cut victory of virtue over vice, Milton presents an impasse.

The Lady's paralysis on the chair is an enduring puzzle in the masque. The text does not directly address why the Lady should come under Comus' spell when she has steadfastly resisted his temptations. But things that aid her disenchantment may provide the clues to the nature of her paralysis. The first solution, the most obvious one that is not available any more, is the wand itself. The enchantment could be reversed with the instrument and charms that put the spell on her. The Attendant Spirit is unable to contain his disappointment when the boys fail heed his instructions about the magic wand:

> What, have you let the false enchanter scape?
> O ye mistook, ye should have snatched his wand
> And bound him fast; without his rod reversed,
> And backward mutters of dissevering power
> We cannot free the Lady that sits here
> In stony fetters fixed and motionless. (813-818)

Earlier the Attendant Spirit had warned the brothers that their youthful venture and physical strength would be of little use against the adversary that they will be fighting. He points out that the nature of the problem that they are dealing with is not one that can be solved by physical force. Although the adversary presents himself as a physical danger, first with the threat of rape and the bodily transformation, then with this paralysis on the enchanted chair, defeating him would require a differently empowered weapon: "But here thy sword can do thee little stead/For other arms, and other weapons must/Be those that quell the hellish charms" (610-612). The other power and the other weapons refer quite directly to magic. She has been magically enchanted and she can only be magically healed.

The "other weapon" that the Attendant Spirit had pulled out to arm the brothers against Comus was the magic herb Haemony. Haemony is one among many herbs "with strange and vigorous faculties" but "amongst the rest small unsightly root/But of divine effect" (627-629). Amongst its vigorous faculties is its power to protect its bearer "gainst all enchantments, mildew, blast or damp/ Or ghastly Furies apparition" (639-640). The Haemony cuts through the "blear illusion" of Comus' "magic dust". The attendant spirits gives the herb to the brothers so that they may "boldly assault the necromancer's hall" (648). "Growing on this soil, unknown and like esteemed" (633) the qualities of the herb are doubly hidden by ignorance and by the herb's darkly blending physical appearance. This powerful herb that is daily trod over by the dull swain is "more med'cinal than that moly/That Heremes once to wise Ulysees gave" (635-40). This "unsightly root of divine effect" goes to the heart of how the early modern period understood Natural magic and pressed it into practical use in the form of sympathetic magic.

In *The Three Books of Occult Philosophy* (1531), one of the most influential early modern magical treatise, Agrippa of Netteshiem defines natural magic as follows: "Natural Magic therefore is that which contemplates the powers of all natural and celestial things, and searching curiously into their sympathy, doth produce occult powers in nature into public view..." (692).[36] Natural magic is inherently neither good nor bad but bends to the practitioner's use. Agrippa ascribes bewitching and even beastly transformations to the realm of natural magic: "There is moreover a kind of natural magic, which they call bewitching, medicinary, which is done by cups, love potions..." (693). To elaborate on this kind of natural magic he describes women in Italy who, like Circe, turned travelers to beasts of burden but with enchanted cheese (693). To Agrippa, this type of magic, though natural is inclined to "goetia, and theurgia, entangled in the wiles and errors of evil spirits" (694). The Attendant Spirit's narrative puts Comus' magic into the realm of natural magic that is entangled in the wiles and errors. It follows, therefore, that the counter magic to it must also come from the realm of natural magic. The Attendant sprit introduces the herb Haemony and Sabrina, the river nymph, as forms of enabling natural magic extended to the functions of healing and restoring.

Agrippa describes the "concatenated sympathy of things" that allows virtues of different objects or bodies in nature to form a powerful networks of influence that can be made to have a very visible effect: "All things are thought to put forth their innate virtue upon other things, draw them to them or expel them from them, no otherwise than the lodestone draws iron, or jet chaff, or a diamond or garlic, bind them so that by this gradual and concatenated sympathy of things...may be received from above..." (694). Sabrina is able to help the Lady because despite her transformation she retains her likeness to the Lady. She "still retains/Her maiden gentleness, and oft at eve/Visits the herds along the twilight meadows,/Helping all urchin blasts, and ill-luck signs that the shrewd meddling elf delights to makes/Which she with precious vialed liquors heals" (841-846). The masque draws on aural and visual imagery to suggest that despite their difference Sabrina and Comus belong in the same realm of nature. For instance, the "glassy, cool, translucent wave", "twisted of lilies knitting" and "amber-dropping hair" (860-862) associated with Sabrina are reminiscent of "braid your locks with rosy twine/dropping odors, dropping wine" (105-106) of Comus' first song. But Sabrina undoes the mischief of elves and reverses enchantments. Scholars who read the masque as an explicitly Christian allegory and even some who do not see the final movement of the masque as redemption made possible through Sabrina's grace. Her "precious vialed liquor" has been read as the baptismal water that gives the Lady a second life. Other scholars read her presence, heralded in with a specific reference to Spenser, as Milton's recourse to poetic art.[37] To these already loaded readings of Sabrina, I suggest that Sabrina represents the healing and restoration attributed to sympathetic magic.

Sabrina can be moved to help the Lady because she retains the memory of her past self, as a mortal she was as a virgin like the Lady. Ken Hiltner thinks that Sabrina's response to the call for help has little to do with the Attendant Spirit's "right invoked warbled song" or "adjuring verse".[38] As a beneficent *genius* of a pastoral landscape she is drawn in sympathy to the Lady in "hard besetting need".

> She can unlock the
> The clasping charm, and thaw the numbing spell,
> If she be right invoked in warbled song
> For maidenhood she loves, and would be swift
> To aid a virgin such as was herself.
> In hard besetting need (851-856).

The basis of the psychological concept of sympathy as the ability to feel compassion for another developed from the magical concept of sympathetic healing. Natural affinity between things was assumed to work even over distances. In the *Archidoxes of Magic*, Paracelcus, the physician who challenged Gallenic medicine, applied the principles of occult virtues for sympathetic healing in the "Oyntment for wounds".[39] In seventeenth-century England, Sir Kenelm Digby whose reputation was even greater than William Harvey's, claimed to have experimented with the weapon salve and the sympathy powder much to the admiration of King James himself.[40] Sympathetic cures and certainly its basis in magical thought was popularly recognized in Milton's time. Sabrina, I suggest, is the literal figuration of the sympathy that the Lady had called upon in her last speech.

But what is the Lady ailing from that she needs healing? Having been steadfastly virtuous why does she come under Comus' spell? The opening stance in the Lady's argument with Comus that her body could be manacled but not her mind comes to pass in a self-fulfilling prophecy. I am not the first to notice that the process of the Lady's self-enclosure was initiated by her substitution of "charity" with "chastity". While charity is premised on the ability to reach outside the boundary of one's self, chastity, as the Lady comes to experience it, is a tightening of the boundaries around her. The absence of sympathy is marked by a hardening of heart and a sense of enclosure protective at first but potentially like a prison. The masque's insistent imagery of imprisonment from the "pestered pinfold" and the "dark and leafy labyrinths" to the "dungeons of the mind" culminates in the Lady's imprisonment in her own body. Chastity without charity produces an insular and solipsistic self that Stephen Orgel points out is evident from the non-responsive song without refrain that she sings for Echo.[41] Sabrina is able to help her because she sympathizes, even as, and perhaps only as "dumb things" do.

In his study of Kenelm Digby's work on sympathetic medicine, Ernest N. Gilman traces the influence of Digby's ideas in a story by Nathaniel Hawthorne called "The Man of Adamant" that is set in a Puritan outpost of the New World.[42] Even if Hawthorne is not referencing *A Masque,* his story is richly illustrative of a possible explanation for the Lady's predicament at the moment of her paralysis on the chair. Richard Digby, Hawthorne's protagonist, has such a narrow and strict understanding of salvation that he secludes himself from community living and begins to live in a cave in order to contemplate his sins and read the scriptures.[43] In the cave, first his heart and then the rest of his body turns slowly to stone. Adamant on his isolated salvation and having rejected the sympathy of human connection, he becomes a man made of adamant. Hawthorne's story turns on connecting the medical and psychological aspects of sympathy that Sir Kenelm Digby was popularizing in early modern England. Hawthorne's Digby turns to stone because he has no sympathy. It could be argued that having substituted chastity for charity the Lady in "stony fetters" physically experiences the absence of sympathy. Hawthorne's protagonist rejects the healing help offered symbolically in the form of some drops of water from a nearby fountain and he is petrified for good. But, Sabrina is able to able to establish a connection with the Lady as she heals her:

> Brightest Lady, look on me
> Thus I sprinkle on thy breast
> Drops that from my fountain pure
> I have kept of precious cure.
> Thrice upon thy finger's tip
> Thrice upon the ruby lip
> Next this marble venomed seat
> Smeared with gums of glutinous heat
> I touch with chaste palms moist and cold
> Now the spell hath lost its hold. (909-919)

Sabrina revives the Lady and returns her to the community of the living. This community, particularly the pastoral community of shepherds and peasants, has an animate and vibrant presence in the masque and not simply because both the Attendant Spirit and Comus disguise themselves as shepherds. One strand of scholarship on *A Masque* is devoted to reading its pastoral elements. Nancy Lindheim argues that the term "pastoral masque harbors paradox if not actual contradiction" (639).[44] She explains why:

> The theory behind both the poetic and moral absolutes of the masques is Neoplatonism, with its sharp dichotomy between body and soul and its clear rejection of this world for another. Pastoral, on the other hand, builds its meanings in this world, most notably on the relationship among the creatures (usually men, shepherds) who are here (639).

This contradiction is resolved, she claims, "by subordinating one or the other" as Lindheim choice of resolution also indicates (639). The mainstay of her argument is that pastoral evokes compassion and keeps the masque from embodying a Neoplatonic aesthetic too completely. Accordingly, she reads the Lady's paralysis, as Sears

Jayne does too, as an enactment of the Neoplatonic frailty of the corporal rind. While Jayne reads the Lady's release as the metaphoric ascension of her soul, Lindheim reads it for the significance of participating nature in drawing attention back to the body and back to Earth.[45] Lindheim's suggestions about the significance of compassion and community as a distinctive feature of Milton's masque enable my claim for Sabrina as a figure of sympathy. However, since the basis of that sympathy is Neoplatonism, it requires a re-envisioning of the contradictory claims of the genres of Masque and Pastoral.

Platonic and Plotinian philosophy of dualism, that results in the kind of contradiction that Lindheim notes, is effectively negotiated by Neoplatonic magic. As a practical application of Platonic ideas, Neoplatonic magic is directed towards the well being of the body in nature that houses the soul, as much of Ficino's practical minded philosophy illustrates. Louis Martz does not name magic, but his use of Ficino to illustrate the power and significance of Orphic music in Milton's pastoral masque forms a corollary to my claim for sympathetic magic.[46] Music is an emanation of the soul, much like sympathetic influence. Martz also argues for the significance of Sabrina in the pastoral, and in his reading the operatic, conclusion to the masque: "the full power of chastity is represented not in the Lady but in Sabrina who combines the spirit of music with the spirit of charity" (29). The Lady's own defense of nature and the even proportion in the distribution of its resources shows her ready to be a part of a magical pastoral world in relation not just to the court culture but also to heaven. The Attendant Spirit's final song describes heaven as a kind of idealized pastoral that Sabrina's sympathetic magic enables on earth.

Conclusion

Milton restores the masque to magic in a philosophically considered and conscious way. The masque does not merely aestheticize magic or subsume it in questions of technology or art as Shakespeare's Prospero negotiates with Ariel. Nor does it take refuge in the antagonistic discourse between religion and magic that Marlowe's

Faustus tried but failed to mediate. Milton's innovations with masque makes use of magic beyond its symbolic functions of what Greene had described as an "aristocratic magic" hinged on its function of panegyric. Ultimately Milton's masque has more in common with Jonson's canny approach to popular magic in *The Alchemist*; Thomas Greene reads Sabrina as a cunning woman whose folk magic is pitted against the black and white ceremonial and ultimately ineffective magic of Comus and the Attendant Spirit (313). The masque, for being a courtly entertainment that routinely turned the anti-masque on grotesque figurations of country folk as well as witches and sorcerers, became in Milton's treatment pastoral, participatory and communal.

The magical epistemologies of the Attendant Spirit, Comus and Sabrina are in the end not about contesting forms of knowledge so much as they are about negotiation and use of the ways of knowing from the full and available gamut of Renaissance epistemologies. What this book hopes to have argued is the negation of a sense of teleological progression from a regressive view of magic to the progressive ways of knowing in science and technology. What a study of early modern magic, such as this, highlights is the simultaneity in the methods of knowing and doing. The modernity of the early modern came precisely from the ability of the early moderns, as evident from all the play texts examined in this book, to reflect on the contestations of the different forms of knowledge that continuously questioned the established credibility and legitimations. The term magic has no defined single definition and the search for one such is futile.

What is available instead are intersections of different traditions of knowledge some reaching back to the past some looking laterally at different geographies, some grounded in the moment of expedience in letter of law or grounding mythologies of local lore to produce rich and intense moments of knowledge formation as has been demonstrated in reading each of the play texts in each of the chapters. Since the premise of the book is that early modern magic is both as forms of knowledge and also one that challenges our modern/post-modern desire to only read it metaphorically, in conclusion it would help to weigh whether such ways of knowing have continued not just in its own times but well into the twenty-first century. What the magical epistemologies require is not faith in super-nature or extra-nature but the willingness to believe that the boundaries of established nature are permeable and ever expanding both materially and metaphysically. If formations of hyper-reality become the hallmark of the twenty-first century and beyond, then it will only be a matter of recognition that keeps a tab on the simultaneous magicality of thought and practice that informs engagement between the fantastical and the real. As this book has hopefully demonstrated, magic as a category of knowledge yields itself not in abstraction but by all the specificities of its location and the intersections of all the different axis on which knowing and doing persistently exist.

NOTES

1. In "The Reformation Masque" David Norbrook alerts us to the artistic achievements of the masques as important artistic achievements in spite of their association with courtly excess (95).
2. "Poet and the Architect: The Intellectual Setting of the Quarrel between Ben Jonson and Inigo Jones". D.J. Gordon. *The Renaissance Imagination: Essays and Lectures*. Collected and Ed. Stephen Orgel. Berkeley: University of California Press, 1975.
3. Georgia B Christopher. "The Virginity of Faith: *Comus* as a Reformation Conceit". *ELH* 43.4 (Winter, 1976): 479-499.
4. Stephen Orgel. *The Illusion of Power: Political Theater in the English Renaissance.* Berkeley: University of California Press, 1975, 39.
5. Thomas M. Greene. "Magic and Festivity at the Renaissance Court: The 1987 Josephine Waters Bennet Lecture". *Renaissance Quarterly*. 4 (Winter, 1987).
6. Tom Bishop. "The Gingerbread Host: Tradition and Novelty in the Jacobean Masque" in *The Politics of the Stuart Court Masque*. Eds. David Bevington and Peter Holbrook. Cambridge: Cambridge University Press, 1998.

7. "This it is hath made the most royal princes and greatest persons (who are commonly the impersonators of these actions) not only studious or riches and magnificence in the outward action or show (which rightly becomes them) but curious after the most high and hearty inventions to furnish the inward parts, and those grounded upon antiquity and solid learnings; which, though their voice be taught to sound to present occasions, their sense or should always lay hold on more removed mysteries." From the Preface to Barriers at Marriage, 1606. David Lindley Ed. *Court Masques: Jacobean and Caroline Entertainment 1605-1640.* Oxford: OUP, 1995, 10.
8. Roy, Strong suggests the connection between the use of music and dance in the masque as a performance of the emblem in the *impresa* tradition and its connection to hermetic magic in *Art and Power Renaissance Festivals 1450-1650.* Berkeley, Los Angeles: University of California Press, 1973.

   E.H. Gombrich has a fuller treatment of both *impresa* and the symbolism of magic in *Symbolic Images: Studies in the Art of the Renaissance*. London: Phaidon Press, 1972.
9. Jonathan Goldberg. *James I and the Politics of Literature: Jonson, Shakespeare, Donne and Their Contemporaries.* Baltimore: Johns Hopkins University Press, 1983.
10. Martin Butler. "Courtly Negotiations" in *The Politics of The Stuart Court Masque*. Ed. David Bevington and Peter Holbrook. Cambridge: Cambridge University Press, 1998.
11. William Prynne's had already acquired the reputation of a "budge doctor of stoic fur" by the time he published *Hisrtio-Mastix* (1633). An index entry entitled "Women actors, notorious whores" was seen as a direct insult to Queen Henrietta Maria for which he was pilloried; his ears were cut off, and he was thrown into the Tower for life.
12. Barbara K. Lewalski. "Milton's *Comus* and the Politics of Masquing" *The Politics of The Stuart Court Masque*.
13. G.F. Sensabaugh argues that Milton's masque is meant to clarify the true doctrine of platonic love in the mileu of a courtly culture that misappropriated the jargon of Henrietta Maria's cult of chastity. "The Milieu of Comus" *Studies in Philology* 41 (1944) 238-249.

14. Maryann Cale McGuire. *Milton's Puritan Masque.* Athens: University of Georgia Press, 1983.
15. Cedric Brown. *John Milton's Aristocratic Entertainments.* Cambridge: Cambridge University Press, 1985.
16. Lewalski, 311.
17. Some of the constraints for Milton were very few and some very young masquers–the three Egerton children aged nine, eleven and fifteen, the costumes were likely borrowed from the production of *Tempe Restored* and the Great Hall at Ludlow was much smaller than the smallest that staged court masques. John Creaser nonetheless makes a case for
18. Ann Coiro. "A Thousand Fantasies': The Lady and the *Masque*" in *The Oxford Handbook of Milton*. Eds. Nicholas McDowell and Nigel Smith Oxford: OUP, 2009. p.90.
19. *Three Books of Occult Philosophy* (1531). Tr. James Freake. Ed. Donald Tyson. Woodbury, MN: Llewellyn Publications, 2010.
20. Marsilio Ficino's *The Book of Life: On Health, Demons and Practical Life.*
21. Angus Fletcher. *The Transcendental Masque: An Essay on Milton's Comus.*
22. Thomas M. Greene. "Enchanting Ravishments: Magic and Counter-Magic in *Comus.*" *Opening the Borders : Inclusivity in Early Modern Studies : Essays in Honor of James V. Mirollo.* Ed. Peter C. Herman.
23. See Chapter 2 for a full range of literary allusions to Comus before Milton.
24. For evil and the nature of matter in Plotinan thought, see Philipus V. Pistorius' *Plotinus and Neoplatonism*.
25. Erin Murphy. "Sabrina and the Making of English History in *Poly-Olbion* and *A Maske Presented at Ludlow Castle*".
26. In "The Milieu of Milton's *Comus*: Judicial Reform at Ludlow and the Problem of Sexual Assault", Leah Marcus argued that the back story of Milton's masque is the rape of Marjery Evans. Earlier in "Comus and the Castlehaven Scandal" Barbara Breasted had already unearthed the Castlehaven sexual scandal as the reason for Milton's particular emphasis on sexual chastity in his masque.

27. Katherine Schawrz. "Chastity Militant and Married: Cavendish's Romance, Milton's Masque".
28. For a feminist recuperation of the Lady in the masque see Lauren Shohet "Figuring Chastity: Milton's *Ludlow Masque*" in Kelly, Kathleen Coyne and Marina Leslie. Eds. *Menacing Virgins: Representing Virginity in the Middle Ages and Renaissance*. Ann Coiro. "A thousand fantasies': The Lady and the *Masque*" in *The Oxford Handbook of Milton*. Eds. Nicholas McDowell and Nigel Smith.
29. For a reading of *A Masque* as a response to and a continuation of *The Tempest* see Mary Loeffelholz "Two Masques of Ceres and Proserpina: *Comus* and *The Tempest*" in *Remembering Milton: Essays on the Texts and Traditions.* Stephen Orgel's "A Case for Comus" also builds on the rich resonance between the two texts.
30. John Arthos. "Milton, Ficino, and the Charmides".
31. Sears Jayne "The Subject of Milton's Ludlow Mas. See also Sensabaugh.
32. John Rogers. "The Enclosure of Virginity" in *Enclosure Acts; Sexuality, Property and Culture in Early Modern England.* Eds. Richard Burt and John Michael Archer.
33. Rogers.
34. Edgar Wind, See Chapter 1 "The Language of Mysteries" in *Pagan Mysteries in the Renaissance.*
35. Peter Walls. "*Comus*: The Court Masque Questioned" in *The Well Enchanting Skill: Music, Poetry and Drama in The Culture of the Renaissance*. 107-113.
36. Henry Cornelius Agrippa of Nettesheim, *Three Books of Occult Philosophy*. Tr. James Freake. Ed. Donald Tyson.
37. Lewalski 31, Martz 29.
38. In a green reading of the masque, Ken Hiltner argues that Sabrina is Milton's way to suggest how paradise may be regained on earth after Adam and Eve lose it. In his reading Sabrina, not the Attendant Spirit, is the real *genius loci* in a pastoral masque. *Milton and Ecology*.
39. Under the heading of "Celestial Medicines, Being the Magnetical and Sympathetical Cure of diseases, as they are appropriated under the Twelve signs ruling the parts of the body", Paracelsus

prescribes "An admirable Oyntment of Wounds" (Ch. IX) and the "Weapon Oyntment" (Ch. X). What makes these cures admirable is that that they heal from a distance by making uses of the active powers of sympathy to brings the occult virtues of objects, the one hurt and the one healing, into alignment. *The Archidoxes of Magic Englished by R. Turner* (1655).

40. Ernest B. Gilman, "The Arts of Sympathy: Dr. Harvey, Sir Kenelm Digby and the Arundel Circle" in *Opening the Borders.*
41. "The Case for Comu*s*".
42. Gilman 271-272.
43. Nathaniel Hawthorne, "The Man of Adamant" (1837). The Project Gutenberg ebook. Accessed August 2, 2011. http://www.gutenberg.org/files/9240/9240-h/9240-h.htm.
44. Nancy Lindheim, "Pastoral and Masque at Ludlow".
45. Jayne 539.
46. See Chapter 1 "Pastoral Music: A Masque Presented at Ludlow Castle".

Bibliography

Agrippa of Nettesheim, Henry Cornelius. *Three Books of Occult Philosophy* (1531). Tr. James Freake. Ed. Donald Tyson. Woodbury, MN: Llewellyn Publications, 2010.

Albanese, Denise. *New Science, New World.* Durham and London: Duke University Press, 1996.

Alwes, Derek. "Service as Mastery in *The Alchemist*" *The Ben Jonson Journal* 17, 1 (May 2010): 38-59.

Apter, Emily and William Pietz. Eds. *Fetishism as Cultural Discourse.* Ithaca and London: Cornell University Press, 1993.

Arthos, John. *On a Masque Presented at Ludlow Castle.* Ann Arbor: University of Michigan Press, 1954.

___, "Milton, Ficino, and the Charmides" *Studies in the Renaissance* 6 (1959): 261-274.

Ash, Eric H. *Power, Knowledge and Expertise in Elizabethan England.* Baltimore and London: Johns Hopkins University Press, 2004.

Bacon, Francis. *The Advancement of Learning.* Ed. G.W. Kitchin. Philadephia: Paul Dry Books, 2001

Bailey, Michael D. "The Age of Magicians: Periodization in the History of European Magic" *Magic, Ritual and Witchcraft* 3.1 (2008) 1-28.

___, "The Meanings of Magic" *Magic, Ritual and Witchcraft* 1.1 (Summer 2006) 1-23.

Baker, Donald C. "The 'Angel' of English Renaissance Literature" *Studies in the Renaissance* Vol. 6 (1959): 85-93.

Barry, Jonathan and Owen Davies. Eds. *Palgrave Advances in Witchcraft Historiography.* New York: Palgrave Macmillan, 2007.

Bartels, Emily C. *Spectacles of Strangeness: Imperialism, Alienation and Marlowe*. Philadelphia: University of Pennsylvania Press, 1993.

___, Ed. *Critical Essays on Christopher Marlowe*. New York: G.K. Hall & Co., 1997.

Barton, Anne. *Ben Jonson, Dramatist*. Cambridge, New York: Cambridge University Press, 1984.

Bate, Jonathan. "Caliban and Ariel Write Back". *Shakespeare and Race*. Eds. Catherine M.S. Alexander and Stanley Wells. Cambridge, CUP, 2000.

Bedford, R.D. "Right Spelling: Milton's a Masque and Il Penseroso" *ELH* 4 (Winter 1985): 815-832.

Belton, Ellen R. "'When No Man Was His Own': Magic and Self-Discovery in *The Tempest*" *University of Toronto Quarterly*, 55.2 Winter (1985/6) 127-140.

Berry, Philippa and Margaret Tudeau-Clayton. Eds. *Textures of Renaissance Knowledge*. Manchester and New York: Manchester University Press, 2003.

Bevington, David. *From Mankind to Marlowe: Growth of Structure in Popular Drama of Tudor England*. Cambridge: Harvard University Press, 1962.

___, "*The Tempest* and the Jacobean Court Masque" *The Politics of the Stuart Court Masque*. London: CUP, 1998.

___, "One Hell of an Ending: Staging Last Judgment in the Townley Plays and in *Doctor Faustus* A and B", in *Bring Furth the Pagants: Essays in Early English Drama Presented to Alexandra F. Johnston* Eds. David N. Klausner and Karen Sawyer Marsale. Toronto: University of Toronto Press, 2007, 292-310.

___, and Eric Rasmussen. Eds. *Doctor Faustus: A- and B-texts (1604, 1616). Christopher Marlowe and Collaborator and Revisers*. Manchester and New York: Manchester University Press, 1993.

___, and Peter Holbrook. Eds. *The Politics of the Stuart Court Masque* Cambridge: Cambridge University Press, 1998.

Bevridge, Henry Esq. Tr. *Institutes of Christian Religion by John Calvin*. Edinburgh: The Edinburgh Printing Company, 1845.

Bier, A.L. "Vagrants and the Social Order in Elizabethan England" *Past and Present* 64 (1974): 3-29.

___, *Masterless Men: The Vagrancy Problem in England in 1560-1640*. London: Methuen, 1985.

Bishop, Tom. "The Gingerbread host: Tradition and Novelty in the Jacobean Masque" in *The Politics of the Stuart Court Masque*. Eds. David Bevington and Peter Holbrook.

Blisset, William. "The Venter Tripartite in *The Alchemist*" *SEL* 8.2 (Spring 1968): 322-334.

Borchardt, Frank L. "The Magus as Renaissance Man" *Sixteenth Century Journal* 21.1 Spring (1990) 57-76.

Brested, Barbara. "Comus and the Castlehaven Scandal" *Milton Studies* 3 (1971): 201-224.

Brown, Cedric. *John Milton's Aristocratic Entertainments*. Cambridge: Cambridge University Press, 1985.

Bruster, Douglass. "Local Tempest: Shakespeare and the work of the early modern playhouse" *Journal of Medieval and Renaissance Studies* 25 (1995) 33-53.

Bryant, J.A. Jr. *The Compassionate Satirist: Ben Jonson and His Imperfect World*. Athens: University of Georgia Press, 1972

Buccola, Regina. *Fairies, Fractious Women, and the Old Faith: Fairy Lore in the Early Modern British Drama and Culture*. Selinsgrove: Susquehanna University Press, 2006.

Burt, Richard and John Michael Archer. Eds. *Enclosure Acts; Sexuality, Property and Culture in Early Modern England.* Ithaca and London: Cornell University Press, 1994.

Butler, Martin. *The Stuart Court Masque and Political Culture.* Cambridge: Cambridge University Press, 2008.

Butterworth, Philip. *Magic on the Early English Stage*. Cambridge: CUP, 2005.

Caldwell, John. Edward Olleson and Susan Wollenberg. Eds. *The Well Enchanting Skill: Music, Poetry and Drama in The Culture of the Renaissance*. Oxford: Clarendon Press, 1990.

Campbell, Lily B. *Scenes and Machines on the English Stage During the Renaissance*. Cambridge, CUP, 1923.

Carlson, Marvin. *Performance: A Critical Introduction*. New York and London: Routledge, 1996.

Cave, Richard Allen. *Ben Jonson*. New York: St Martin's Press, 1991.

____, Elizabeth Schafer and Brian Wooland. Eds. *Ben Jonson and Theater: Performance, Practice and Theory*. London, New York: Routledge, 1999.

Chambliss, William J. "A Sociological Analysis of the Law of Vagrancy" in *Social Problems, Law and Society*. Eds. A. Kathryn Stout, Richard A. Dello Buono and William J. Chambliss. Maryland: Rowman and Littlefield Publishing, 2004.

Chickering Howell. "Hearing Ariel's Songs" in *Shakespeare and the Arts*. Shakespeare: The Critical Complex Series. Eds. Stephen Orgel and Sean Keilen. New York and London: Routledge, 1999.

Christensen, Ann C. "Reconsidering Ben Jonson and the "Centered Self" *South Central Review* 13.1 (Spring 1996): 1-16.

Christopher, Georgia B. "The Virginity of Faith: Comus as a Reformation Conceit" *ELH* 43.4 (Winter, 1976): 479-499.

Clark, Stuart. *Thinking with Demons: The Idea of Witchcraft in Early Modern Europe*. Oxford: Oxford University Press, 1997.

Cobb, Christopher J. *The Staging of Romance in Late Shakespeare: Text and Theatrical Technique*. Newark: University of Delaware Press, 2007.

Cohen, Adam Max. *Shakespeare and Technology*. New York: Palgrave, 2006.

Coiro, Ann. "A Thousand Fantasies: The Lady and the *Masque*" in *The Oxford Handbook of Milton*. Eds. Nicholas McDowell and Nigel Smith. Oxford: OUP, 2009.

___. "Anonymous Milton, or, a Maske Masked" *ELH* 3 (Fall 2004): 609-629.

Cole, Douglas. *Suffering and Evil in the Plays of Christopher Marlowe*. New Jersey: Princeton, 1962.

Corfield, Cosmo. "Why Does Prospero Abjure His "Rough Magic"? *Shakespeare Quarterly* 36.1 (1985) 31-48.

Cox, John. *The Devil and the Sacred in English Drama, 1350-1642*. Cambridge: Cambridge University Press, 2000.

Craig, D.H. *Ben Jonson: The Critical Heritage 1599-1978*. London and New York: Routledge, 1999.

Craigie, James and Alexander Law. Eds. *Minor Prose Works of King James VI and I*. Edinburgh: The Scottish Text Society, 1981.

Crane, Mary Thomas. "What was Performance"? *Criticism* 43.2 (2002): 169-87.

Danson, Lawrence "Jonsonian Comedy and the Discovery of the Social Self" *PMLA* 99.2 (1984): 179-93.

Davies, Owen. *Popular Magic: Cunning-Folk in English History*. London and New York: Hambledon Continuum, 2003.

Deats, Sara Munson. *Placing the Plays of Christopher Marlowe: Fresh Cultural Contexts*. Hampshire, Burlington: Ashgate, 2008.

___, Ed. *Doctor Faustus: A Critical Guide*. London: Continuum, 2010.

___, and Robert A. Logan. Eds. *Marlowe's Empery: Expanding His Critical Contexts*. Newark: University of Delaware Press, 2002.

Demaray, John G. *Milton and the Masque Tradition: The Early Poems, "Arcades" And Comus*. Cambridge: Harvard University Press, 1968.

___, *Shakespeare and the Spectacles of Strangeness: The Tempest and the Transformation of Renaissance Theatrical Forms*. Pittsburgh: Duquesne University Press, 1998.

Dessen, Alan C. *Elizabethan Drama and the Viewer's Eye*. Chapel Hill: University of North Carolina Press, 1977.

Dionne, Craig and Steve Mentz. Eds. *Rogues and Early Modern English Culture*. Ann Arbor: University of Michigan Press, 2004.

Dods, Marcus. Tr. *The City of God by Saint Augustine*. New York: The Modern Library, 1950.

Dollimore, Jonathan. *Radical Tragedy: Religion, Idelogy and Power in the Drama of Shakespeare and His Contemporaries*. Chicago: University of Chicago Press, 1984.

Donaldson, Ian. *Jonson's Magic Houses: Essays in Interpretation*. Oxford: Clarendon Press, 1997.

Downie, J.A and J.T. Parnell. Eds. *Constructing Christopher Marlowe*. Cambridge: Cambridge University Press, 2000.

Drakakis, John. Ed. *Alternative Shakespeares*. London and New York: Routledge,1986._

Duffy, Eamon. *The Stripping of the Altars: Traditional Religion in England 1400-1580*. New Haven: Yale University Press, 1992.

Duncan, Edgar Hill. "Jonson's Alchemist and the Literature of Alchemy" *PMLA* 61.3 (1946): 699-710.

Dunn, Catherine M. "The Function of Music in Shakespeare's Romances". *Shakespeare Quarterly* 20.4 Autumn (1969) 391-405.

Dutton, Richard. Ed. *Ben Jonson*. Essex: Longman, 2000.

Duxfield, Andrew. ""Resolve Me of All Ambiguities": *Doctor Faustus* and the failure to unify". *Early Modern Literary Studies* Special

Issue 16 (October, 2007): 71-21. Accessed on July 25, 2011. http://extra.shu.ac.uk/emls/si-16/duxfdrfs.htm#_ednref31.

___, "*Doctor Faustus* and Renaissance Hermeticism" in *Doctor Faustus: A Critical Guide*. Ed. Sara Munson Deats.

Dyke, Joyce Van. "The Game of Wits in *The Alchemist*" *SEL* 19.2 (1979): 253-269.

Eamon, William. "Technology as Magic in the Late Middle Ages and the Renaissance" *Janus* 70 (1983) 171-212.

Easlea, Brian. *Witch-hunting Magic & the New Philosophy: An Introduction to the Debates of the Scientific Revolution 1450-1750*. Sussex and New Jersey: The Harvester Press and Humanities Press, 1980.

Edwards, Karen L. *Milton and the Natural World: Science and Poetry in Paradise Lost*. Cambridge: Cambridge University Press, 1999.

Egan, Robert. "This Rough Magic: Perspectives of Art and Morality in *The Tempest*" *SQ*, Vol. 23. No 2 (Spring, 1972) 171-182.

Eggert, Katherine. "*The Alchemist* and Science" in *Early Modern English Drama: A Critical Companion*. Eds. Garett A. Sulivan Junior, Patrick Cheny and Andrew Hadfield. Oxford: Oxford University Press, 2006.

Elmer, Peter. "Science, Medicine and Witchcraft". *Palgrave Advances in Witchcraft Historiography*. Eds. Jonathan Barry and Owen Davies. New York: Palgrave Macmillan, 2007, 33-51.

Empson, William. *Faustus and the Censor: The English Faust-book and Marlowe's Doctor Faustus*. Ed. John Henry Jones. Oxford: Basil Blackwell, 1987.

Enck, John J. *Jonson and the Comic Truth*. Madison, University of Wisconsin Press, 1957.

Ericksen, Roy. "The Epilogue in *Doctor Faustus*: The Petrarchan Context" *The Nordic Journal of English Studies* 9.1 (2010): 1-16.

Ferguson, Margaret W., Maureen Quilligan and Nancy J. Vickers. Eds. *Rewriting the Renaissance: The Discourses of Sexual Difference in Early Modern Europe*. Chicago: The University of Chicago Press, 1986.

Ferreira-Ross, Jeanette D. "Jonson's Satire of Puritanism in *The Alchemist*" *Sydney Studies in English* Vol. 17 (1991) 22-42.

Ficino, Marsilio. *The Book of Life: On Health, Demons and Practical Life*. Tr. Charles Boer. Woodstock: Spring Publications, 1994.

Filotas, Bernadette Pagan. *Survivals, Superstitions and Popular Cultures in Early Medieval Pastoral Culture*. Toronto: Pontifical Institute of Medieval Studies, 2005.

Finnigan, David F. "The Role of Surly in *The Alchemist*" *Papers on Language and Literature* 16.1 (1979): 100-4.

Flachmann, Michael. "Ben Jonson and The Alchemy of Satire" *SEL* 17.2 (1977): 259-80.

Fletcher, Angus. "*Doctor Faustus* and the Lutheran Aesthetic". *English Literary Renaissance* 35.2 (March 2005): 187-209.

Fletcher, Angus. *The Transcendental Masque: An Essay on Milton's Comus*. Ithaca and London: Cornell University Press, 1971.

Foucault, Michel. *The Order of Things: An Archaeology of Human Sciences.* New York: Vintage Books, 1994.

Fox-Good, Jacquelyn. "Other Voices: The Sweet, Dangerous Air(s) of Shakespeare's Tempest" *Shakespeare Studies* 24 (1996) 241-74.

French, Peter J. *John Dee: The World of an Elizabethan Magus*. London: Routledge and Kegan Paul, 1972.

Fumerton, Patricia. *Unsettled: The Culture of Mobility and the Working Poor in Early Modern London*. Chicago: University of Chicago Press, 2006.

——. "Making Vagrancy (In)Visible: The Economics of Disguise in Early Modern Rogue Pamphlets" *English Literary Renaissance* 33.2. (2003) 211-227.

Gatti, Hilary. *Renaissance Drama of Knowledge: Giordano Bruno in England*. London and New York: Routledge, 1989.

Gaukroger, Stephen. *Francis Bacon and the Transformation of Early Modern Philosophy*. Cambridge: Cambridge University Press, 2001.

Gibson, Marion. *Witchcraft and Society in England and America 1550-1750*. London: Continuum, 2003.

Gieskes, Edward. *Representing the Professions: Administration, Law and Theater in Early Modern England*. Newark: University of Delaware Press, 2006.

Goebel, Julius. "The Etymology of Mephistopheles" *Transactions and Proceedings of the American Philological Association*, 35 (1904): 148-156.

Goldberg, Jonathan. *James I and the Politics of Literature: Jonson, Shakespeare, Donne and Their Contemporaries*. Baltimore: Johns Hopkins University Press, 1983.

Golinski, Jan. *Making Natural Knowledge: Constructivism and the History of Science*. Cambridge: Cambridge University Press, 1998.

Gombrich, E.H. *Symbolic Images: Studies in the Art of the Renaissance*. London: Phaidon Press Limited, 1972.

Gordon, D.J. *The Renaissance Imagination*. Collected and Ed. by Stephen Orgel. Berkeley: University of California Press, 1975.

Gouk, Penelope. *Music, Science and Natural Magic in Seventeenth Century England*. New Haven and London: Yale University Press, 1999.

Grafton, Anthony. *Magic and Technology in Early Modern Europe*. Washington DC: Smithsonian Institute Libraries, 2005.

Grantley, Darryll and Peter Roberts. Eds. *Christopher Marlowe and English Renaissance Culture*. Aldershot: Scolar Press, 1996.

Greenblatt, Stephen. *Shakespearean Negotiations: The Circulation of Social Energy in Renaissance England.* Berkeley, Los Angeles: University of California Press, 1988.

Greene, Thomas M. "Enchanting Ravishments: Magic and Counter-Magic in *Comus*." *Opening the Borders: Inclusivity in Early Modern Studies : Essays in Honor of James V. Mirollo.* Newark: University of Delaware Press, 2003.

___, "Magic and Festivity in the Renaissance Court" *Renaissance Quarterly* 40.4 (1987) 646-647.

Gurr, Andrew "Who is Lovewit? What is He?" (5-19) in Richard Cave, Elizabeth Schafer and

___, *The Shakespearean Stage 1574-1642*. Cambridge: CUP, 1970.

Brian Wooland. Ed. *Ben Jonson and Theater: Performance, Practice and Theory*. London, New York: Routledge, 1999.

Gurr, Andrew. *Playgoing in Shakespeare's London.* Cambridge: CUP, 1987.

Hakansson, Hakan. *Seeing the Word: John Dee and Renaissance Occultism.* Ugglan Minervaserien, University of Lund, 2001.

Halpern, Richard. "Marlowe's Theater of Night: *Doctor Faustus* and Capital" *ELH* 71 (2004): 455-495.

___, "Puritanism and Maenadism in *A Masque*" in *Rewriting the Renaissance: The Discourses of Sexual Difference in Early Modern Europe*. Eds. Ferguson, Margaret W., Maureen Quilligan and Nancy J. Vickers Chicago: The University of Chicago Press, 1986, (65-87).

Hamilton, Donna B. *Virgil and The Tempest: The Politics of Imitation.* Columbus: Ohio State University Press, 1990.

Hamlin, William H. "Casting Doubt in Marlowe's *Doctor Faustus*" *SEL* 41 (2001): 257-275.

Harkness, Deborah E. *The Jewel House: Elizabethan London and the Scientific Revolution*. New Haven, London: Yale University Press, 2007.

Harp, Richard. Ed. *Ben Jonson's Plays and Masques*. New York, London: W.W. Norton and Company, 2001.

Harraway, Clare. *Re-citing Marlowe*. Aldershot: Ashgate, 2000.

Harris, Jonathan Gil and Natasha Korda. *Staged Properties in Early Modern English Drama.* Cambridge: CUP, 2002.

Haynes, Jonathan. "Representing the Underworld: *The Alchemist*" *Studies in Philology* 86 (1989): 18-24.

Hiltner, Ken. *Milton and Ecology*. Cambridge: Cambridge University Press, 2003.

Hirsh, James. Ed. *New Perspectives on Ben Jonson*. Madison, Teaneck: Farleigh Dickinson University, Associated University Press, 1997.

Hochschild, Arlie Russell. *The Commercialization of Intimate Life.* Berkeley: University of California Press, 2003.

Howard, Jean E. *The Stage and Social Struggle in Early Modern England.* London and New York: Routledge, 1994.

Hunter, Robert Grams. *Shakespeare and the Comedy of Forgiveness*. New York and London: Columbia University Press, 1965.

Jardine, Lisa. *Francis Bacon: Discovery and the Art of Discourse*. Cambridge: CUP, 1974.

Jayne, Sears. "The Subject of Milton's Ludlow Mask" *PMLA* 74.5 (December, 1959): 533-543.

Johnson, Stacy W. "The Genesis of Ariel" *Shakespeare Quarterly* 2.3 (1951): 205-10.

Johnstone, Nathan. "The Protestant Devil: The Experience of Temptation in Early Modern England" *Journal of British Studies* 43.2 (April 2004): 173-205.

Jolly, Karen. "Medieval Magic: Definitions, Beliefs and Practices" in *Witchcraft and Magic in Europe: The Middle Ages*. Eds. Bengt Ankarloo and Stuart Clark. Philadelphia: University of Pennsylvania Press, 2001.

Jones, John Henry. Ed. *The English Faust Book.* Cambridge: Cambridge University Press, 1994.

Judges, A.V. Ed. *The Elizabethan Underworld: A Collection of Tudor and Early Stuart Tracts and Ballads.* London: Routledge and Kegan Paul, 1930.

Kearney, James. "The Book and the Fetish: The Materiality of Shakespeare's Text" *Journal of Medieval and Early Modern Studies.* 32.2 (2002) 433-468.

Kelly, Kathleen Coyne and Marina Leslie. Eds. *Menacing Virgins: Representing Virginity in the Middle Ages and Renaissance.* Newark: University of Delaware Press, 1999.

Kent, E.J. "Masculinity and Male Witches in Old and New England, 1593-1680" *History Workshop Journal* 60 (2005) 69-92.

Kernan, Alvin B. *The Playwright as Magician: Shakespeare's Image of the Poet in the Public Theater.* New Haven and London: Yale University Press, 1979.

___, *The Cankered Muse: Satire of the English Renaissance.* New Haven and London: Yale University Press, 1959.

Kieckhefer, Richard. *European Witch Trials.* Berkeley: University of California Press, 1976.

___, *Magic in the Middle Ages.* Cambridge: Cambridge University Press, 1989.

Kiefer, Frederick. *Shakespeare's Visual Theater: Staging the Personified Characters.* Cambridge: CUP, 2003.

Kinney, Arthur F. *Rogues, Vagabonds and Sturdy Beggars.* Amherst: University of Massachusetts Press, 1990.

Knapp, Peggy. "The Work of Alchemy" *Journal of Medieval and Early Modern Studies* 30.3 (Fall 2000): 575-599.

Knights, L.C. *Drama and Society in the Age of Jonson.* New York: W.W. Norton and Company, 1937.

Lachmann, Richard. "State Church and the Dis-establishment of Magic" in *The Production of English Renaissance Culture.* Eds. David Lee Miller, Sharon O' Dair and Harold Weber. Ithaca and London: Cornell University Press, 1994.

Latham, Jacqueline E.M. "The Magic Banquet in *The Tempest*" *Shakespeare Studies* 12 (1979) 215-227.

Lawrence, Christopher and Steven Shapin. Eds. *Science Incarnate:*

Historical Embodiment of Natural Knowledge. Chicago and London: University of Chicago Press, 1998.

Lenz, Joseph. "Base Trade: Theater as Prostitution" *ELH* 60.4 (Winter 1993): 833-855.

Levack, Brian P. *The Witch-Hunt in Early Modern Europe.* London and New York: Longman, 1995.

Levao, Ronald. "Bacon and the Mobility of Science" *Representations* 40 Special Issue: Seeing Science, Autumn (1992) 1-32.

Levin, Harry. *The Overreacher: A Study of Christopher Marlowe.* Cambridge: Harvard University Press, 1952.

Lindheim, Nancy. "Pastoral and Masque at Ludolow" *University of Toronto Quarterly* 67 (1998): 639-668.

Lindley, David. *Shakespeare and Music.* Arden Critical Companions. London: Arden Shakespeare, 2006.

___, Ed. *The Court Masque.* Manchester: Manchester University Press, 1984.

Long, Pamela O. *Openness, Secrecy, Authorship: Technical Arts and the Culture of Knowledge from Antiquity to the Renaissance.* Baltimore and London: Johns Hopkins University Press, 2001.

Loomba, Ania and Martin Orkin. Eds. *Post-Colonial Shakespeares.* London and New York: Routledge, 1998.

Lopez, Jeremy. *Theatrical Convention and Audience Response in Early Modern Drama.* Cambridge: Cambridge University Press: 2003

Lovelock, Julian. Ed. *Milton and Samson Agonistes.* A Casebook. London: Macmillan, 1975.

Loxley, James. *The Complete Critical Guide to Ben Jonson.* London: Routledge, 2002.

___, *Performitivity.* The New Critical Idiom. London and New York: Routledge, 2007.

Lucking, David "Carrying Tempest in his Hand and Voice: The Figure of the Magician in Jonson and Shakespeare" *English Studies* 85.4 (2004): 297-310.

___, "Our Devils Have Now Ended" *Dalhousie Review* 80.2 (Summer 2000): 151-168.

Mandel, Jerome. "Dream and Imagination in Shakespeare" *Shakespeare Quarterly* 24.1 (1973) 61-68.

Marchitello, Howard. *Narrative and Meaning in Early Modern England: Browne's Skull and Other Histories.* Cambridge: Cambridge University Press, 1997.

Marcus, Leah Sinanoglou. "The Milieu of Milton's *Comus*: Judicial Reform at Ludlow and the Problem of Sexual Assault". *Criticism* 25.4 (1983): 293-327.

___ , *Unediting the Renaissance: Shakespeare, Marlowe and Milton.* London and New York: Routledge, 1996.

Mardock, James D. *Our Scene is London: Ben Jonson's City and the Space of the Author.* New York: Routledge, 2008.

Marshall, Peter. *Reformation England 1480-1642.* London: Arnold, 2003.

Martin, Catherine Gimelli. "Angels, Alchemists and Exchange: Commercial, Ideology in Court and City 1596-1610" in *The Witness of Times: Manifestations of Ideology in Seventeenth Century England.* Eds. Katherine K. Keller and Gerald J. Schiffhorst. Pittsburgh and Pennsylvania: Duquesne University Press, 1993.

Martin, Catherine Gimelli. Ed. *Milton and Gender.* Cambridge: Cambridge University Press, 2004.

Martin, Matthew R. *Between Theater and Philosophy: Skepticism in the Major City Comedies of Ben Jonson and Thomas Middleton.* Newark, London: University of Delaware Press, 2001.

Martz, Louis L. *Milton: Poet of Exile.* New Haven and London: Yale University Press, 1980.

Marx, Karl. *The Capital* Vol. 1 Tr. Ben Fowkes. London: Penguin Books in Association with the New Left Review, 1976.

Matthews, Charles T. *Evil and the Augustinian Tradition.* Cambridge: Cambridge University Press, 2001.

Mauss, Marcel *A General Theory of Magic* Tr. Robert Brain. London, Boston: Routledge and Kegan Paul, 1970. First published in French 1950.

Mazzio, Carla and Douglass Trevor. Eds. *Historicism, Psychoanalysis and Early Modern Culture.* New York: Routledge, 2000.

McAdam, Ian. *Magic and Masculinity in Early Modern English Drama.* Pittsburgh, Pennsylvania: Duquesne University Press, 2009.

McAlindon, Tom. "The Discourse of Prayer in *The Tempest*" *SEL* 41.2 (2001) 335-355.

McEvoy, Sean. *Ben Jonson, Renaissance Dramatist*. Edinburgh: Edinburgh University Press, 2008.

McGuire, Maryann Cale. *Milton's Puritan Masque.* Athens: University of Georgia Press, 1983.

McManus, Caroline. "Queen Elizabeth, Dol Common, and the Performance of the Royal Maundy" *ELR* 32.2 (2002): 189-213.

McNamara, Kevin. "Golden Worlds at Court: *The Tempest* and its Masque" *Shakespeare Studies* 19 (1987) 183-202.

Meads, Chris. *Banquets Set Forth: Banqueting in English Renaissance Drama*. Manchester and New York: Manchester University Press, 2001.

Mebane, John S. *Renaissance Magic and the Return of the Golden Age: The Occult Tradition and Marlowe, Jonson and Shakespeare*. Lincoln and London: University of Nebraska Press, 1989.

Melnikoff, Kirk. ""[J]ygging vains" and "riming mother wits": Marlowe, Clowns and the Early Framework of Marlowe's Dramatic Authorship" *Early Modern Literary Studies* Special Issue 16 (2007): 1-37. Accessed on July 25, 2011. http://extra.shu.ac.uk/emls/si-16/melnjygg.htm.

Mikics, David. "Psychoanalysis, Idealizing and Magic: Reading *The Tempest*" *Shakespeare International Yearbook* 5: Special Section, Shakespeare and the Bonds of Service. Ed. Michael Neill. England and Burlington: Ashagate, 2005.

Miles, Margaret R. *Plotinus on Body and Beauty*: *Society, Philosophy, and Religion in Third Century Rome.* Malden: Blackwell Publishers, 1999.

Miles, Rosalind. *Ben Jonson: His Craft and Art*. New York: Routledge, 1990.

Montrose, Louis Adrian. ""Shaping Fantasies": Figurations of Gender and Power in Elizabethan Culture" *Representations* 2 (Spring 1983): 61-94.

Moore, Mary. "Wonder, Imagination, and the Matter of Theater in *The Tempest*" *Philosophy and Literature* 30.2 (2006) 496-512.

Moran, Bruce T. *Distilling Knowledge: Alchemy, Chemistry and the Scientific Revolution*. Cambridge: Harvard University Press, 2005.

Mousely, Andy. *Renaissance Drama and Contemporary Literary Theory.* New York: St. Martin's Press, 2000.

Mowat, Barbara A. "Prospero, Agrippa, and Hocus Pocus" *English Literary Renaissance* 11.2 (1981): 281-303

___, "Prospero's Book" *Shakespeare Quarterly* 52.1 Spring (2001) 1-33.

___, "The Role of the Visual on the Elizabethan Stage, 1576-1600" in *The Elizabethan Theater 1X*. Ed. G.R. Hibbard. Ontario: PD Meany, 1981

Muldrew, Craig. *The Economy of Obligation: The Culture of Credit and Social Relations in Early Modern England.* New York: Palgrave, 1998.

Mundhenk, Rosemary Kramelich. "Dark Scandal and the Sun-Clad Power of Chastity: The Historical Milieu of Milton's *Comus*". *SEL*. 15.1 (Winter 1975): 141-152.

Murphy, Erin. "Sabrina and the Making of English History in *Poly-Olbion* and *A Maske Presented at Ludlow Castle*" *SEL* (winter 2011): 87-110.

Neuse, Richard. "Metamorphosis and Symbolic Action in *Comus*". *ELH* 34.1 (March 1967): 49-64.

Newman William R. and Anthony Grafton. *Secrets of Nature: Astrology and Alchemy in Early Modern Europe.* Cambridge Mass, London: The MIT Press, 2001.

Nicora, Falminia. "'This is as strange a maze as e'er man trod': The Semiotics of Labyrinth in

Niell, Michael. "Noise, Sound and Sweet Airs": The Burden of Shakespeare's *The Tempest Shakespeare Quarterly* 59.1 (2008): 36-59.

Norbrook, David. "'What Cares These Roarers for the Name of King?': Language and Utopia in *The Tempest*" in *The Politics of Tragicomedy*. Eds. Gordon McMullan and Jonathan Hope. London and New York: Routledge, 1992.

___, and Roy Strong. *Inigo Jones: The Theater of the Stuart Court*, Vol. 1&2. Berkley and Los Angles: University of California Press, 1973.

___, "The Reformation Masque" in *The Court Masque*. Ed. David Lindley.

Nummedal, Tara. E. *Alchemy and Authority in the Holy Roman Empire* Chicago: University of Chicago Press, 2007.

___, "The Problem of Fraud in Early Modern Alchemy". In *Shell Games: Studies in Scams, Frauds and Deceits 1300-1630.* Eds. Mark

Crane, Richard Raiswell and Margaret Reeves. Toronto: Center for Reformation and Renaissance Studies, 2004.

Nuttall, A.D. *The Alternative Trinity: Gnostic Heresy in Marlowe, Milton and Blake*. Oxford: Clarendon Press, 1998.

Nyquist, Mary and Margaret W. Ferguson. *Re-membering Milton: Essays on the Texts and Traditions.* London and New York: Methuen, 1987.

O'Brien, Margaret Ann. "Christian Belief in *Doctor Faustus*" *ELH.* 37.1 (March 1970): 1-11.

O'Dair, Sharon. *Class, Critics and Shakespeare: Bottom Lines on the Culture Wars*. Ann Arbor: University of Michigan Press, 2000.

Oesterle, Jean. Tr. *St. Thomas Aquinas On Evil*. Indiana: University of Notre Dame, 1995.

Oldridge, Darren. *The Devil in Early Modern England*. Gloucestershire: Sutton Publishing, 2000.

Oram, Willam. "The Invocation of Sabrina" *SEL* 24.1 (Winter 1984): 121-139.

Oremerod, David and Christopher Wortham. Eds. *Dr Faustus The A-Text*, Nedlands: University of Western Australia Press, 1985.

Orgel, Stephen. *The Illusion of Power: Political Theater in the English Renaissance.* Berkeley: University of California Press, 1975.

____, "The Case for Comus" *Representations.* 81.1 (Winter 2003): 31-45.

Orkin, Martin. *Local Shakespeare: Proximations and Power*. London and New York: Routledge, 2005.

Ornstein, Robert. "The Comic Synthesis in *Doctor Faustus*" *ELH* 22.3 (September 1955): 165-172.

____, "Marlowe and God: The Tragic Theology of *Doctor Faustus*" *PMLA* 83.5 (October 1968): 1378-1385.

Ouellette, Anthony J. "*The Alchemist* and the Emerging Adult Private Playhouse" *SEL* 45.2 Spring (2005) 375-399.

Oz, Avraham. Ed. *Marlowe*, The New Casebook Series. New York: Palgrave Macmillan, 2003.

Pack, Robert. *Willing to Choose: Volition & Storytelling in Shakespeare's Major Plays*. Idaho: Lost Horse Press, 2007.

Paracelcus. *The Archidoxes of Magic Englished by R. Turner* (1655). Ed. Stephen Skinner. London: Askin Publishers and New York: Samuel Wesier, 1975.

Partridge, Edward B. *The Broken Compass: A Study of the Major Comedies of Ben Jonson*. New York: Columbia University Press, 1958.

Pask, Kevin. "Caliban's Masque" *ELH* 70.3 (2003) 739-756.

Pearson, D'Orsay W. ""Unless I be Relived by Prayer": *The Tempest* in Perspective" *Shakespeare Studies* 7 (1974) 253-281.

Pierce, Robert B. "Understanding *The Tempest*" *New Literary History* 30.2 (1999) 373-388.

Pistorius, Philippus Villiers. *Plotinus and Neoplatonism: An Introductory Study*. Cambridge: Bowes & Bowes, 1952.

Poole, Kristen. "The Devil's in the Archive: *Doctor Faustus* and Ovidian Physiscs" *English Renaissance Drama* 35 (2006): 191-219.

___,"*Doctor Faustus* and Reformation Theology" in Early *Modern English Drama: A Critical Companion*. Eds. Garrett A. Sullivan Jr. Patrick Cheney and Andrew Hadfield. Oxford: Oxford University Press, 2006.

Pugliatti, Paola. *Beggary and Theater in Early Modern England* Burlington: Ashgate, 2003.

Pye, Christopher. *The Regal Phantasm: Shakespeare and the Politics of Spectacle.* London and New York: 1990.

Randolf, Mary Claire. "Celtic Smiths and Satirists: Partners in Sorcery" *ELH* 8.3 (1941) 184-197.

Ravelhoffer, Barbara. *The Early Stuart Masque: Dance, Costume and Music.* Oxford: OUP, 2006.

Regan, Richard J. Tr., Ed. *Thomas Aquinas: A Summary of Philosophy*. Indianapolis: Hackett Publishing Company Inc. 2003.

Reynolds, Bryan and William N. Nest. Eds. *Rematerializing Shakespeare: Authority and Representation on the Early Modern English Stage*. Hampshire and New York: Palgrave Macmillan, 2005.

Ribton-Turner, C. J. *A History of Vagrants and Vagrancy* London: Chapman and Hall, 1887.

Riener, A.P. *Antic Fables: Patterns of Evasion in Shakespeare's Comedies*. Manchester: Manchester University Press, 1980.

Riggs, David. *The World of Christopher Marlowe*. New York: Henry Holt and Company, 2004.

Roberts, Gareth. "Necromantic Books: Christopher Marlowe, Doctor Faustus and Agrippa of Nettesheim" in *Christopher Marlowe and English Renaissance Culture*. Eds. Darryll Grantley and Peter Roberts.

___, *The Mirror of Alchemy*. Toronto: University of Toronto Press, 1994.

___, "Marlowe and the Metaphysics of Magicians" in *Constructing Christopher Marlowe*. Eds. J.A Downie and J.T Parnell.

Robinson, Fred Norris. "Satirists and Enchanters in Early Irish Literature" (95-130) in *Studies in the History of Religions*. Eds. David Gordon Lyon and George Foot Moore. New York: Macmillan Company, 1912.

Ross, Cheryl Lynn. "The Plague of *The Alchemist*" in Dutton, Richard Ed. Ben Jonson Essex: Longman, 2000.

Rossi, Paolo. *Francis Bacon from Magic to Science*. Trans. Sacha Rabinovitch. London: Routledge and Kegan Paul, 1968.

Rushton, Peter. "A Note on the Survival of Popular Christian Magic" *Folklore* 91.1 (1980): 115-118.

Russell, Jeffrey Burton. *The Devil: Perceptions of Evils from Antiquity to Primitive Christianity*. Ithaca and London: Cornell University Press, 1977.

Sachs, Arieh. "The Religious Despair of Doctor Faustus" *Journal of English and Germanic Philology* 63 (1964): 625-647.

Schwarz, Katherine. "Chastity Militant and Married: Cavendish's Romance, Milton's Masque" *PMLA* 118.2 (March 2003): 270-285.

Scott, Charlotte. *Shakespeare and the Idea of the Book*. Oxford: OUP, 2007.

Semon, Kenneth J. "Fantasy and Wonder in Shakespeare's Last Plays" *Shakespeare Quarterly* 25.1 Winter (1974) 89-102.

Sensabaugh, G.F. "The Milieu of Comus" *Studies in Philology* 41 (1944) 238-249.

Shakespeare. "*The Tempest*" *Textus* XVII (2004) 275-290.

Shanahan, John. "Ben Jonson's *Alchemist* and Early Modern Laboratory Space" *The Journal for Early Modern Culture Studies* 8.1 Spring/ Summer (2008): 35-66.

Shapin, Steven. *The Scientific Revolution*. Chicago and London: University of Chicago Press, 1996.

___, *A Social History of Truth: Civility and Science in Seventeenth-Century England.* Chicago and London: University of Chicago Press, 1994.

Sherman, William H. *John Dee: The Politics of Reading and Writing in the English Renaissance*. Amherst: University of Massachusetts Press, 1995.

Shohet, Lauren. "Figuring Chastity: Milton's *Ludlow Masque*" in Kelly, Kathleen Coyne and Marina Leslie. Eds. *Menacing Virgins: Representing Virginity in the Middle Ages and Renaissance*.

___, "*Reading Masques*" *The English Masque and Public Culture in the Seventeenth Century*. Oxford: Oxford University Press, 2010.

Shullenberger, William. *Lady in the Labyrinth*. Madison: Farleigh Dickinson University Press, 2008.

Simkin, Stevie. *A Preface to Marlowe*. Harlow: Longman, 2000.

Simonds, Peggy Munoz. "Staging The Tempest as an Alchemical Experiment in Theater" *Shakespeare: Text and Theater: Essays in Honor of Jay L. Halio*. Eds. Lois Potter and Arthur F. Kinney. Newark: University of Delaware Press, London: Associated University Presses, 1999.

Sinfield, Alan."Reading Faustus's God" in *Marlowe* New Casebooks. Ed. Avram Oz.

Sleights, William W.E. *Ben Jonson and the Art of Secrecy*. Toronto, Buffalo, London: University of Toronto Press, 1994.

Slover, George. "Magic, Mystery and Make-believe: An Analogical Reading of *The Tempest*" *Shakespeare Studies* 11 (1978): 175-206.

Smith Jr., George William. "Milton's Revisions and the Design of Comus" *ELH*, 46.1 (Spring, 1979), 56-80.

Smith, Hallett. Ed. *Twentieth Century Interpretations of The Tempest: A Collection of Critical Essays*. New Jersey: Prentice Hall Inc., 1969.

Sokol, B.J. *A Brave New World of Knowledge: Shakespeare's The Tempest and Early Modern Epistemology*. Madison, Teaneck: Fairleigh Dickinson University Press: 2003.

Spiller, Elizabeth. "Shakespeare and the Making of Early Modern Science" *South Central Review* 26.1&2 (2009): 24-41.

Stallybrass, Peter. "The Value of Culture and the Disavowal of Things" in *The Culture of Capital*. Ed. Henry S. Turner. London and New York: Routledge, 2002.

Steadman, John M. *Milton's Haemony: Etymology and Allegory PMLA* 77.3 (June 1966): 200-207.

Stevens, Paul. "Magic Structure: *Comus* and the Illusion of Fancy." *Milton Quarterly* 17 (1983): 84-87.

Stillman, Robert E. Ed. *Spectacle and Public Performance in the Late Middle Ages and the Renaissance*. Leiden, Boston: Brill, 2006.

Streete, Adrian. ""Consummatum Est": Calvinist Exegesis, Mimesis and Doctor Faustus" *Literature and Theology* 15.2 (2001): 140-157.

Strong, Roy. *Art and Power: Renaissance Festivals 1450-1650.* Berkeley, Los Angeles: University of California Press, 1973.

Sullivan, Garrett A., Patrick Cheney, Andrew Hadfield. Eds. *Early Modern English Drama: A Critical Companion*. New York and Oxford: Oxford University Press, 2006.

Summers, Montague. Tr. Ed. *The Malleus Maleficarum of Heinrich Kramer and James Sprenger*. New York: Dover Publications, 1971.

Sweeny III, John Gordon. *Jonson and the Psychology of Public Theater*. Princeton: Princeton University Press, 1985.

Szonyi, Gyorgy E. *John Dee's Occultism: Magical Exaltation Through Powerful Signs*. Albany: State University of New York Press, 2004.

Thomas, Catherine. "Chaste Bodies and Poisonous Desires in Milton's *Mask*" *SEL* 46.2 (Spring 2006): 435-459.

Thomas, Keith. *Religion and the Decline of Magic*. New York: Charles Scribner and Sons, 1971.

Thomas, Vivien and William Tydeman. *Christopher Marlowe: The Plays and their Sources*. London and New York, Routledge, 1994.

Thompson, N.S. *Controversy Between the Puritans and the Stage*. New York: Scribner and Company, 1903.

Thorndike, Lyn. *A History of Magic and Experimental Science*. New York and London: Columbia University Press, 1941.

Tomlinson, Gary. *Music in Renaissance Magic: Toward a Historiography of Others*. Chicago: University of Chicago Press, 1993.

Totaro, Rebecca. *Suffering in Paradise: The Bubonic Plague in English Literature From Milton.*

Traister, Barbara Howard. *Heavenly Necromancers: The Magician in English Renaissance Drama*. Columbia: University of Missouri Press, 1984.

Tromly, Fred B. *Playing with Desire: Christopher Marlowe and the Art of Tantalization*. Toronto: University of Toronto Press, 1998.

Turner, Henry S. *The English Renaissance Stage: Geometry, Poetics, and the Practical Spatial Arts 1580-1630*. Oxford, New York: Oxford University Press, 2006.

Ulreich Jr., John C. "A Bright Golden Flow'r: Haemony as a Symbol of Transformation" *The English Renaissance* (Winter 1977): 119-128.

Valetta, Frederick. *Witchcraft, Magic and Superstition in England, 1640-70.* Aldershot and Burlington: Ashgate, 2000.

Vaughan, Virginia Mason and Alden T. Vaughan. Eds. *Critical Essay on Shakespeare's The Tempest*. New York: G.K. Hall & Co., 1998.

___, Virginia Mason, Vaughan and Alden T. Vaughan. Eds. *The Tempest*. The Arden Shakespeare. Surrey: Thomas Nelson and Sons Ltd., 1999.

Versnal, H.S. "Some Reflections on the Relationship of Magic-Religion" *Numem* 38.2 (1991): 177-197.

Vikers, Brian. *Occult and Scientific Mentalities in the Renaissance.* Cambridge: Cambridge University Press, 1984.

Walker, D.P. *Spiritual and Demonic Magic From Ficino to Campenella.* Notre Dame, London: Notre Dame Press, 1975.

Walker, D.P. *Spiritual and Demonic Magic: From Ficino to Campanella.* Notre Dame: University of Notre Dame Press, 1975.

Wall-Randell, Sarah. "*Doctor Faustus* and the Printer's Devil" *SEL.* 48 (2008): 259-81.

Warner, Rex and Vernon J. Bourke. *The Confessions of St. Augustine*. New York: New American Library, 1963.

Warren, Michael. "*Doctor Faustus*: The Old Man and the Text" *English Literary Renaissance*. 11.2 (1981): 111-147.

Waters, Douglas D. "Milton's Use of the Sorcerer-Rhetorician" *Milton Quarterly* 8 (1974): 113-116.

Wells, Headlam Robin. *Elizabethan Mythologies: Studies in Poetry, Drama and Music.* Cambridge: CUP, 1994.

Welsford, Enid. *The Court Masque.* New York: Russell & Russell, 1927.

Willby, Emma. *Cunning Folk and Famililar Spirit: Shamanistic Visionary Traditions in Early Modern British Witchcraft and Magic.* Brightton, Portland: Sussex Academic Press, 2005.

Wilson, Eric. "Abel Drugger's Sign and the Fetishes of Material Culture" in *Historicism, Psychoanalysis and Early Modern Culture.* Eds. Carla Mazzio and Douglas Trevors. New York: Routledge, 2000.

Wilson, Richard. "Voyage to Tunis: New History and the Old World of *The Tempest*" *ELH* 64.2 (1997) 333-357.

Wind, Edgar. *Pagan Mysteries in the Renaissance.* New York: W.W. Norton and Company, 1958.

Witmore, Michael. *Culture of Accidents: Unexpected Knowledges in Early Modern England.* California, Stanford University Press, 2001.

Wolfe, Jessica. *Humanism, Machinery and Renaissance Literature* Cambridge: Cambridge University Press, 2004.

Woodbridge, Linda. *Vagrancy Homelessness and English Renaissance Literature* Urbana: University of Illinois Press, 2001.

Woolley, Benjamin. *The Queen's Conjurer : The Science and Magic of Dr. John Dee, Adviser to Queen Elizabeth I.* New York: Henry Holt, 2001.

Yates, Francis A. *Shakespeare's Last Plays: A New Approach.* London: Routledge and Kegan Paul, 1975.

____, *Occult Philosophy in the Elizabethan Age.* London, Boston: Routledge and Kegan Paul, 1979.

Zambelli, Paola. *White Magic, Black Magic in the European Renaissance: From Ficino, Pico, Della Porta to Trithemius, Agrippa and Bruno.* Leiden: Brill, 2007.

Zimbardo, Rose. "Form and Disorder in *The Tempest*" *Shakespeare Quarterly* 14.1 (1963) 49.

Index